A PLUME BOOK

BOOZE FOR FREE

ANDY HAMILTON lives in Bristol, where he is founder of the Bristol Brewing Circle and runs brewing workshops and an allotment. He forages and regularly takes groups on wild food walks, sharing his extensive knowledge of edible wild foods, plant folklore, and herbal medicine. Andy is a cocreator of the hugely successful website selfsufficientish.com (winner, Nigel's Eco Awards 2009) and writes a wild drinks blog for guardian.co.uk. He also writes a brewing column for *Home Farmer* magazine, brewing and foraging features for the BBC's *Countryfile* magazine, and features for the *Guardian* (London), the *Ecologist, Tow Path Talk, Kitchen Garden* magazine, selfsufficientish.com, and the New York–based website Civil Eats. He has also written a survivalist column for wired.co.uk. He has been a consultant survival/wild-food expert for various TV shows and makes regular TV and radio appearances both in the UK and abroad, on shows that include the BBC's *Countryfile* and *Autumnwatch*. Andy is coauthor of *The Self-Sufficientish Bible*.

For more information on Andy Hamilton and his books, see his website at www.selfsufficientish.com

Booze for Free

The Definitive Guide to Making Beer,
Wines, Cocktail Bases, Ciders,
and Other Drinks at Home

Andy Hamilton

A PLUME BOOK

PLUME
Published by the Penguin Group
Penguin Group (USA) Inc., 375 Hudson Street, New York, New York 10014, USA
Penguin Group (Canada), 90 Eglinton Avenue East, Suite 700, Toronto, Ontario M4P 2Y3, Canada
(a division of Pearson Penguin Canada Inc.)
Penguin Books Ltd, 80 Strand, London WC2R 0RL, England
Penguin Ireland, 25 St Stephen's Green, Dublin 2, Ireland (a division of Penguin Books Ltd)
Penguin Group (Australia), 707 Collins Street, Melbourne, Victoria 3008, Australia
(a division of Pearson Australia Group Pty Ltd)
Penguin Books India Pvt Ltd, 11 Community Centre, Panchsheel Park, New Delhi – 110 017, India
Penguin Group (NZ), 67 Apollo Drive, Rosedale, Auckland 0632, New Zealand
(a division of Pearson New Zealand Ltd)
Penguin Books, Rosebank Office Park, 181 Jan Smuts Avenue, Parktown North 2193, South Africa
Penguin China, B7 Jaiming Center, 27 East Third Ring Road North,
Chaoyang District, Beijing 100020, China

Penguin Books Ltd., Registered Offices: 80 Strand, London WC2R 0RL, England

Published by Plume, a member of Penguin Group (USA) Inc. Previously published in the
United Kingdom by Eden Project Books, an imprint of Transworld Publishers.

First American Printing, March 2013
1 3 5 7 9 10 8 6 4 2

Ⓟ REGISTERED TRADEMARK—MARCA REGISTRADA

LIBRARY OF CONGRESS CATALOGING-IN-PUBLICATION DATA

Hamilton, Andy, 1974-
Booze for free : the definitive guide to making beer, wines, sherries, cordials, ciders,
and other drinks at home / Andy Hamilton.
p.   cm.
Includes bibliographical references and index.
ISBN 978-0-452-29880-4
1. Brewing—Amateurs' manuals.   2. Wine and wine making—Amateurs' manuals.   I. Title.
TP570.H2275 2013
641.2'2—dc23
2012028865

Printed in the United States of America

PUBLISHER'S NOTE

This book is dedicated to all those people I have
enjoyed a drink with,
and to those I have yet to enjoy a
drink with. Cheers!

This book is dedicated to all those people I have
enjoyed a drink with,
and to those I have yet to enjoy a
drink with. Cheers!

CONTENTS

Introduction   ix

Part One: The Basics

A Short History of Booze   3
Homebrewing Equipment   11
Homebrewing Ingredients   29
Best Practice   39
Notes on Foraging   49
Notes on Growing Your Own   57

Part Two: The Recipes

Cider-making   69
Beer-making   83
Wine-making   91
Spring   99
Summer   149
Autumn   193
Winter   249
Problem-solving   277

Part Three: Further Information

Directory of Homebrew Equipment
    Suppliers   287
Further Reading   299
Useful Websites   305
Glossary of Brewing Terms   309
Glossary of Gardening and Botanical
    Terms   327
Acknowledgments   329
Index   331

INTRODUCTION

W HEN IT COMES to making your own alcohol, everybody's first experiences are similar. You might make a few bottles of root beer, sarsaparilla, lemonade, beer from a kit, or even a country wine. Your lemonade might be divine, but it's the only drink you make; your root beer is only drunk by you and the neighbor's dog; and your sarsaparilla doesn't, as you thought it would, so much capture the taste of the forest in a glass as the syrupy taste of a long-forgotten something at the back of a medicine cabinet.

Despite these setbacks something still pulls you in to watch the bubbles rise into the airlock and gurgle out into the air, to see the mist inside your demijohns dissipate to reveal a crystal-clear translucent hue of outstanding beauty. Every step of the process seems magical, a moment of alchemy, and you experience a thirst to find out more. You want to make something that rivals your favorite brand of ale or wine; you gaze longingly at apple trees in the autumn and dream of turning those rotting orbs at your feet into cider. You even begrudge buying your kids packed-lunch drinks as you're sure you could do better at a fraction of the cost and with much more wholesome ingredients.

Making your own alcohol places you in a sensuous world full of new aromas and tastes, many of which are often ancient aromas and tastes reborn. What's more, these aromas and tastes can be tailored entirely to your liking. For example, by using bay and rosemary in your beer a warming, fragrant, almost gingery beer can be created; by altering slightly the way you ferment a wine in terms of letting air in, you can change the flavor of a parsnip wine into a sherry; less sugar could be used in the brewing to produce a clear, crisp, dry wine.

A hands-on approach to our drink can go beyond smells and flavors. Over the last decade an awareness of provenance has been growing. We are now more than ever questioning how our food is produced and what goes into it, but sadly, all too often a blind eye is turned when it comes to what we drink. This is fairly understandable: eating five carrots one after another does not make me care less about where those carrots came from, but by the fifth consecutive beer sometimes it's easy not to care whether you've even got your trousers on. But that's not to say we shouldn't question what goes into our booze.

Due to a hangover from Prohibition times, home brewing was

illegal in the United States until 1978. At the time of this writing, most states permit the brewing of beer with the exceptions of Alabama and Mississippi. There is a limit on how much you can brew, and this has been set at 100 gallons a year—although there are moves toward changing the laws, so people get lobbying!

Up in Canada it is a more complicated business and there is little information for the would-be brewer to ascertain whether they are breaking the law, and many, especially in remote areas, will actively ignore the law. It would appear that it is legal in most provinces except Nova Scotia. As it is locally regulated, though, it will be worth checking first if you don't want to break the law. The law gets even more backward, as in all Canadian provinces kegging is illegal, but there is nothing to stop you from bottling hundreds of beers in one go.

Current legislation dictates that alcoholic drinks containing less than 7% alcohol are exempt from compulsory labeling, which means that if a brewer wishes to put his cock (a male chicken) into his beer then he can. In fact many beers contain isinglass, a substance derived from collagen taken from the swim bladders of fish (it is used to clarify the brew), which makes for tricky ground for vegetarians and vegans. The commercial brewer may (and regularly does) decide to put in a selection of chemicals to change the color, taste, or shelf life of his drink. Many of these chemicals fall under the general heading of permissible ingredients and can even be found in pure beers that masquerade as fully natural. This could be reason enough to stop and think about what you are drinking, without even considering what may have been sprayed on the grapes, hops, and barley before they ended up inside your wine or pint glass.

Making your own booze is just like growing your own vegetables or baking a cake: *your* hand has put in each ingredient so you can be sure of its purity. And it is possible to take this a logical step further and ensure that you know each ingredient that goes into your booze from seed. There is no reason why your drinks, like your meals, cannot be wholly organic and completely seasonal. There is a joy among homebrewers who brew to the seasons: we all know that our sloe gin made with sloes picked in the early autumn will be ready by Christmas but will taste better if we leave it for a year; we all know our wine ferments quicker in the spring; we all know there is no such thing as a summer or autumn overabundance of vegetables as all of them can be made into some kind of drink; and many of us tend to make parsnip wine in the first months of any given year, mainly because it is delicious and partly because it blows your socks off. Moreover, it's a gentle, ancient, simple craft.

It's easy to misjudge this craft and consider it the refuge of small, rotund, bespectacled men with mustaches, small pocket books, and tons of equipment stashed away in their garages. Indeed, I sometimes feel I am turning into such a man with each passing year. As with all stereotypes, it's not an accurate picture: of those who turn up to my homebrewing classes or to the local brewing circle that I founded, the only strange man with a pocket book is me. Those attracted to this craft cannot be categorized, apart from by their love of alcoholic beverages. They are as diverse a bunch as you might find in a good traditional village pub.

Many of my friends have been shocked that anything home-made can be not only palatable but also delicious. Once you start brewing you will no doubt encounter such reactions. At first I was offended: I always try to give my guests good food, why would they think things would be any different when I give them a drink? But it's an understandable reaction and you can't blame your guests. I too, once upon a time, had a somewhat derogatory opinion of home-brewed drinks, born of my first experiences of homebrew.

I can still almost taste my first ever sip of homebrewed beer. I was twenty-one, and my friend John had brewed some from a kit. "Here, try this," he said, grinning as he passed me an orange-colored liquid in a plastic pint glass. "It tastes like petrol." He wasn't far wrong. It did the job so far as inebriation was concerned, but it did nothing for the taste buds. This is by no means a slight on John: most of my initial attempts at brewing beer were fairly disastrous too. Some of the drinks I created were more akin to something typically found flowing through drains, and only slightly more alcoholic. And it wasn't just the beer I made that was terrible. I remember making a cider that tasted more like a very, very sweet German wine, and wines that tasted like cough medicine.

This is one of the aspects of homebrewing *Booze for Free* aims to address. Each recipe in this book has made it on to the page either for taste or curiosity value. You will find here classic wines that can accompany even the most gourmet of meals, curious beers using recipes that have been in existence since the dawn of time, soft drinks that could be sold by the million, powerfully individual liqueurs, and instructions to make a cider that will rival anything bought from a shop. My favorites include a beer brewed using the stalks of a maize crop, a sort of wine made by prisoners, and parsnip sherry. The world of homemade alcohol need not be populated with mediocre beverages made just because something is in season; if you have waited twelve months for a particular fruit or veg then you want to be darn sure that the drink you make with it tastes good.

You also want to be sure that you are going to make a great-tasting brew before you go out and spend a fortune on equipment—though this is an act that almost defeats the object of booze for free. It's like bringing your own sandwiches to a free lunch. Prisoners brew their own alcohol using little more than trash bags and leftovers so there's no reason why you too can't adopt a simplistic method, perhaps "poshing it up" a bit by putting the trash bag in a cardboard box, and using fruit from the garden (or foraged fruit) instead of leftovers, and decanting the brew into bottles saved from the recycling. It will still cost you next to nothing. For the biggest skinflint—sorry, for the most frugal among you—this book even contains alcoholic drinks that will cost nothing at all, apart from your time. Of course you can buy plenty of equipment, some expensive stuff too, and it is great to add to your collection as your interest and knowledge grows.

There is a lot of knowledge out there. Topics such as home-brewing and fermentation can attract the sort of people who like to overcomplicate things; as a result, the wealth of literature on these subjects can be daunting. I have read chapters, even whole books, that concentrate on nothing but yeast. It is important to know about the right yeast, but for the novice it is more important simply to learn how to make something you can happily drink. If we are listening to the radio, our pleasure is not diminished by the fact that we don't know specifically which transmitter the signal is coming from. It is more than possible to make a great-tasting beer, wine, or cider with hardly any knowledge of what you are doing, save perhaps what to look for if it all goes wrong—and problem-solving forms an important part of this book (see Part Two).

One of the greatest pleasures I have in life is the process of starting a wine, beer, or cider. Such a process can begin weeks, months, sometimes even years before the drink is tasted. It can begin by pressing a foot into the earth to secure a newly planted apple tree; leaning over a fence to swipe a handful of your neighbor's rosemary; pushing a seed down into a pot of freshly prepared compost; or boiling up a handful of hops and stinking out your kitchen.

The beauty of homebrewing is that this pleasure extends beyond the crafting process. Parties can be thrown just to "test-run" a new barrel of beer; bottles can be given out at Christmas; you'll never need to turn up anywhere empty-handed again. But most of all, the pleasure resides in making a drink that is specifically designed for your own personal taste and that contains nothing but produce picked from your favorite spot or grown by your own fair hand.

The whole of life can flow from drink. Marriages and friendships can be forged over a glass or two of wine or beer; babies can be conceived after a glass or two more. Why shouldn't homebrew be this drink? It really is the nectar of the gods—a fact you will discover the more you dip into the pages of this book.

Booze for Free will take you by the hand and lead you into this homebrewing world. The opening part acts as an introduction for the beginner to foraging and growing your own, and more importantly discusses the equipment and knowledge you will need to get on and make your own drinks.

Because, as I've mentioned, one of the joys of homebrewing is its seasonality, Part Two is divided into sections by season, and in each of these you will find the natural produce that is either at its best or only available at that time of year. Each of the hundred or so featured recipes is set out simply so that at a glance the reader will know exactly what ingredients and equipment are needed and what steps to take. Alongside the recipes, each fruit, herb, nut, or vegetable mentioned carries details on where and how to forage for it, or grow it (or both, if appropriate), a brief description, and a Latin name to help with identification. Beer-, wine-, and cider-making have a lot more depth to them, so this seasonal breakdown is preceded by articles devoted entirely to these crafts.

On some occasions it has been impossible to avoid using jargon. If you are unsure of any of the terminology, turn to the extensive glossaries at the end of the book. Drink-making is an expansive subject so these lists have been extended beyond the terms used in this book so that the reader can gain more from further reading or Internet browsing. Selected lists for both books and websites can also be found in Part Three.

Experienced drink-makers rarely agree on how to make things, which is partly why we have so many wines, beers, ciders, and soft drinks on the market. Most will adopt their own style over time, even if this style is to continue to follow recipes. This book does not adhere to one particular style; instead it offers a variety. After a time you may prefer to, for instance, make beer only from malt extract, use smaller amounts of sugar, use larger amounts of sulphites, or start adding your own ingredients to adapt these recipes. This will become easier as your drink-making experience grows. That was certainly the case for me and the other drink-makers I know.

Above all, this book is supposed to bring joy to the reader and to get you to go out into the wilds and literally sample the seasons.

To ease identification, the Latin name of each plant has been added. In some cases, where all types of a particular species can be used, I have only used the Latin name for the species (for example, *Fagus* for beech) but when only a specific species can be used I have also referenced the species (for example, horseradish, *Armoracia rusticana*).

PART ONE

The Basics

A SHORT HISTORY
OF BOOZE

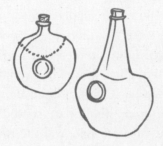

MAKING ALCOHOL is a process as familiar to our species as flight is to a bird or prize lettuce eating to a slug. It is impossible to know when the first alcoholic drinks were made as precious little evidence has been left behind. Perhaps stored crab apples were crushed into a crude cider; maybe crushed grapes fermented into wine, or naturally fermented fruit was picked off the ground and eaten. We can't be sure, then, about the origins of alcohol consumption in general, but we can with more certainty follow the history of specific drinks such as beer and grape wine.

BEER

Some ten to twenty thousand years ago humans inhabiting the Near East began to farm cereal crops such as barley as they stored for longer than any other foodstuff. It was the storing of these grains that forced hunter-gatherers to build communities where the crops grew in order to protect their supply of food.

Barley can't be eaten raw, therefore it would have been crushed, pounded, and soaked in water, then eaten with other food such as fish to make a kind of gruel. It was this simple practice of soaking cereals in water that would have roused the interests of the early homebrewer as the grains would have started to taste sweet—they were embarking on what we now call the malting process, which turns starches into sugars. They would have thought this a magical process, especially as there were so few natural sources of sugars.

Quite by accident, some of this malting grain would have been left in water for a few days, perhaps by someone who couldn't be bothered to wash up. Who knows what happened next; maybe someone was so hungry they decided to eat this fizzing gruel. This person would not have had much of a tolerance for alcohol—this is something we have evolved over time—so even having ingested a small amount of this weak solution they would have been drunk very quickly.

So the first ever beer, albeit accidental, was made by a home-brewer. Neolithic man would have rejoiced in this drink and thought it a gift from the gods. Beer brewing in some isolated communities is still considered sacred.

Fast forward to around 3400 BCE, to Mesopotamia (now Iraq)

where a crude written language was beginning to evolve: tokens were pressed into clay tablets and lines were scratched to denote physical goods—early administrative documents depicting, among other things, the allocation of beer as a wage. Four hundred years later these rudimentary pictograms had evolved into more abstract lines that started to look more like what we now would recognize as words. Tablets dating from around 2000 BCE tell the story of the god of agriculture, Enki, and include a cryptic but unmistakable recipe for beer. Of course, this means the first ever recipe was for homebrew—and I mean the first ever written recipe for *anything*.

The brewing tradition was refined by the Babylonians, who made at least twenty different types of beer. The beer flag was then flown by the Egyptians, who passed the tradition on to the Greeks, and from there, perhaps surprisingly, to the Romans. The Roman Empire was so huge that it was not feasible to make wine in each corner of it so beer became popular in some regions, modern-day Germany and the UK being two examples. Beer was still considered to be a barbarian drink, which no doubt fueled the notion that Britons and Teutons were too.

In the centuries after the Romans left Britain Saxons and Vikings invaded, bringing with them their ale. Alehouses began to appear across the country. By the Middle Ages ale was being drunk with every meal, partly due to the impurity of the water: beer, having gone through the fermentation process, was considered safer to drink. It is thought that every man, woman, and child was drinking about 1 liter/2 pints of beer a day, albeit a weaker version of the ones we know today.

From medieval times right up to the industrial revolution,

brewing would have been a task for the women of the household, who were known as "brew wives." There was an ale for almost every occasion: a lamb ale for lambing time; church ale, a potent brew made by the church wardens and sold on Whitsun to raise funds for the church; and even a bride ale (the origin of the word "bridal"). These ales would have likely been made with rosemary, yarrow, ground ivy, nettles, and various other mixtures of herbs.

Despite the fact that hops grew in the UK, beer was not flavored with them for a long time. The Low Countries started to use them from around 800, and by 1400 the first hopped beers had made it to our shores. Herbal ales might still have as strong a relevance in our society as ever had it not been for European laws banning the use of them. For example, in Bavaria in 1533 severe penalties were imposed on anyone *brewing ale with herbs and seeds not normally used for ale*. In Norway and Holstein (Germany), the use of bog myrtle and other herbs was also outlawed. In the UK the fight against herbal ales had religious connotations, since the Puritan Protestants thought the use of "stimulating herbs" self-indulgent, lavish, and ultimately un-Christian.

Paradoxically, by around the fifteenth century beer brewing in Britain had started to become an artisan activity undertaken initially by monks. The scale of this practice grew steadily and the bigger brewer slowly but surely began to be favored. By the nineteenth century beer was being made on a huge scale: in 1814 a tank containing 3,500 barrels of beer (135,000 gallons) ruptured in London causing an alcoholic tidal wave that killed nine people and demolished two houses.

There were a few dalliances into beer making in the United

States and Canada by the early settlers, but nothing that really lasted more than a season. In 1609, this started to change as the settlers in Jamestown were growing their own barley and employing a couple of East London brewers. Up in Canada the French were following suit in Quebec.

Brewing gathered pace with settlers and it became as common to brew some beer as it did to bake an apple pie (well, almost). At this time, brewing was a task mostly undertaken by women, with a most notable exception of George Washington. Perhaps he chopped down that cherry tree in order to get more light on his hops or to make room for some barley?

Universities noticed that students would enjoy the taste of a pint or two of beer, and not being shy of the free-market economy, they made the most of it. For around a hundred years, from the early part of the eighteenth century to the early nineteenth century, universities had brew pubs close by; indeed Harvard went a step further and had its on-campus brew pub.

Americans' love of beer saw no bounds and by 1810, there were around 120 breweries; by 1860 this had leaped to around 1,300 breweries, before reaching a peak of more than 4,000 in 1873. It must have been a boozy time to be alive and drinking in United States. A dark shadow, however, was forming in the guise of the temperance society formed in 1826; in three short years it had 100,000 members. This would later lead to Prohibition in 1919, a dark time indeed for the brewer, when, until April 7, 1933, by law no one could brew anything.

Despite it being legal to brew commercially from 1933, it wasn't until October 14, 1978, that President Jimmy Carter created an exemption from taxation for beer brewed at home for personal or family use. The law took effect in February 1979, and soon after the American Homebrewers Association in Boulder, Colorado, was set up by a couple of Charlies: Matzen and Papazian. The latter is still considered somewhat of a god in homebrew circles.

Presently, both home and commercial brewing in the United States are the envy of the world. There are estimated to be more than 1 million home brewers and more than 200 million barrels brewed commercially every year. Much of the commercial beer is fairly generic, bland lager, but beer lovers are voting with their feet and sales are declining in favor of lovingly produced craft beer. Conversely, sales of craft beer in 2010 were selling an estimated $7.9 billion, the size of California's state deficit. It looks as if America's golden age of beer is right now!

WINE

The earliest archaeological evidence for wine dates back to around 6000 BCE—vinous residues found on a jug in Georgia. It is highly likely that wine was made long before this but the archaeological evidence has so far eluded us. However, as the fermentation process takes time it is unlikely that a nomadic people would have stayed in one place long enough to make wine, nor did they have clay pots to store it in. Successful wine-making would only have been possible when settled communities were making their own pottery, which first happened about ten thousand years ago. Some even suggest that we started farming in order to grow grapevines.

Wine-making spread through Greece and the Middle East before arriving (by 3000 BCE) in Egypt, where some of the first documented evidence of the cultivation of grapevines was found. The Egyptians must have really prized the drink as King Scorpion I, one of their earliest rulers, was buried with seven hundred jars of expensive imported wine (what a waste!).

It was not until around 2500 BCE, when we know grapevines were being grown in Greece and Crete, that wine made it to the Mediterranean countries. At this time it was a drink for the elite only. The Greeks took wine production to southern Italy and Sicily where they found the climate most agreeable to the cultivation of vines. From there, the Romans, synonymous with wine drinking, took the baton and ran with it to new heights. In contrast to the Greeks, they thought everyone from the pauper to the aristocrat should have wine, believing that it was a necessity of life. Although they didn't drink it as we do, often mixing it with seawater—not something I would recommend.

The Romans were keen to extend viniculture to the far reaches of their empire so that established garrisons could enjoy wine without the expense of transporting it across Europe (the great Roman poet Horace noted that "No poem was ever written by a drinker of water," and no doubt no battle was ever won by one either). They planted vines from Colchester through Germany and France to southern Spain, so it was they who brought the now famous wine-producing regions into being (not including Colchester). Even if they couldn't conquer the world, wine drinking could.

HOMEBREWING EQUIPMENT

THERE ARE SOME basic items of equipment you will need to get you started and, luckily, some of these can be substituted for items that won't cost you a penny. It is possible to spend several weeks' wages on equipment to make beer, wine, and cider, but that's not necessary for the beginner. Learning the craft before you jump right in is the natural path. You should know how to use such items before investing significant amounts of money in them. You wouldn't buy a Formula One car after finding out you like driving on the freeway in your mom's station wagon.

All the equipment listed here can be found at specialized home-brew shops (see Directory, p. 287); sometimes an item will have to be ordered in.

FERMENTATION BUCKET

A fermentation bucket is rather self-explanatory: it's a bucket-shaped vessel in which you ferment your beer, wine, or cider. They normally come in three different sizes, for different jobs:

- 10 liters/2.2 gallons—generally used for fruit wines

- 15 liters/3.3 gallons—generally used for making small amounts of beer and cider

- 25 liters/5.5 gallons—generally used for making kegs of beer and cider

Professional fermentation buckets often come with a measurement scale in liters or gallons running up the side, making it far easier to top up with the correct amount of water. They can also come with an airlock (see p. 14), meaning that you can use them as a giant carboy, or demijohn (see p. 13). Top-of-the-range buckets can come with a fitted tap, which makes it much easier to decant the resulting brew.

If you are short on cash or unsure about the wisdom of making a big investment in making your own beer, wine, or cider, then all you need to produce a makeshift fermentation bucket is a little bit of imagination. However, a word of warning about colored plastic: the chemicals used in the coloring process can leach into the wort or must (names for beer or wine liquid during the fermentation process—see Glossary, p. 309), so if you intend to use the same vessel frequently it should be clear or white.

Trash bag in a cardboard box

This is simplicity itself. Wash a trash bag with a sterilizing solution and fit it inside a stout cardboard box. Once filled with the wort or must it can be loosely secured with an elastic band. Don't use cheap trash bags for this job as they have a tendency to split, which is not something you would wish to happen when the bag is full of sweet liquid.

A plastic storage box

These can be picked up from bargain stores at very little cost and come in all sorts of shapes and sizes, making them ideal for home-brewing. The downside is that they are often made from cheap plastic and there can be a danger of splitting, so they may make for a false economy if you intend to reuse.

Plastic food containers

When I buy my malt extract, I quite literally get it by the bucket load. This not only makes economic sense, but, as it comes in a small white bucket with a plastic lid, it means I also have one more vessel to brew with. Many food items when bought in bulk come in food-grade plastic buckets with sealable lids. If you have a contact within the catering industry it is always worth asking for any spares. You might also ask in your local health food shop; I have found mine to be most generous with their buckets. Local cafés and restaurants are another option.

SECONDARY

These are 4.5-liter/1-gallon plastic or glass containers normally used in the secondary stage of fermentation (the stage before bottling).

They are essential items when making wine and the beginner should buy at least one. Most of my collection have been obtained very cheaply second hand, even for free. Check auction websites such as eBay, decluttering ones such as ilovefreegal.org and freecycle, and also charity/second-hand shops.

Makeshift secondaries

I have successfully turned a 5-liter plastic juice container into a secondary. Get a sharp implement such as a Stanley knife and make two small incisions in the shape of a cross in the lid. Next, push your airlock (see below) into this cross. As long as the cross is small enough, it should be airtight; if not, some duct tape will help to secure it. The lid can then simply be screwed into place when needed.

AIRLOCKS AND BUNGS

An airlock allows the carbon dioxide created during the brewing process to escape while keeping out the outside air, which can contaminate the contents. The bung seals the airlock in place on the secondary.

Airlocks have become fairly standard in recent years and will always be made of plastic rather than the much more delicate glass. To use, half-fill with water and half a crushed Campden tablet (see p. 36 and Glossary). The water and tablet act as a barrier, keeping any airborne contaminants from infecting the brew yet still allowing CO_2 to escape. During the early stages of fermentation they bubble away very quickly and it is highly satisfying to know that with every bubble some more alcohol is being created. Which brings us to the secondary use for the airlock: it helps you see how your fermentation is coming along. The fermentation process will eventually slow down until few or no bubbles at all are produced.

A rubber or sometimes cork bung seals the airlock on the mouth of the secondary. Both the bung and airlock can be purchased very cheaply (see the Directory for details of suppliers).

BOTTLES

Both beer and wine bottles are available from homebrew shops, or online. The beauty of store-bought bottles is that you know they will be made of thick glass and will be perfect for the job. However, a cheaper and much more fun way of collecting bottles is to throw a bring-a-bottle party. I threw a beer-tasting party three years ago and all my friends turned up with bottled beers. After they left I made good use of their empties. You can also nip out early on a recycling morning and collect some of your neighbors' bottles, or simply keep your own. You'll soon have a big enough collection.

There are a few things to know if you are going to reuse beer or wine bottles. First, try not to use plastic as it can easily change shape and can also taint the contents with a plastic flavor. Also, avoid very thin glass bottles as these have a tendency to explode.

CORKS, CAPS, CAPPERS, AND CORKING MACHINES

When it comes to sealing beer bottles, you have two options. Either you go the professional route and buy a capping machine and crown caps, which always looks impressive when offering friends a drink; or you can use self-sealing swing-top bottles similar to the ones used by Grolsch (or just use old Grolsch bottles). They can be bought from larger health food shops, homebrewing suppliers, and over the Internet (see directory).

There is a similar choice to be made when it comes to sealing wine bottles. I don't use large swing-top bottles when I intend to age a wine for a few years, as air will get in eventually and begin to oxidize the wine. They are just about fine to use if you intend to drink your wine within a year, but still not advisable. They are, however, fine to use when making non-alcoholic drinks as these are often drunk not long after they are made.

Corks are the preferred and age-old method, and they allow the wine to breathe a little. I also believe that the experience of drinking wine should start in a tactile way when you first pick up the smooth glass bottle and open it with a pop! Which is why I prefer to use corks. The downside is getting them into the bottle in the first place. For that you will need an extra bit of equipment known as a corking machine.

At the cheap end of the scale is a hand corker, which can be hard work to use, and ironically you need to use a mallet to hammer the cork home. Next up the food chain is a two-handed machine that mechanically pushes the cork in for you. Last, and most expensive, is the floor-standing corker—a dream to use and well worth considering if you intend to bottle vast quantities of wine.

To finish off corked wine you can also buy a thin plastic sheath that shrinks to fit over the neck of the bottle when placed over boiling water, making the wine look much more professional.

When making larger amounts of wine the plastic push-in cork is an attractive option because of its ease of use and price tag. They can be bought cheaply in packs from most homebrew suppliers and are easy to sterilize then push into the bottles. The downside is that they are not very attractive to look at—enough, sometimes, to put people off homebrew (a plus, actually, if you want to drink it all yourself). Another drawback is getting them out of the bottle—once they're wedged in you need a cast-iron grip to dislodge them.

For ease of use you could also consider plastic screwcaps (generally only available over the Internet, or by reusing the caps from soft drink bottles) or metal ones. But in my experience, reusing any screwcaps has led to the wine being tainted.

For sparkling wine and cider, champagne corks are available. These are also made of plastic and are simply pushed into the bottle. Cider can be stored in champagne bottles and secured with push-in corks surrounded by a wire cradle, which not only adds an element of ceremony to the opening, it also keeps the sometimes volatile cider firmly inside the bottle.

Soft drinks can safely be placed in reused bottles, and although these do have to be sterilized, they don't have to be glass. What's more, cordials can be frozen if kept in plastic bottles. If placing the "champagne"-type drinks in plastic bottles, do keep them refrigerated and keep an eye on them as the bottles tend to expand, then explode.

BEER BARREL

When making quantities of cider or beer it can be easier to store the liquid in a specialized homebrewer's beer barrel—a fairly standard plastic container that holds 25 liters/5.5 gallons, with a tap on the bottom for pouring beer. Of course there are other barrels available made from stainless steel and in other sizes, but these plastic ones are the most common and are perfectly adequate for the home-brewer.

HYDROMETER

Only very experienced brewers, who through some kind of super-human ability can see the level of sugar in everything, will argue that you don't need a hydrometer. I think it is an invaluable piece of equipment. (As they test the level of sugar in a wort or must, they really should be called saccharometers—but I'm getting a bit geeky there.) It's important to be able to gauge the sugar level as not only does the information give you a good idea of the potential level of alcohol in your liquor at the start of the process, it also helps you know when the fermentation process has finished.

A hydrometer can be used in conjunction with a trial jar, which allows you to pour out a small amount of your wort or must to measure its density, thus avoiding the messy task of poking around in a secondary with some tweezers or your fingers trying to pull out the hydrometer.

Hydrometer readings should be taken over a few days and fermentation vessels should be moved to a warmer area (as cooler temperatures can halt a ferment), to assess whether or not fermentation has completed.

FUNNEL

Can I assume that you know what a funnel is? If you need a reminder, it's a tube with a wider top than bottom that allows you to pour liquid from a bigger vessel into a smaller vessel. They are not essential, but pouring without one, especially if you undertake homebrewing on your own, will help your carpets change color fairly quickly. They can be bought from homebrew or local hardware shops. I have three funnels of different sizes: a very large one for decanting fruit wines into secondaries; a medium-sized one that is useful when decanting flower wines into secondaries; and a smaller one that is ideal when decanting sloe gin/vodka, or when bottling beer.

MUSLIN/CHEESECLOTH

This is placed on top of the aforementioned funnel, or across a fermentation bucket, and is used to filter out any debris or plant matter. Fabric shops are often the cheapest source for muslin, and they sell it by the meter or yard. It is often thin so you will need to fold it over at least once; 2 meters/yards should be enough to start with. You could also consider using an old (clean) T-shirt.

NYLON BRUSH / BOTTLE CLEANER

Very useful when reusing bottles as it helps clean off any solid matter that may have collected on the insides of bottles. They generally come in two styles: a bendy one that helps reach all sides of a secondary, and a straight one for cleaning bottles.

SIPHONING TUBE

When your drink has finished fermenting it will leave some sediment at the bottom of your fermenting container. With a siphoning tube, liquid can be transferred without disturbing this sediment.

A length of rubber or plastic hose will do the job perfectly well. However, you can buy specialized siphoning tubes with small taps on them to help control the flow and with convenient little holes that rest above the line of sediment and prevent it from being sucked up without your having to hover your tube above it.

Of course there is a high end even when it comes to siphoning tubes. You can get what's known as an auto-siphoning tube. One end is submerged into your liquid and then you pull the tube out to start the pump action, which causes enough suction to start siphoning. I use the more expensive pump action as it eliminates any bacterial infection transmitted from the mouth, and once set in action you can just leave it and do something else. You don't have to stand around like a lemon holding the tube. (By the way, the traditional way of sterilizing your mouth is to take a glug of the finest whisky money can buy and gargle with it before sucking.)

SAUCEPAN / CAULDRON

There is no real need to run out and buy a specialized saucepan; whatever you already have should suffice. When faced with the larger-quantity recipes, using one, two, or three saucepans together will do the job of one large saucepan.

SCALE

It pays to have an accurate scale. A set with a bowl on top and a dial from 10g to 10kg (.5oz. to 20lb.) is all you need, and I have found that mechanical scales are better than electronic as you never need to replace a battery. They can often be picked up in thrift/second-hand shops for a steal.

LIQUID MEASURING CUPS

Two sizes of measuring cups are useful, one for big measures and one for small. Cups come in sizes from 1 cup/250ml and beer glasses are often 1 pint; using a combination of these you can measure pretty much anything you need to. Also, a standard-sized measuring cup generally holds 1 cup/250ml.

MEASURING SPOONS

Standard cutlery spoons tend to be of varying sizes, and as the amount of various additives to wine can make a difference to the final product it is well worth (although not essential) using professional measuring spoons, which can be bought fairly cheaply at kitchenware shops. I use a stainless-steel set as they can be easily cleaned.

LARGE SPOON

Believe it or not there is a specialized brewing spoon that you can buy from homebrew suppliers. The beauty of this spoon is that it is made of plastic and so is easy to sterilize. You can use a normal stainless-steel serving spoon or even a plastic ruler to do the same job. Wooden spoons can harbor bacteria, wild yeast, and other nasties that will contaminate so they are best avoided.

THERMOMETER

Various thermometers are available and all will help you to ensure your wort or must is at the ideal temperature before adding yeast, or while mashing. They range from normal ones made of glass to adhesive ones that stick to the side of your fermentation bucket and models that fit on the side of a mash tun.

LABELS

Either small stickers or more elaborate labels will save you from that head-scratching moment when you are simply not sure what beer you are drinking, or exactly what is bubbling away in your secondaries. Small adhesive labels can be bought very cheaply from a stationery shop, or cut-out bits of paper and glue will do the same job. I use old envelopes and glue.

As you progress in your homebrewing career you will start to wonder about acquiring more advanced equipment. The following are items you might use in an ideal world.

CIDER PRESS

Actually, if you want to make cider then a cider press is more of a necessity than a luxury: there really is no other way of crushing the apples. A cider press works by applying pressure on to the cut apples, which forces out their juice down a spout. Some use a juicer, but unless you have an industrial-sized one it can be easy to burn them out when making a gallon or more.

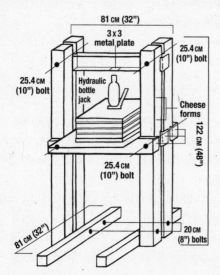

It's a rather expensive bit of kit, and beware: it is a false economy to buy cheap ones as they break. The cost can be reduced if you buy yours with a group of friends or with neighbors, as part of a brewing circle. In some villages men still go round door to door crushing apples in return for a share of those apples so that they can make their own cider for free. It would be possible to make your money back by reviving this tradition, and you could end up with enough cider for a year to boot.

Some brewing shops will hire a press out for a reasonable cost. See Directory, p. 287, to find your local supplier.

A host of presses are available at the high end, hydraulic ones that will press every last drop of juice from the apples. At the other end are simple screw presses that push down on the apples as you turn the screw—slightly less efficient, but they will get the job done.

There is, of course, one other option open to you: make your own press. You can find more information at

http://tinyurl.com/boozeforfreepress
http://tinyurl.com/boozeforfreepress2
http://tinyurl.com/boozeforfreepress3
http://tinyurl.com/boozeforfreepress4

WORT CHILLER

Made from copper piping, a wort chiller reduces the temperature of your brewed beer so that you can add yeast as soon as you have finished the boil (making your beer). This reduces the chance for rouge, wild yeasts, and bacteria to infect your brew.

There are two types of wort chiller available, a counterflow and an immersion chiller. They both do the same job but the counterflow does it more efficiently. The immersion chiller is made from a simple copper pipe that is bent into a spiral; as its name suggests, it is dunked into the wort and the cold water that runs through the

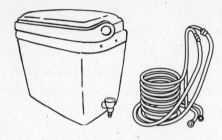

piping cools it. The counter-flow is also made from a copper spiral but it is housed in a hose pipe. Water is passed through the hose and wort is passed through the copper in the opposite direction. The wort comes out the other end at a similar temperature to the water going in.

Both chillers are available from homebrew stockists, but the DIY enthusiast would make a considerable saving by making one. Plans can be found on many of the specialized beer brewing websites featured in Part Three (see p. 305).

BOTTLE RINSER

Once you decide you love making your own booze or soft drinks you might want to upscale and start making a hundred bottles at a time, or more. Upscaling has its advantages, but the bottling stage can quickly become tedious and boring. Using a rinser can really help. It's a simple device that fits on to a tap. Water is forced into a jet stream (rather like a garden hose) whenever a bottle is pushed on to the device, and it is rinsed in seconds.

WARMING DEVICES

Much more popular in the days before central heating, heating pads plug in and either wrap around your secondary or fermentation bucket or heat it from below. They can be great to ensure your booze has fully fermented as they can kickstart a brew that has stopped due to low temperatures.

Many people instead wrap up their secondaries in a duvet or sleeping bag. Some even knit secondary-shaped sweaters to keep their fermentables warm through the coldest months.

BOTTLE RACK

Bottle racks are necessary when you start to make wine or beer on a larger scale: they not only keep your wine neat, they are also an ideal place to age wine. They can often be found very cheaply second-hand.

LITMUS STRIPS

Can be very useful to determine the level of acidity when making wine or cider. Simple litmus strips like the ones you had in science class at school will do the job.

MASH TUN

To release the sugars from a grain and grist a regular temperature must be maintained for an allotted period of time. The cheapest way of doing this is to use an insulated cooler. Some people will affix a little tap on the bottom of the cooler in order to be able to drain out the liquor.

Another, far cheaper, option is just to use a large saucepan and an oven or microwave. Basically all you need to do is keep the grains at the same temperature for an hour or so. This means you need an insulated box: an oven or a microwave!

MASHING AND SPARGE BAG

This is a bag that fits into your boiler/mash tun and holds the grain and/or hops. It has a mesh bottom, which means water can freely flow through it and the grain and/or hops do not end up in your mash tun/boiler.

HOMEBREWING INGREDIENTS

THE WRONG CHOICE of ingredients can drastically affect your final drink. Sometimes what would have been a perfectly good drink has been ruined for the sake of one small ingredient. It is undoubtedly true that getting to know your ingredients and using the best will yield great results. For example, Pinot Noir, Chardonnay, and Pinot Meunie grapes grown in the Champagne region are the best grapes for making white wine, and Burton-on-Trent has the best water for making beer.

These are two statements that many will nod at and a few will get angry about. Brewers and wine-makers are just like great chefs (and should be held in the same esteem): they will all swear by their preferred ingredients. Try telling Guinness that the Trent's water is better than the Liffey's, or someone from Asti in Piedmont, Italy that any sparkling wine made from the Moscato Bianco is inferior to a wine made from a mix of grapes from northern France. You might have a fight on your hands.

WATER

The one ingredient that all of your drinks will share is water, and it will matter to a greater or lesser extent what type of water you have depending on the type of drink you are making. I have found no great differences when using different waters to make wine or soft drinks. You should avoid using extremely hard water, heavily chlorinated water, and distilled water, and, of course, seawater or saltwater and stagnant water. By all means experiment with different waters if you have access to them and keep note of the results, but the changes will be subtle.

It will make a difference when making beers. A lot of talk in pubs has revolved around which water is best for which beer. The novice brewer need not worry too much about this unless their water has a high chlorine content (this should be filtered or boiled before use), and as with wine-making, very hard water is a problem too. As a crude rule of thumb, soft water works well for lagers and hard for ale, but both can be adjusted.

SUGAR

White refined cane sugar or sucrose is cheap and colorless, and there is nothing wrong with using white cane sugar for most of the wine and soft drink recipes in this book.

Unrefined sugar cane is another option I use. It is a brown-, almost gray-colored sugar that can be purchased from health food shops. I have used it with no discernible ill effects.

Brown sugars are not recommended when making white wines,

pale ales, or even lightly colored cordials. Both can lend your drinks a distinctive taste and a golden color. They can, however, be useful to add a little extra body to a wine.

Beer-makers often replace sugar with dried malt extract when brewing as it creates more body. Some even use it to prime their beer, reporting great results.

Corn sugar can be used and is widely available. Use in the same way as white sugar.

Honey can be used as a sugar, but it can impart a very strong flavor, depending on what the bees have been feeding on. A light flower honey is often used when the maker wants the flavors of other ingredients to be discernible.

YEAST

The basic function of yeast, as charmingly described to me one rainy afternoon by a Scottish brewer in Bo'ness, is that it eats sugar, pisses alcohol, and farts out carbon dioxide. Which is sort of true, and it is the very least a homebrewer needs to know. Ensuring that your yeast is happy means you will be able to make alcohol. Just having this knowledge of yeast already means you know more than everyone who made booze pre-1680, who thought the fermentation process had more to do with the gods.

What actually happens during fermentation is that at least twenty-five enzymes secreted by yeast cells through a series of chemical reactions act as catalysts to turn sugar molecules into alcohol and carbon dioxide gas.

Yeast is added to wort or must in a process that is known as pitching the yeast. The first thing this fungus does is start to multiply vigorously, and for this it needs energy, hence the addition of sugar. Yeast first enters what is known as a lag period; like some sci-fi foe they first test an area to see if it is suitable for colonization. After this period they start to reproduce. If the environment is optimal they can theoretically double in number every hour, becoming 4 in three hours, 64 in twelve hours, and 4,096 in a day until they reach a density of 150,000,000 per milliliter of liquid. At this point a steady population is maintained until all remaining oxygen and nutrients are used up or the alcohol they have produced kills them off.

Your job is to make sure the yeast has the best conditions when multiplying. In the initial stages of fermentation this means keeping your must or wort at 21–23°C (70–75°F), which will favor the yeast you have added; during secondary fermentation the ideal temperature is above 14°C (57°F). In practice this means moving your fermenting booze from a warmer room to a cooler room, depending on at what point it is fermenting.

Yeast is normally supplied in a silver foil packet in a dormant state. Ideally you need to make a yeast starter to wake it up rather than just sprinkle the yeast over the top. A starter will get to work quickly and result in rapid fermentation, ensuring that all the flavors and aromas from your ingredients are captured and don't have time to dissipate. It also means you can check that your yeast is still viable. If you just sprinkle the yeast on the top and it has died due to poor storage in the warehouse or any other factor beyond your control you might not know until your wine, beer, or cider has become infected. Making a starter is like growing plants from seed you have saved; it will have time to acclimatize to its new environment and will be much healthier for doing so.

To make a starter, first boil enough water for two mugs of tea in a kettle. Make one cup for yourself, then third-fill another cup and top it up with cold water. If you want to get your thermometer out and measure it you are ideally looking for a temperature of about 38°C (100°F). Gently stir your yeast into the water, adding half a teaspoon of sugar. Leave covered in a warm place for between fifteen minutes and an hour, then add to your must or wort.

Do not underestimate the importance of yeast when making booze. It can make a huge difference in terms of taste. Two identical drinks with this one ingredient altered can be worlds apart. An example of this is baker's yeast v. ale yeast. The first time I made nettle beer I used baker's yeast and ended up with horrible-tasting beer that looked like muddy water. Baker's yeast does not settle down in the wort and clouds form every time it's moved; it also has a low alcohol tolerance and starts to die before it has fermented all the sugars.

Strangely enough, bread, ale, and wine yeast are variants of the same sugar fungus, namely *Saccharomyces cerevisiae* (and S. *cerevisiae* var. *ellisoideus*, the variant wine form). The difference comes from the fact that each strain has been cultivated over time to do a specific job and to work in various environments. Baker's yeast does not need to cultivate flavors or ferment all the sugars as it is only active for a short while, not even a day. Ale yeast, on the other hand, needs to be active for a week or more, must ferment all the sugars, and also needs to impart as much flavor as possible. Wine yeast needs to be active for months, sometimes years.

These differences are only the tip of the iceberg: there are over six million strains of yeast, all of which do slightly different things. The home booze-maker need not worry about knowing their names, but it does help to get the right yeast for the right job. There are wine yeasts that have been cultured to make a port, a sherry, a red wine, a dry white wine, a champagne; there are yeasts that can make the whole spectrum of beers; then again many craft brewers will have cultured their own specific yeast. Luckily, life has been made a lot easier by homebrew suppliers. Instead of learning the Latin names, all we need to know is what is printed on the packet. Match up what you are fermenting with the right yeast for the job, give it the perfect conditions, and you will make the best booze possible. Most booze-makers will be happy with results from straightforwardly matching ale yeast with ales, white wine yeast with white wines, cider yeast with ciders, and red wine yeast with red wines.

It is possible not to use yeast in a recipe—that is, it is possible to rely on wild yeasts, which are omnipresent in our atmosphere. Many wine-makers in the old world won't add yeast. They crush the grapes, get the juice, and let the wild yeasts get on with it. Each year they take the grape skins and place them as a mulch around the vines. Over time this changes the natural mix of wild yeasts in the area, favoring the *Saccharomyces* strain above all else. This process has taken centuries, however; the home booze-maker who endeavors to create the same in his back garden in just a couple of years is hopeful at best. Reliance on wild yeast is like going drunk to a loud, packed nightclub in the hope of finding the future Mr. or Mrs. Right: it might happen, but the chances are minimal.

Having said that, whenever I make non-alcoholic champagnes

wild yeasts do seem to take hold very quickly and work very well. For the champagnes it doesn't matter so much whether or not the yeast "eats" all the sugar as the only reaction you are looking for is it eating some and therefore getting some carbonation, and many wild yeasts do at least that.

YEAST NUTRIENT

Grapes and some cider apples have everything in the perfect balance needed to feed yeast and therefore make the perfect alcohol. All other fruits, vegetables, and flowers don't, and this needs to be compensated for.

When yeast does not have enough food it will grow for a while then give up. Once that happens the wine or beer will not reach its full alcohol potential and it becomes vulnerable to spoilage. Adding yeast nutrient gives your yeast the nitrogenous matter it needs to continue functioning.

Yeast nutrient can be purchased as a powder, and one teaspoon per 4.5 liters/1 gallon is normally enough to prevent yeast malnutrition. Some also use malt extract for red wines, Marmite, or even vitamin B tablets.

PECTOLASE

Also known as "pectolaze" and "pectinol," or by its actual name "pectic enzyme," this additive is deployed when using fruits and vegetables with a high pectin content to help rid the must of a pectin haze.

Pectin is a gelling agent; it's what sets jam. So pectin is great for jam-making, but who wants any kind of solid in a wine, or rather solids clumping together in suspension in your otherwise perfect wine? What pectolase does is eat this haze. To be more accurate, it breaks down the pectin, converting the haze into sugars, which are then turned into alcohol. Buy from good homebrew stockists.

CAMPDEN TABLETS

Campden tablets provide a measured amount of sulfur dioxide, which helps kill off any wild yeast or bacteria that might be present in your must or wort. This helps the yeast you have added to get to work without any competition and also reduces spoilage. One Campden tablet contains around 0.44g (or 50ppm in 4.5 liters/ 1 gallon of liquid) of sulphite. When you pick up a wine bottle and it reads "contains sulphites," this is what it means.

It can be a contentious issue when wine- and cider-makers meet. Some will add up to three tablets per 4.5 liters, others just half a tablet. Many will use none. They are normally added to the must before fermentation at a rate of half to one tablet per 4.5 liters, then sometimes after the first racking (see p. 43) at the same rate. Some also add between half and two tablets to a finished wine to halt fermentation.

The recipes in this book don't enforce the use of Campden tablets as I believe it is up to the individual to find his or her own path when it comes to sulphite use.

CITRIC ACID

All fruits contain a certain amount of acid. Vegetables, herbs, and leaves don't contain any, therefore it has to be added. Citric acid works as a natural preservative, and in wine-making it inhibits the development of hostile bacteria and encourages the activity of wine yeast. It can be found naturally in citrus fruits, hence their addition to many recipes. It can also be bought in a powdered form from all good homebrew stockists. One teaspoon of citric acid is roughly equivalent to four tablespoons of lemon juice, or the juice of one lemon.

OTHER ACIDS

Tartaric and malic acids are found naturally in grapes, and malic acid is the predominant acid in apples. They also act as a natural preservative and give extra tartness to wines and ciders.

TANNIN

Tannin is present in the skins of fruits such as grapes, apples, plums, and elderberries and imparts bite and zest to a good wine. It is responsible for that impression of dryness you get after drinking wine. Without tannin many wines can become flat and insipid; too much can make a wine taste astringent—rather like biting into an acorn (which contains high levels of tannin) or drinking an overly stewed cup of tea. Tannin is a useful addition to flower wines, lending them a depth they would otherwise lack.

Tannin can be bought from all good homebrew stockists in a powdered form. Although for many of the recipes I have recommended using half a cup of strong tea instead, and there is one simple reason for this: its availability. I have a girlfriend who frequently leaves half-drunk cups of tea around the house and it seems a shame to let them go to waste. Of course it's a much cheaper option too. Half a cup of strong tea is roughly equivalent to a teaspoon of tannin in powdered form.

BEST PRACTICE

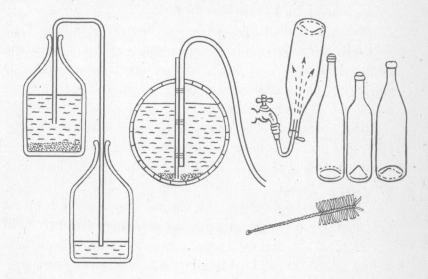

BACK IN THE MISTS of time when it was thought that fermentation was a gift from the gods, brewing practices must have been enough to give present-day beer-, cider-, and wine-makers heart palpitations. These days there are best-practice guidelines that if followed should decrease the chances of something going wrong.

THE JOYS OF CLEANING AND STERILIZING

There are no two ways about it, most problems with the making of alcoholic and non-alcoholic drinks can be put down to one specific practice being rushed or ignored: sterilization. It certainly pays to start enjoying the cleaning process. Doing it in company or putting on the radio can really help pass the time.

Bacteria is everywhere. We are hosts to millions of them. If all the bacteria in and on our bodies upped sticks and left one morning we would fall apart. A tiny colony from such an abundance can easily find its way into your fermenting booze, so observing good cleanliness is vital to avoid problems.

The lower the alcohol content the more strenuously you have to clean your stuff. That is not to say you can be lackadaisical because you are making wine instead of beer, just that you don't have to be quite so meticulous.

Before you sterilize you must clean your equipment. It is best practice to clean straight after use, but in reality it can often be an afterthought; sometimes you return to your equipment months later to find a family of mold has taken up residence. Scrub your equipment with a soft clean cloth and soapy water and be careful not to scratch it. Check the outside of secondaries and fermentation buckets: you can be scrubbing away on the inside of glass secondaries only to discover it's the outside that's filthy. Specially shaped nylon brushes can be used to get to the hard-to-reach parts of your equipment. Check all over your equipment for deposits and make sure it is all visibly clean. For really stubborn stains you may need to soak overnight using 25g (1 fl. oz) of bleach in 4.5 liters/1 gallon of water, or a sterilizing solution as directed. If deposits build up on a piece of equipment and cannot be washed off despite repeated soaking, that item should not be used for brewing again as it might harbor harmful bacteria. And once you have cleaned, make sure you rinse thoroughly.

Household bleach (but *not* thick toilet bleach) can be used to sterilize as described above, but most homebrewers use Star San or Iodophor. Fermentation buckets can be filled with solutions of either (not both), and the rest of your utensils can be put inside. Both Star San or Iodophor need to be handled properly, and you will need to follow the instructions as provided.

Once sterilized and rinsed, if left for a day or longer, rather than go through the whole sterilizing process again a trick I have adopted from iconic wine-maker C. J. J. Berry is to keep a squeeze-action spray bottle full of this solution to squirt onto equipment when you need to be doubly sure. You will of course need to rinse thoroughly again as any residue bleach can impart horrible metallic flavors to your booze.

When not in use, your secondaries can be lightly plugged with cotton balls to stop any insects from getting in (whatever you may think, they will always find a way to your booze). Bigger bits of equipment can be covered with plastic sheeting to prevent any contamination—but remember, if left for any length of time, equipment should be re-cleaned and sterilized as directed above.

A useful recap:

- Clean then sterilize everything that touches the fermenting booze, such as secondaries, thermometer, hydrometer, spoons, and bottles.

- Always rinse after cleaning and sterilizing.

- Beware of scratches as they can harbor bacteria.

STRAINING WINES

Many fruit wines at some point will require straining. This means getting a piece of finely woven cloth and pouring the must through it. It can be a very messy and awkward job with bits of fruit splattering all over the place, and there's the possibility of losing some, maybe most of your must. The job can be made easier with the right equipment and a bit of forethought. It also helps to have someone else there.

If straining from one large fermentation bucket to another a square of thick muslin cloth or cheesecloth can be pegged onto the bucket. At least eight clothespins should keep even the heaviest fruits or vegetables from falling in.

Fruits with high pectin levels should not be squeezed (as tempting as this might be) as this can cause a pectin haze inside the bottle.

By the way, don't expect wine-making to be a neat process. Even if you think you have a hand steadier than the world's greatest brain surgeon, don't think you will be able to pour elderberry wine from a fermenting bucket into a secondary without some splashes. Our land-lord will probably charge us a small fortune for all the stains I've made over the years from homebrewing—stains that could have been avoided if I'd put down some plastic sheeting or even newspaper. Sometimes, too, a fermenting bucket or secondary full of fermenta-bles can get overly excited and froth out, taps on beer barrels can leak, and bottles can explode. Think carefully about where you are making your booze and try to minimize possible damage.

If spills do happen on carpet, blot out as much as you can with paper towels or a dishcloth, then dilute with water, push the liquid into one area, blot, and repeat if necessary. Clothes should be soaked as soon as possible to minimize damage. On other surfaces such as linoleum and wood, diluted bleach might have to be used.

After a while muslin cloths will discolor. To avoid this, try washing off as much sediment, pulp, detritus, or debris as you can, then soak in water. They can then be thrown in with your towels and other whites on a hot wash and hung out to dry. The UV of sunlight can help as a bleaching agent.

RACKING

The word "racking," derives from the Provençal *raca*, meaning the debris of pressed grapes, and *arraca*, meaning to draw wine off, and is the process of drawing wine or beer off the dead yeast or sediment and other deposits, also known as the lees, left by the fermentation process. Wine or beer left on the lees can take on an unpleasant taste. This is why we siphon booze, to get as much as we can out of the fermentation vessels while leaving behind the dead stuff.

Beers are OK to rack just the once from the fermentation bucket to the bottles or keg, but as wine stays on its lees for longer it needs to be racked a few times. Racking wine should take place in the first four weeks, then again as required. Racking is required when the sediment builds up to anything over 5mm (quarter of an inch).

To rack, place the secondary or fermentation bucket higher than the container you wish to transfer your liquor to and place the end of a siphoning tube just above the lees (often siphoning tubes will have a hole just above where the lees sit making this job easier).

Suck on the other end and allow the liquor to pour into the container. You will need to tip the secondary toward the end of the process so that all the clear liquor is transferred. Throughout be very careful not to disturb the lees as doing so will defeat the objective of the process.

BOTTLING

When bottling you should siphon the booze off the lees and into bottles. It can be easier to siphon into a large sterilized pitcher and then pour the booze into the bottles. Fill wine bottles up to the base of the neck to ensure that a cork can be pushed in without disturbing the wine. Beer bottles should be filled to leave 2cm (1in) of room in the neck.

LABELING

If you have the sort of mind that can remember pi to a hundred decimal places you really don't have to worry too much about labeling. You will no doubt be able to recall what is in every bottle by the subtle differences in the light as it refracts through the liquid and reflects off each contour of the bottle neck; you will remember the day you bottled it, even the hour, by a mere whiff of the pollen grains, undetectable by the eye but not the nose, stuck to the side of the bottle.

For everyone else, finding an unlabeled bottle can be a real pain. A label can tell you if it is sweet or dry wine, a good or bad bottle, if it's wine or vinegar, beer or cider, if it's ready or could do with another month to mature, and whatever other details you might choose to record. Furthermore, labels can make an immediate impact in terms of the appearance of a bottle. The French say that the first taste is in the eye. The palate expects something different from a wine served from a bottle with half a moldy label hanging off it and the words "Elderflower '08" scratched on with ballpoint pen than from a wine served with a pristine label supporting an image of elderflowers blowing in the breeze and the words "Elderflower wine, made from elderflowers growing next to the flowing waters of the River Avon, picked on a bright, dew-soaked spring morning in 2008."

In a bygone age, to get a decent label you would have to buy a job lot; these days all you need is some imagination, a computer and printer, and a tube of glue. If using a Word document, a page can be set into two columns by clicking on Page Layout/Columns, which will then hold four labels at a size of 10cm by 12cm (4in by 5in)—a perfect size for any beer or wine bottle. I have found that using PVA glue makes peeling the labels off, when the time comes, much easier.

The level of detail you wish to put on the label is up to you. The name of the drink and the month and year in which it was bottled is the minimum requirement.

KEEPING RECORDS

After tucking into a vintage elderberry port that you have slightly adapted, your friend turns to you and says, "This is great, can I have he recipe?" It's all in my head, you think, until you sit to write it down, which is when the cold realization hits you and you have to admit that your head is not such a great storage device.

Taking accurate notes allows you to recreate successful recipes; it also means you can learn by mistakes and start to experiment a little more. Keeping a little notebook or a spreadsheet filled with details about what ingredients you used and when you picked something and where will make next year's task so much easier. I have even heard of a woman who kept notes on how much she was paying for sugar so that she could get it for the cheapest price possible.

STORING YOUR FERMENTING BOOZE

It can be tricky to find a suitable place for your fermenting booze, especially if you live in a small apartment. Ideally the fermentation bucket or secondary needs to be somewhere warm for the initial stages of fermentation, then somewhere slightly cooler for secondary fermentation. My secondaries are on shelves in my hall, and my fermentation buckets sit in my warm office.

The most important thing is that you choose a site that does not experience big fluctuations in temperature, which means a loft or attic is a daft place and a cellar a better one (have you ever heard of a wine loft?). Also, think of others who live in your house. The continual bubbling of airlocks might get rather annoying if the noise is coming from right outside their bedroom door.

STORING YOUR DRINKS

A wine rack is the traditional place to store wine, and crates for beer. Liqueurs should be kept in a cool dark place such as a drink cabinet, herbs for herb teas should go into airtight containers, and soft drinks generally go in the fridge.

NOTES ON FORAGING

WHEN I AM OUT foraging I often drift away and start to daydream about how our ancestors lived. I can almost see them with bags made from lime bark over their shoulders picking nuts and berries. What was so commonplace centuries ago has become an activity enjoyed by just a few. It is my hope that this will be reversed, that over the next few decades the numbers out foraging will increase, if only so that others can share in the joy I feel when undertaking this most primeval of activities.

GETTING OVER THE FEAR OF FORAGING

Unfortunately, our world seems to have taken a turn toward being scared of anything that does not come to us wrapped in cellophane. One of the first steps potential foragers have to take is to rid themselves of this fear. I have encountered people who were fearful of picking cherries from a tree, and when I was seen picking and eating them I was informed that I was eating poisonous fruit! It would seem that in just a few short generations we have gone from hunter-gatherers to sedentary idiots. Of course, it is not the fault of the individual. Busy lives mean it's easier to teach children to be wary than to learn about what is growing around them. Even I was taught not to eat from trees. Also, years of consumerism mean that we now recognize logos before leaf patterns and jingles before smells, making it somehow easier to trust something that is being sold to us than it is to pick something "a dog might have peed on."

The first step to getting over this fear is to acknowledge that we do know more than we think we do about our native plants. I always ask the people who come on my educational foraging walks if they have ever foraged before. Most of the time half the group will say that they haven't. I then ask if they have ever picked a blackberry or an apple, and everyone says yes, they have. Indeed most of us as children will have picked and eaten something wild.

That is not to say there are no plants out there that will make you ill or kill you. Dichotomous thinking has to be adopted by the forager, and knowing what will kill you and what won't is a good first step. Don't forget the little saying that goes, "There are old foragers, there are bold foragers, but there are no old bold foragers."

Of the many wild plants mentioned in this book there are only two that I think could be mistaken for something deadly, namely yarrow and alexanders, both of which flower in a similar way to hemlock. However, when you start to think carefully about the differences you will soon see that alexanders generally flower much earlier than hemlock, and when it does its flowers are yellow; that yarrow has very distinctive feathery leaves; and that hemlock smells like mouse urine. It's only when you learn about the differences that you can start to be confident about what you pick.

For the really nervous forager, or the forager who knows nothing, it is advisable only to pick plants that can't be mistaken for anything else. The easiest way to do this is to stick to picking plants that are already familiar, and this will help to increase confidence and knowledge. Blackberries and apples fall into this category for most, and both make excellent drinks. Apples and blackberries have countless varieties, so to begin with, why not set your sights on learning the differences between just some of them? You'll soon find yourself becoming more familiar with the plant world.

If you are then hooked, the next stage in teaching yourself would be to look at more common plants, ones that grow almost all year round. Perhaps try to tell the difference between a dead nettle and stinging nettle, or correctly identify a dandelion (which is harder than it sounds: many plants, such as sow thistles and hawkweeds, can easily be mistaken for dandelions). The more you put yourself out there and do this, the more you will familiarize yourself with the plants around you and the more confident you will become to pick them and turn them into booze. Finding a good field guide is, of course, essential (see Further Reading for suggestions) as you should *never* put something in your mouth unless you are 100 percent sure you know what it is.

WHERE TO LOOK

Most of the plants, berries, and nuts mentioned in this book can be found in parks, on wasteground at field edges, and even (with permission) in people's gardens. One of the biggest mistakes people make when first going out foraging for food is to go to a woodland or out into the countryside: both are great for a walk but not always the best when it comes to finding things to brew. Woodlands are great places for fungi, wood avens, and wood sorrel, but for the would-be brewer there are only a handful of trees worth looking out for and all of them can be found in municipal parks. All of the produce mentioned in this book can be found growing in unkept corners of suburban and urban neighborhoods. So unless you live near or in the woods, have a look round your local area before you go further afield—unless, of course, you just want an excuse to spend a day out in the country.

Successful foragers are opportunists and will always have their eyes open, scanning their surroundings. I find that whenever I go to a new town or city and point out fruit trees or other food to the locals they often say they have never noticed them before, despite walking past them every day. I have found that the best places to look for fruit are parks, people's gardens (again, with their permission), abandoned gardens, country parks, and wasteground. Other food such as herbs and shrubs can be found on river banks, at the edges of woodlands, on organically farmed field perimeters, along the coast, and on disturbed soil.

POLLUTION

Older wild food books will warn against foraging by roadsides due to higher levels of lead in the plants. Some foragers took this further and advocated not picking nettles in any town or city. Thankfully, nowadays, due to the use of unleaded gas, lead is less of a problem. I do forage on roadsides but not on very busy roads and never on freeways. This is partly due to higher levels of pollution but also because foraging near traffic is slightly dangerous and not the most comfortable of experiences.

Of the pollutants foragers are much more likely to come into contact with, pesticides rank pretty high. Weeds (or wild plants) are often sprayed in early spring, so look out for white marks on the plants and leave withered-looking plants. I have experienced mild pesticide poisoning, which left me very weak with flu-like symptoms for a fortnight; it wasn't the most pleasant of experiences. I now make sure the areas I forage have not been sprayed before I go there. On farmland, even organic farmland, it is a little more difficult as farmers can sometimes be less than willing to share that information with you. Rather than approach them with an e-mail or a phone call I have found them a lot more willing to tell you face to face where and when they spray, especially if you offer them a bottle of booze in return.

Another potential hazard you have to watch out for may lie hidden. Plants growing on old industrial sites, old gas stations, and even old mines can accumulate chemicals from contaminated soil, some, such as nettles, more than others. Local knowledge is the key to finding out about what an area used to be. Failing that, history books or the laminated plaques you often see in country parks or by river walks can contain enough relevant information.

FORAGING AND THE ECOSYSTEM

Foraging in the same places year after year helps you to observe your impact on an area. Novice foragers may not be aware of their impact in the first year, but over time, as there is less and less to pick, it will become very clear. The forager should be putting back as much as he or she is taking, quashing the shouts of "Foragers strip the countryside bare"—a nonsense considering there are countries where many people forage and have done so for years without harming the ecosystem. Industrial farming with all its pesticides and herbicides and destruction of habitat to create ever larger fields has had a much bigger impact than foraging ever will.

That is not to say that foragers shouldn't be mindful of what they are picking. A great rule of thumb to ensure that there is enough of your plant is to look for four of them and only pick the leaves or parts of the fourth. If you can't find four then try elsewhere, or don't pick. You could then return to the spot next year and you might find the plant is settling in nicely and has spread out. Therefore there will be at least four of the plant. When digging up roots, try planting the seeds of whatever you have dug up, and only pick about a third of the leaves of a plant. When picking fruit, think of the birds and leave the fruit that you can't reach easily.

It is also possible to have a positive impact on the environment when foraging. For instance, most sources will agree that only the top leaves of nettles should be harvested as these are the tastiest. Only it goes beyond that, as by leaving the rest of the plant you are also leaving a potential home for over forty species of insect, including butterflies, that live their whole lifecycles on a nettle. Also, as the nettle will grow two "heads" in place of the one you picked you will actually be increasing insect habitat.

Plants such as Japanese knotweed and Himalayan balsam are well-known as invasive species. They are like that irritating friend; once they have appeared somewhere, they are very difficult to eradicate. If you wish to try to rid yourself of knotweed, then it can be a costly business—knotweed will even grow through asphalt and concrete. This plant has spread across much of Europe and the United States so imagine what it would cost to rid the *world* of it. Harvesting the plant year after year—and it can be used to make a decent ale and wine (see p. 131)—will start to weaken it. It normally takes about five to ten years of constant harvesting to weaken the plant sufficiently for it to die off, and in the meantime you are keeping it from growing. Knotweed is still legal in some states, but I'd advise heavily against planting it. In the United Kingdom, it is impossible to get a mortgage on a house with knotweed growing in it. I assume it's only a matter of time before a similar practice will befall North American mortgage lenders.

FORAGING AND THE LAW

There are some state laws that prohibit foraging in certain areas, so check before foraging in municipal parks and other state-owned areas. Mind you, Steve Brill was arrested in Central Park before being employed by it; it was enough to be the making of him. Also, always ask permission before foraging on someone's land.

NOTES ON GROWING YOUR OWN

E VEN THE TINIEST GARDEN or community plot can be used to grow crops that can be turned into booze for free or at practically no cost.

SEED COLLECTING

Harvesting seeds from your plants is the best way to ensure a free crop year after year. Plants start to naturalize to the area they are grown in, therefore collecting seeds also means better crops will be produced year after year, and by selecting seeds from the biggest, most disease-resistant, most prolifically cropping plants you really will be on track to get maximum yield from your crops.

The process of seed collecting will deepen your plant knowledge, if only because you'll be witnessing the whole magical lifecycle of your plants. What's more, if you collect seed from old and heritage breeds you can play a part in the conservation of strains that would otherwise disappear. However, you should not save seed from F1 hybrids as these are plants that are produced by crossing two specific parent plants and their offspring do not generally grow true to the original plant.

All plants want to reproduce and it is just a question of knowing how and when they do this in order to collect seed. The following table gives some pointers for some commonly used crops; others can easily be researched.

Plant name	What it looks like when the seed is ready	Season	Notes	Seed lifespan
Broad beans (fava beans)	Pods will go brown/black	Late summer/ autumn, first year	Look out for insect holes	5 years
Burdock	Spiky "burrs" will appear during the second year and will become loose on the plant	Late summer to early winter	Burrs are very sticky and just walking through a field full of burdock is the easiest way to harvest seed	5 years
Carrots	When the large umbels that appear from the carrot have gone brown and dry	Summer/ autumn, second year	In colder areas, dig up carrots, cut off foliage, and store in sand before replanting the following year	1–3 years
Chilies	When fully grown	Summer/ autumn	Wash hands after handling chilies!	5 years
Squash/ pumpkin	When grown to full size	Autumn	Separate carefully from the pulp	5 or more years
Parsnips	As with carrots	Summer, second year	Short shelf life	1–3 years

STORING SEED

Once collected, the seeds will need to be cleaned of all plant debris and dried in order to be stored before planting out the following year. To dry, place on newspaper in a well-ventilated room, turning once. Plants such as carrots and parsnips can be dried by hanging the whole plant upside down and letting the seeds drop off.

Once you have harvested your seeds they should be kept in airtight containers away from sunlight in a cool, dry area. Carefully label your seeds and include the harvest date so that you don't end up trying to plant seeds that simply won't germinate due to their age.

PROPAGATING FROM CUTTINGS: SOFTWOOD

When taking softwood cuttings, the morning is the best time because that's when the plant has a higher moisture content. A softwood cutting is basically a cutting from the fresh new growth. Take a 15cm (6in) shoot, pull off the lower leaves, and clean below the leaf joint. Put the stem into a growing medium of perlite, coir, and sand. Water very well and tie a clear plastic bag around the pot—this helps to keep heat and moisture in. Keep warm and re-pot after about six weeks, by which time you should be rewarded with a brand-new plant. If you take a number of cuttings it should increase your chances of success.

PROPAGATING FROM CUTTINGS: HARDWOOD

Grapevines and fruit bushes can be multiplied using hardwood cuttings taken from perennials that have grown all they will for that season (this is normally during late autumn to midwinter).

Make a cut at a slight angle with your secateurs just below a node (the angle is for no reason other than to help you remember at a glance which way up your cutting should be). A typical hardwood cutting, after trimming of the thin tip, should be about 20cm (8in) long.

Take off a 1–2cm (half-inch) sliver of bark from the bottom of your cutting and dip it into hormone rooting compound. This is optional, but results will be more consistent if you do so. Dig a trench and plant your cuttings to a depth of about 15cm (6in), back-fill with a good-quality compost, and heel them in. The area should be free-draining and sheltered.

After heavy frosts check that the ground has not cracked and come away from your cutting. Keep well watered throughout the spring.

TREE PLANTING

The first thing to think about when planting trees is how the tree will look when it is fully grown. This may sound obvious, but you'd be surprised by how many people plant a tree too close to the house, so that as it grows it blocks out light, or simply slap-bang in the middle of a small garden so that it eventually swamps everything else.

The best time to plant a tree is from the autumn to the spring, although in harsh winters waterlogged or frozen ground should be avoided at all costs. I have found autumn the best time as the tree still has a bit of growth and will set some roots to see it through the winter months.

Trees need soil that is free-draining, which means avoiding any wet or waterlogged patches. They will also benefit from good rich soil, free of weeds and containing plenty of compost. Native trees such as beech and birch should be fine on most soils, apart from very dry soils, so they should not be left to dry out.

Before planting, soak the root ball in water and dig a hole that is a little deeper than the soil mark where the tree was originally grown. Spread out the roots and drive in a stake close to the tree. Backfill, adding some fresh compost. Tread in firmly and water well. Add mulch around the tree to keep back weeds.

SOIL

The soil is by far the most important part of your garden or allotment. Poor soil means poor plants, so it is essential to keep your soil as healthy as possible. To do so you must first find out what type of soil you have and ascertain if any changes are necessary. The easiest way to do this is to ask your neighboring gardeners. If the first reaction is a sound, especially if that sound takes the form of a long guttural groan, followed by a few expletives, you will know you have some work ahead of you. If you can't find out your soil type from your neighbor, take a handful of moist soil and squeeze it to the size of a golf ball. If it feels smooth and slippery you have the most common soil type, clay. If it feels silky and powdery you have silty soil. If it feels gritty you have sandy soil.

Clay soil holds on to nutrients but can be tough to work with. Hard, compacted clay soil should be dug over in the winter months so that the frosts can help break it down. Manure and/or compost (see next section) should be incorporated into the soil during the autumn (this also helps to remove any weeds). Clay soil should not be worked when it's wet. Not only is it a heavy, hard job, it can break your tools (and your back) and damage the soil structure.

Sandy soil does not hold on to nutrients, but plants such as carrots and parsnips quite like it as they can easily push their roots down. For other plants the soil texture can be improved by adding compost and manure. As sandy soil does not hold on to moisture either, mulching around your plants will really help.

Silty soil can be mineral-rich as it's made from ground-down rocks. Small amounts of clay will improve composition.

You'll also need to be familiar with your soil's acidity level, which is key to whether certain plants suffer or thrive. You can use a simple pH test kit from your garden center, or perhaps a quick look at the weeds that are growing will suffice. Nettles, bracken, marestail, and daisies all like acidic soil whereas sow thistles, henbane, and black mustard are lovers of alkaline.

COMPOSTING

A good gardener will always have a compost heap. As my Australian mate Nev always says, "Anything that once lived can be composted"—which often makes me wonder what's in his compost. Many books have been written on the subject of composting, but if you keep to these few simple rules, you can't really go wrong:

- If your heap gets too wet, add dry material such as ripped-up cardboard.

- Try not to add too much of one thing.

- From time to time, wee on your heap.

- Turn your compost as much as possible.

- Don't add cooked food as this can attract vermin.

- Don't add too much woody material as it won't break down.

- Leave out weed seeds and roots unless mashed up so that they can never germinate again.

- Don't put too much citrus fruit into your bin as worms hate it.

And beware: the homebrewer, after adding fruit and other sticky material, may end up attracting his worst enemy, the vinegar fly. If they do become a problem and make their way into your brewery there are two solutions. The quickest and easiest is to wet some newspaper and place this over the top of your heap or bin, but don't do this too often as it affects the compost. The second, which can be employed simultaneously, is to get a carnivorous plant such as a sundew, pitcher plant, or a Venus fly trap that will munch up all the flies. I keep such a plant in my brewing area at all times and it does noticeably keep down the number of flies.

Compost bins can be made by nailing four pallets together, or they can be bought cheaply from local municipal authorities.

PESTS AND DISEASES

Every gardener at some point in his or her gardening life will harbor thoughts about mass genocide of the slug population. It is inevitable that some of your fruit and veg will get eaten by them. Indeed, the garden or allotment can be a very unforgiving place for plants: it's not just the slugs that can destroy them but a whole array of insects, diseases, and fungi. This trio sometimes seems to have it in for us, trying to turn our best efforts into compost or disease-ridden rubbish. Fortunately, it is not all one-sided. We can fight back.

The first line of offense, as has just been discussed, is keeping your soil as healthy as possible. Healthy soil means healthier plants less prone to infections and disease. You will need to feed your soil from time to time, and the easiest and cheapest way to do this is to compost comfrey leaves and to top-dress your growing fruit and vegetables. Comfrey is a very effective plant feed, containing many of the minerals plants need to be healthy.

The next step is to work with nature rather than against it by attracting insect-eating predators and beneficial insects. This can be achieved by growing the right plants around your crops. Plants that will attract beneficial insects include Phacelia, dill, fennel, cilantro, tansy, dandelion, yarrow, lemon balm, parsley, lavender, spearmint, Queen Anne's lace, and buckwheat. To attract bigger predators such as frogs, small mammals, and birds to your garden or allotment you could consider putting in a small pond, or hanging up a bird feeder.

Over the winter months hedgehogs will be appreciative of twig and leaf piles and the occasional unkempt area around your plot.

Last, most plants will benefit from crop rotation. This basically means ensuring you are not growing plants of the same family in the same spot year after year. Host-specific pests and pathogens tend to build up in an area when this happens. More established perennial plants will over time find their own natural balance. A prime example of this in action is my hops. The first year they were fine, but in the second year the greenfly had obviously had words with one another and they swamped the plant. Then in the third year (and in subsequent years) they were covered in ladybugs, which finished off the greenfly before they got a chance to do any damage.

Talking of hops, that's enough of Part One. Let's move on to the actual booze-making, shall we?

PART TWO

The Recipes

ElderFlower cordial

Ingredients

20 Elderflower heads
1.5 Kg/3lb sugar
1.2 litres/2.5 litres boiling water
1 sliced lemon

CIDER-MAKING

I T IS RIDICULOUSLY simple to make hard cider, known simply as cider. Here's the recipe:

INGREDIENTS

apples

EQUIPMENT

knife

cider press

secondary

airlock and bung

METHOD

Cut apples up and press into a secondary. Attach airlock and leave until fermented.

This is how cider has been made since mankind first appreciated the apple's qualities. This is how many people still make cider, including many of the cider-makers I know. And why not? It works and it produces a perfectly acceptable alcoholic drink at the end. It may be cloudy, it may be a bit rough-tasting, but it will be perfectly acceptable cider.

If instead of perfectly acceptable cider you wish to make good cider or even bloody great cider then a little more care and attention are needed. Notice I say a *little* more care and attention: it remains a pretty simple exercise.

CHOOSING THE RIGHT APPLES

Non-commercial or amateur cider-makers often end up choosing the "whatever you can get your hands on" method of obtaining apples, thus your average haul is a mixture of cider, dessert, crab, and cooking apples. There is nothing wrong with this method, but care must be taken when mixing the apples to get the right blend of acids and tannin. Indeed, some commercial cider producers in Kent don't use cider apples at all: dessert apples are mixed with cookers.

Achieving the right blend can also be a question of taste, but there are a few simple rules to follow:

- Too many cooking apples makes for a very sour-tasting cider.

- Too many sweet dessert apples can produce a bland cider.

- Single-variety ciders are not as full-flavored as a good mix (though some perfectly good ciders can be made from a single variety of cider apple; the best is thought to be the Kingston Black).

- It is OK to use up to 20 percent pears in cider-making (this might make the purists' blood boil, so don't tell them).

- A blend of two dessert apples to one cooking apple should be fine. The ideal blend is four sweet, two sharp, and one bitter apple.

- Weak-flavored apples make weak-flavored cider.

- About three typical-sized carrier bags full of apples will make 4.5 liters/1 gallon of juice.

One of the downsides of using a mixture of apples is that they will mature at different times (see below for details on storing apples).

CIDER APPLES

If you can get hold of a single variety of cider apples—such as Golden Russet, Ribston Pippin, Roxbury Russet, or Nonpareil—then great. If you can blend a few of these varieties, even better. I suspect, as they are rather rare, that you might have to find a specialty nursery to obtain some, and even then you'll have to wait a while for them to grow. Most cider makers recognize four categories of cider apple according to the relative proportion of malic acid and tannin: bittersharp, sharp, bittersweet, and sweet. The following list is by no means exhaustive, but it will help you to select your cider apples:

Bittersharp (high acidity, high tannin) varieties: Kingston Black, Porter's Perfection, Stoke Red.

Sharp (high acidity, low tannin) varieties: Brown's and Tom's Putt.

Bittersweet (low acidity, high tannin) varieties: Chisel Jersey, Dabinett, Harry Master's Jersey, Michelin, Yarlington Mill.

Sweet (low acidity, low tannin) varieties: Amere de Berthecourt, Sweet Chopin, Taylor's Sweet.

The blend you use is entirely up to you and your tastes and is something some cider producers annoyingly keep to themselves. Keep accurate notes and don't stress too much about getting that mixture right as you can blend the juice or even the finished cider later.

OBTAINING APPLES

The law differs from state to state, but often it is legal to pick fruit from someone's tree if it overhangs onto either your property or public property. However, if you damage the tree and it subsequently dies, you will have broken the law. It is, however, courteous and best practice to ask permission before taking apples from someone's land, and most people are not going to turn down a bottle of free cider in return for keeping their perimeters or lawn neat. There are apple-picking groups around the country, often called harvesting groups—a great, enjoyable way of getting some apples and making new friends to boot.

And remember, if you have the space you may also wish to grow your own (see p. 60). Ideally you want more than one tree to achieve an appropriate blend. Make as many ciders as you can over one year, keep accurate notes of which apples you thought successful, then grow these varieties.

WASHING APPLES

There has been some debate about whether or not you should wash apples before pressing; some have suggested the wild yeasts are reduced by such a practice. As apples can be covered in mud, bird crap, and who knows what else, in my opinion they should be washed. This can be done in a bath or sink with a hose. Or, for a real pampering, put them in the shower.

At the washing stage apples should be inspected for mold and rot. You can cut off mold or rot if it hasn't engulfed the apple, but those beyond redemption should be discarded. Bruised fruit is OK unless it is covered in spores. Another debate arises when it comes to insect damage: some cut this out, others suggest that some insects are good for the yeast and it means you don't have to throw in a dead rat (a process some traditional cider-makers apparently still adopt). A rat, or any other piece of meat for that matter, was thought to add nutrients to the cider, imparting a greater flavor. The rat or meat would completely dissolve in the process.

When cutting, use a stainless-steel knife if possible to avoid metal contamination.

STORING APPLES

The traditional method used by Somerset cider-makers is to bag up all the apples as they fall in hessian sacks, which protects them from the worst of the weather. The reason this keeps the apples is that they are kept cold. Another, more modern, way would be simply to put them in the fridge, if you have space. They can also be boxed up in cardboard boxes and placed in a cool area, such as down in a cellar or in a garden shed. Check your pile from time to time and take out any bad apples, as it really is true that one bad one will infect the whole lot, and very quickly too.

CUTTING APPLES

Apples need to be cut before they can be crushed as the amount of pressure needed to extract juice from a whole apple is immense. The smaller the apple piece the less pressure is needed to extract the juice.

Some invest in scratters, which are specialized apple cutters, and when making large amounts of cider they are a godsend. They can even be homemade. For the smaller cider-maker, cutting the apples into quarters with a stainless-steel knife works absolutely fine. If there are a few of you a half-barrel/strong bucket and a small tree trunk/thick gate post with handles on either side can be used as a giant mortar and pestle with great results. Our ancestors would have done something similar, and using this method means you will be pressing the apples too, but there are far more efficient ways of doing so as discussed below.

PRESSING APPLES

A nylon bag filled with cut-up apples is tied shut and placed inside the press. Pressure is applied to the apples and out pours the juice. If using a hydraulic press the apples are loaded into a number of slotted racks each lined with a nylon press cloth. The apples are wrapped up and another layer is placed on top. Normally about six to eight "cheeses" are placed on top of one another.

Whether you use a hydraulic press or a simple screw press, the juice will pour out into a glass secondary, a fermentation bucket, or a stainless-steel container. Juice from different varieties and types of apples may be kept in different containers if blending before fermentation, but these should be sealed with an airlock as the longer juice is exposed to air the greater the chance of contamination. (Some blend before and some after fermentation, but it is easier for the beginner to blend after fermentation as he or she can do this by taste, which has the advantage that you get to drink the cider!)

Once the pressing is over you will be left with a load of dry apple. The high acid content of this "pomace" means it can be used as an effective garden mulch to inhibit weed growth. Traditionally it was fed to the pigs, or water was added and it was pressed again to make a light apple juice that was given to children. These days it often just gets composted.

STRAINING AND FERMENTATION

Once pressed, the juice should be strained into a fermentation bucket or secondary. Simply pouring your juice through a piece of muslin cloth will be fine.

The next stage is fermentation, and here you have two choices: either to allow wild yeasts to do their job or to kill them and any other bacteria that might be lurking with chemicals. Many people pop in a Campden tablet, which adds to the juice a measured amount of sulfur dioxide. The practice of using SO_2 in cider-making dates back to at least Elizabethan times, but to some it is sheer heresy. Rob from my brewing circle has a very pragmatic approach to his annual 450-liter/800-pint cider-making operation: he sulphites half of his cider and makes a "wild brew" with the other half. He argues that this way he always has at least 225 liters/400 pints of cider a year to drink should anything go wrong. Martin, a friend from Cider punk, a cider blog and delivery service, suggests sulphating at a rate of 50ppm, which is half the recommended dose (this works out at about 1 Campden tablet per 4.5 liters/1 gallon). This allows a succession from wild yeasts, which die when the cider reaches about 2–2.5%, allowing the *Saccharomyces* yeast to take over and take the cider to its full strength. In other words, Martin allows two yeasts to get to work and has the best of both worlds.

Sulfur simply inhibits the growth of weaker strains of yeast that can leave the cider tasting bad and allows beneficial added yeasts to dominate the process. It also kills off harmful bacteria that will ruin the flavor of your finished cider.

Despite all the talk of wild yeasts, many choose to add their own, which will get to work very quickly on the sugars. Again, this is down to personal taste. I swear by using champagne yeast, others simply use an all-purpose wine yeast; ale yeast and baker's yeast should be avoided. If you have sulphited your juice then wait overnight before adding any yeast as it will die off.

You may wish at this stage to take a pH reading to see how much acid is in your juice. The ideal value for cider is between 3.2 and 3.8. You can buy pH strips that are the right range for cider from your homebrew stockist. If using mostly cooking apples your juice could be above this level; add some potassium carbonate or precipitated chalk to calm it down. If the acidity is too low you can buy malic acid or an acid blend and add this to hot water, then put a tiny amount in a specimen of your juice. Take a taste test before adding the same proportion to the rest of your juice. There is also another option recommended by the much-respected and sadly missed Long Ashton cider research: a higher dose of sulphite if the acid is too low.

The level of tannin might also be wrong. Again, take a taste test, and if after a drink your mouth resembles a cat's bum there is too much tannin. This can be adjusted by adding proprietary gelatin finings. A weak, thin cider is the result of not enough tannin, and this can be counteracted by adding powdered grape tannin, which is available from homebrew shops; alternatively, as mentioned earlier, you could just add a tablespoon of cold tea per 4.5 liters/1 gallon, although this practice is considered by craft cider-makers a manipulation too far.

Once fermentation is under way the open stages can be rather violent as the yeast rapidly multiplies. If you are fermenting in a secondary with an airlock and cider has burst up through the airlock and forced out the water inside it, the secondary should be cleaned and filled again with water. If loads of juice has escaped and the level inside the secondary has dropped you can top it up with sugary water or apple juice.

Once this initial fermentation has calmed down, cider will enjoy temperatures of around 15°C (60°F) when fermenting. As cider is often made throughout the winter months when temperatures can plummet, fermentation may halt. Some cider-makers suggest that this slower fermentation helps create a better cider, so if it does happen then don't panic as it will start again and perhaps even improve the finished product.

Cider will benefit from racking (see p. 43) a couple of times throughout this fermentation process.

After about six months you should have dry cider, which can be siphoned into sterilized bottles and then enjoyed!

MAKING SWEET CIDER

There are a few ways of turning your dry cider into sweet cider. First, a "fermentation stop" packet can be bought, which contains the potassium sorbate and benzoate (naturally occurring in rowan berries) that will halt the fermentation before all the sugar has fermented. You will need to taste your cider and take a hydrometer reading to ensure that it is as sweet as you like it. The downside to using fermentation stoppers is the "geranium-like" off-taste.

I've come across recipes dating back to the 1860s that add saccharine to their cider. Saccharine is a non-fermentable sugar but it does have a noticeable, some say unpleasant, aftertaste.

Another way of sweetening is to do it a glass at a time by stirring in sugar at 10g (0.4oz) per liter/quart to turn a dry into a medium.

MAKING CARBONATED CIDER

Cider can be naturally carbonated by bottling just before fermentation has finished. The reading on your hydrometer should be 1010. Strong bottles such as champagne bottles should be used, along with champagne corks.

Carbonated cider can also be produced by adding 5g (0.2oz) of sugar per 500ml/1 pint bottle when bottling.

The French and some West Country producers also make a clear sparkling cider using an old and fairly complex process known as keeving. If you are brave enough to try it, the process is explained in full at cider.org.uk/keeving.html.

BLENDING FERMENTED CIDERS

If you are thinking about blending, you should do so as soon as your cider has fermented fully and before you bottle. Take the taste test and pour ciders into each other. This is best done a glass at a time. You should also ensure that your ciders are stable before blending as they can start to re-ferment, which may result in exploding bottles or unexpected flavors.

PROBLEM-SOLVING

Problems can start right at the beginning, when pressing the apples. If you're using a lot of dessert apples, slimy pulp can clog up the material covering the cut-up apples and stop juice from pouring out. This happens due to the high level of pectin in the fruit, so it can be counteracted by adding pectolase to the pulp. The natural way of counteracting this phenomenon is to alter your mix of apples by adding more cider apples.

The next problem you might face is the non-fermentation of the juice—see Stuck Fermentation on p. 279.

If your juice ends up smelling like nail polish and has a

white/yellowish film crusted over the surface I'm afraid to say air has been allowed to get in and it has been infected, which isn't good news. These "film yeasts" will start to break down the alcohol. As soon as a problem like this arises, add Campden tablets and top up to exclude any air. You might save your cider, but it will be touch and go. This problem crops up more often when making a wild cider and can be put down to poor storage or unsanitized equipment.

Another common problem is acetification, or acetic acid bacterial infection, which will turn your lovely cider into vinegar. The tell-tale signs are jelly-like sheets on the surface of your cider. Treat as above. Again, this is a problem that arises when air gains access to your juice. It is often carried by the fruit fly, *Drosophila melanogaster*, but can also be caused by off yeast, crap corks, broken seals, or improperly rinsed-out bottles.

A condition known as "ropiness" can occur when you have a low-acid cider. This happens in the bottle, and when you pour your glass of cider a slimy, ropy fluid almost like frogspawn emerges. It is still perfectly drinkable, but only those who have made drinking an all-day-every-day activity would want to. The addition of bentonite finings, vigorous stirring, and filtering can help but often not much can be done. Prevention is better than cure: ropiness rarely happens in sulphited cider.

Ever tasted a mouse cage? Well, you might taste the equivalent in cider terms—a taste that apparently some people like. It arises when a rogue wild yeast of the *Brettanomyces* family infects your juice, and the problem can be avoided by sulphiting and by ensuring that your apples are clean before pressing. Apparently some people can't detect these flavors; taking a mouthwash of bicarbonate of soda can allow such people to detect it.

Last, a hazy cider can be a problem for people. I must admit to not being too fussy when it comes to cider haze, but some will insist on a bright, clear cider, which actually isn't too much to ask for. Haziness is due to too much pectin, so adding pectolase can help, but it is far more effective pre-fermentation. Tannin can also haze after refrigeration, and this can be removed by fining, although the process can affect the flavor and is best avoided.

BEER-MAKING

ONE OF THE FIRST steps you should take when it comes to making beer is to drink some. It may sound like odd advice, but getting to know your finished product before you try to make it yourself is essential. It really helps to know your ingredients. Look at the color, flavor, taste, and smell as these aspects are what you will try to recreate. Most towns and cities have a bar serving craft ale hidden away somewhere and the beer they have on tap is usually changed on a regular basis. If you don't have one nearby, bottled beers can be obtained from good liquor stores. After trying a beer, look it up and find out what goes into it, which hops are used, which grains. Some brewers readily share this information on their websites; some even offer tours of their breweries, which can really help you to know great beer. You can then think about making your own.

When I first started doing it I would only make beers using malt extract—beers similar to the simple hop beer on p. 229. A malt extract beer is pretty simple to make. Boil a bittering agent such as hops or whatever herbs you are using, mix with malt extract (and sometimes sugar too), allow to cool, pitch, leave to ferment, then bottle or keg. That's it! The beauty of this process is that you can make different beers in small amounts using a saucepan if you wish.

As with all drink-making the level of expertise you wish to attain is entirely up to you. Many homebrewers continue to use malt extract for the rest of their brewing days. If all you want is a barrel for a party every now and then, or you are perfectly happy with your beer, then read no further. Indeed, just playing around with different levels of hops and different herb mixes, and changing your malt extracts or sugars, can keep you busy indefinitely, and with excellent results.

The level up from making beer using malt extract is known as grain brewing. Grain brewing involves heating up the grains (such as barley) in a liquid and keeping it at a steady temperature for a certain amount of time so that the starches from the grains turn to sugars. This process is known as mashing. The variety of ingredients available, and therefore the variety of beers achieved by this method, are exponential.

Grain brewing is broken up into two categories: partial mash and all-grain brewing. A partial mash is when you use grains but make up the sugar difference using malt extract or another sugar.

All-grain brewers use, well, all grains. Again some people carry on making beer using the partial mash method and never move on to the full mash. If you get decent results or simply don't have the space to progress, there is no shame in making beer using only the partial mash method.

MASHING

There are a number of ways to get the (normally barley) grains to release sugars, but it's essential to keep the grain at the ideal temperature of around 65°C (149°F) for at least an hour. The correct balance of sugars is created at this temperature and you will get a great beer.

It is still possible to mash grains at lower temperatures, you will just have to mash them for longer. For example, when mashing at 64°C (147°F) you will have to mash for an hour and a half rather than an hour. There are reasons for mashing at this lower temperature: you will end up with a more fermentable wort but with less body. Mashing at a higher temperature will give you less fermentable sugars and thus a weaker beer but with more body. The highest mashing temperature that is recommended is 75°C (167°F). Any higher and the enzymatic activity needed to turn starch to sugars simply won't happen.

Many brewers use a modified cooler (or any other insulated box, see equipment, p. 26) to mash their grains. They work perfectly: despite being designed to maintain cold temperatures, they will hold higher temperatures too. Water (known as "strike water") that has been heated to approximately 72°C (162°F) is poured into the cooler (this temperature can fluctuate depending on how efficient your cooler is). The grains are poured in at a water:grain ratio of anything from around 1:2 to 1:5 depending on what type of beer you are making. They are stirred and the temperature is taken. Due to heat loss it should be close to that magic number of 65°C (149°F); in fact it should be a little higher as you will expect some more heat loss throughout the mashing process. If it is lower, some boiling water can be added. The lid is then put on the box and sometimes a towel, a duvet, or anything else that will keep the box insulated. The box is then left for the required mashing time.

Another method of mashing uses a boiler on a gas burner or a specially built boiler with a thermostatic control and an element inside. The water is heated to the required temperature and the grains are added. A mashing bag, which holds the grain in the liquor, can be used, which has the added benefit of making the process much easier to clean up after.

SPARGING

When grains are mashed they release their sticky sugars. Unfortunately around 60 percent of this sugar can stick to the husks of the grain. They must be rinsed off or you will not get the maximum yield of beer from your grains. Huge breweries have an automatic sprinkler-like system that is highly efficient. Some, such as the famous Fuller's brewers in London, England, employ a no-sparge technique—which is worth researching but which I won't go into here as it might take me a whole chapter to explain it to you.

The homebrewer (apart from ones with lots of space and money) does not have access to such equipment and therefore has to improvise, and as with most techniques, there are many ways to sparge. Some homebrewers make an elaborate contraption using a bucket with a hose coming out of it and a watering can rose or a sprinkler system on the end. The bucket is placed higher than the fermentation bucket with the grains in it so that hot water can be poured into the bucket and directed all over the grains.

Another easy way of sparging, especially if you don't have all the equipment, is to put the spent grains into a sieve and place the sieve over a large saucepan. Heat an amount of water equaling half the volume of beer you are making to 77°C (171°F)—which helps to halt any unwanted enzymatic activity—and pour this over the grains. Recycle that water over the grains at least twice more, then mix into the water from the mash and move on to the boil.

However you sparge your grains, just remember the golden rule: you want to use the least amount of water to get the biggest amount of sugars off the grains.

THE BOIL

This is where the flavor is added, and you can use hops or bittering herbs. It is also the process that helps boil off certain unwanted volatile compounds. The full volume of beer is boiled for around an hour (or whatever the recipe suggests). Longer boils can aid color development.

Adding hops or bittering herbs at the start of the boil will yield a greater bitterness, adding hops at the end will release aroma. Some IPAs are made by adding hops every five minutes over a two-hour boil, resulting in a powerfully hoppy beer.

The boil is also the time to add Irish moss (if using), a seaweed that will help clear your beer. Put it in during the last fifteen to twenty minutes of a boil.

THE COOL

Although not essential, the next step is to cool your beer down as rapidly as possible to 18°C (64°F) before pitching your yeast. There are some yeasts that will work at higher temperatures, but many yeasts get to work at around 18°C (64°F) and a hotter temperature will kill them before they get a chance to turn your hard work into delicious beer. By cooling quickly, so you can inoculate with yeast, you greatly lessen the chance of your beer getting infected. So while you can just wait for your beer to cool, it is better practice to chill it.

Beer can be cooled using a wort chiller (see p. 24), or by placing the fermentation bucket into an ice bath.

THE FERMENT

Once the yeast is pitched, your beer needs to stay at a steady temperature. That temperature will depend on your yeast strain. A steady 18–21°C (64–70°F) is ideal for an ale yeast and therefore all the beers in this book. Which temperature mark on this range your beer is fermenting at will denote how long your beer will ferment, for it can be anything from four to fourteen days.

CONDITIONING

After fermentation has finished you then need to put your beer into bottles or a keg. The choice is yours. You need to put in a little bit of sugar—around 10g (0.4oz) in each 500ml/1-pint bottle—to restart fermentation and give your beer a little fizz. This can be done by making a little funnel shape with a piece of paper (you could even use a small funnel) and pouring a teaspoon at a time of normal sugar into each bottle. You could also boil similar amounts of sugar, dried malt extract, molasses, or honey with water, allow to cool, then pour this liquid into your bottles or keg. Then, siphon your beer onto it. It is much less messy and gives better carbonation.

After that, the beer must be left upright to develop (or condition) for at least a week for lower alcohol beers and up to three months for stronger barley-wine-type beers. Some prefer to condition for a short time only, but it can be said that beer that is too young will be sharp and slightly astringent like unripe apples, a flavor that will diminish with time.

WINE-MAKING

TRADITIONAL WINE-MAKING from grapes is a pretty straight-forward process: crush grapes into a container, then strain and leave the juice to ferment. This is because grapes contain the perfect balance of acids, sugars, nutrients, and tannin. Country wine is also pretty straightforward, and the whole process can be broken down into a few steps:

- Extracting flavor, aromas, and other nutrients

- Adding tannin, other acids, and sugars

- Primary fermentation

- Secondary fermentation

- Bottling (see p. 44)

- Aging/conditioning

However, some of the steps differ slightly, depending on what you are using to make your wine from. Unlike grapes most fruits, vegetables, and flowers don't contain anything like the right balance of sugars, acid, and tannin. Luckily, we can cheat: countless varieties of yeast can be bought from our homebrew shops (see Part Three for your nearest shop), along with tannins and acids. Sugar will need to be added to all country wines, unless you boil down huge quantities of tree sap or fruit sugars.

EXTRACTING FLAVOR, AROMAS, AND OTHER NUTRIENTS

Flower, herb, or leaf wines

The first thing to realize about flower, herb, and leaf wines is that the flavor imparted can be subtle, and therefore should not be overpowered by adding ingredients with strong flavors. That is, unless you want to use flowers just as a hint of flavor in a recipe.

How you extract the flavor is a matter of taste, and there are a few options. Some like to use a hot water infusion technique, which involves putting the flowers into a fermentation bucket and pouring over hot water, like making a massive cup of herbal tea. Alternatively, you can put the flowers into a pan with some water, bring it to a boil, simmer (as per the recipe), and then strain off the liquid. Last, flavors can be extracted by fermentation—in other words, by putting the plant material into the fermentation bucket along with the other ingredients and allowing that to ferment.

Only use flowers that you know are edible. These include apple blossom, broom, chamomile, coltsfoot, clover, thistle, dill, dandelions, elderflowers, evening primrose, gorse, hawthorn, hibiscus, hollyhocks, lavender, lime blossom, meadowsweet, mustard, nasturtiums, pansies, plum blossom, radish, roses, rosemary, and sage. Flowers that are considered toxic include bindweed, bluebells, buttercups, daffodils, dogbane, foxgloves, henbane, ivy, marsh marigold, periwinkle, potato, nightshade, tobacco, water hemlock, and wolfsbane.

Neither list is by any means exhaustive, and careful research should be done before deciding to make a new recipe using flowers. Some wild flowers are protected and shouldn't be picked: if you are unsure, leave the flower in its place.

Fruit and vegetable wines

Before you start, all fruit and vegetables should be washed, and checking for mold and damage doesn't go amiss, either. Don't think you can get away with using dodgy old fruit or vegetables: I'm afraid they should be as ripe as possible (but not overripe) to get the best results. I also like to put my fruit and vegetables in the freezer overnight before using, since this helps to break down the cell structure thus helping to release more juice.

There are a few different ways to extract flavors from fruit and vegetables. Choosing your method really depends on which fruit or vegetable you're making your wine from: hard root vegetables always need boiling but wines made from soft fruit can be made using cold water. Whichever method you use, it will involve crushing, chopping, or slicing your fruit or vegetables first. This will then be followed by:

- Hot water extraction: place the fruit or vegetables into your fermentation bucket along with sugar, and cover with boiling hot water.

- Cold maceration: place the fruit or vegetables into your fermentation bucket along with sugar, cover with cold water, bucket and leave overnight. Then add pectolase and leave for up to two days.

- Boiling extraction: place the fruit or vegetables into a pan of boiling water and then strain into your fermentation bucket.

- Fermentation extraction: place the fruit or vegetables into your fermentation bucket along with all the other ingredients.

Juice wines

Juice wines are perhaps the easiest wines to extract flavor and aromas from, as the hard work has already been done for you. If using concentrates you might need to top up with water, but other than that you will be able to move on to step 2.

ADDING TANNIN, OTHER ACIDS, AND SUGARS

All flowers, herbs, and leaves are lacking in everything bar flavor, which means you will always have to add other acids and sometimes tannin. Fruit and vegetables can contain the right acids, including tannin, but sometimes they have to be adjusted. These additives are added during the primary fermentation stage.

Tannin

Throughout this book I have used half a cup of cold tea to impart tannin into my wines, since this is a readily available source. However, many wine-makers prefer to use tannin that is bought as a powder (see p. 37): about half to one teaspoon per 4.5 liters/1 gallon of wine will suffice for most flower wines. If neither tea nor tannin powder are available or you wish to make your wine as natural as possible, you can use a couple of fresh (green) oak leaves, which contain high amounts of tannin.

Tannin is useful in helping a wine (generally a red wine) to keep and will also give it a boost, causing the slight dryness of the mouth you are after with a good wine: without tannin wine can taste insipid. Fruits that are high in tannin include sloes, damsons, elderberries, grapes, and gooseberries; fruit and vegetables that don't contain tannin include carrots, lemons, limes, pineapples, parsnips, and squashes.

Other acids

Acid needs to be contained in all wines or they can taste medicinal, dull, or simply off. The ideal balance of acids in a wine should give a pH of 3.4–3.6. Acid can be imparted by adding the juice of citrus fruit—four teaspoons per 4.5 liters/1 gallon will suffice—or using citric acid power (1 teaspoon). An acid blend is preferred at the measure of 1 teaspoon per 4.5 liters/1 gallon. If you are developing a recipe and you wish to check the acidity level, it is possible to buy an acid test kit or litmus papers.

Sugars

All wines will need sugar (see p. 30) in order to ferment, but the question is how much? This is answered by your hydrometer (see p. 18). As some fruits will contain sugar already you will need to measure the sugar content of your must using your hydrometer. The reading on the side will indicate how much more sugar needs to be added in order to create a wine at your required strength. The higher the amount of sugar, the higher the potential volume of alcohol. But don't think that by adding a vast amount of sugar you will end up with a very strong wine, since most yeasts will not tolerate a level over 16 percent and often they will stop working before then.

PRIMARY FERMENTATION

Primary fermentation is a rapid initial fermentation during which process between 60 and 75 percent of the sugar content is turned into alcohol. At this stage all of your ingredients should be sitting in your fermentation bucket, bubbling away like there is no tomorrow. Primary fermenting needs oxygen for the first three days (or so), which is why recipes often ask for a dish towel to be placed over the top of the fermenting bucket. This process can last up to ten days, often depending on the temperature of your fermentation bucket. At this stage you want your fermentation bucket to be somewhere fairly warm: around 21°C/70°F will be fine.

SECONDARY FERMENTATION

Once primary fermentation has finished, secondary fermentation will begin. It is characterized by being a much slower process, normally taking around three months, often longer. The must is filtered from the fermentation bucket and into a secondary, and an airlock and bung attached. They are added since no oxygen is needed at this stage; indeed oxygen can actually ruin a wine before you've even had a chance to drink it.

The optimum temperature for secondary fermentation is 15–18°C (60–65°F). It is important to keep your must fairly cool at this stage as the cooler temperature slows fermentation. Most wine-makers will agree that a slower fermentation will create a superior wine as the flavors from the fruits, flowers, herbs, or vegetables have more time to develop.

BOTTLING

When bottling, it is very important to ensure that the wine has finished fermenting. To do so, first check that your hydrometer readings are consistent. Also move your secondary to a warmer place and re-check your readings.

If you are sure your wine has finished fermenting, you should then siphon the wine off the lees (see Glossary) and into wine bottles. They should then be firmly sealed and placed upright for a week before setting down on a wine rack.

AGING/CONDITIONING

It's easy to get overly excited and want to open your wines within days of making them. If you want to drink just to get a bit drunk then there is nothing to stop you. If, however, you wish to savor the flavor of your wine then it is well worth leaving it to age for a while in a cool place. It makes all the difference and I find a few extra months can utterly transform a wine.

White wines will benefit from at least six months aging and red from at least a year. If it is difficult to age your wine as you can't resist drinking it then try to make twice or three times as much (although I can't help thinking that this sounds like a recipe for disaster for some)!

SPRING

Beech leaf noyau

Birch sap wine

Broad bean (fava bean) wine

Broom flower wine

Cherry wine

Cherry brandy/gin

Cherry cordial—Vissinada

Cleavers juice 1

Cleavers juice 2

Dandelion wine

Dandelion champagne

Dandelion and gorse wine

Elderflower champagne

Elderflower cordial

Elderflower wine

Gorse flower cordial

Gorse flower wine

Gorse et al: First flower champagne

Horseradish vodka—Khrenovukha

Japanese knotweed ale

Japanese knotweed wine

Dandelion and knotweed mead

Golden lime sap wine

Lime et al: Relaxing bedtime tea

Nettle ale 1

Nettle ale 2

Nettle wine

Nettles et al: Hair of the dog tea

Pine needle cordial

Japanese rose petal vodka

I T HAPPENS ALL of a sudden, slowly creeping up on you. You realize you haven't put the heating on in weeks, you only have on two layers of clothes, and better still, things have started growing. Spring is an exciting time for me: it is when nature declares a New Year.

Being a forager helps the gardener side of me at this time of year. As Brian, my 70-year-old gardening guru always says, "If everything is growing it's time to start planting." Tender plants can wait, but others can certainly go in now. In early spring you may hear the term "hungry gap" in relation to the garden—the time when roots and brassicas have finished but it's still not time to harvest early crops such as salad leaves and beans. Again, this is when it helps to be a forager as lime leaves, hawthorn buds, and other edible flowers and plants are ready.

Wine racks can be troublesome in the spring. If you thought that wine bottled in the autumn was stable then you could be proved wrong. Look at your bottles and check for bubbles. If one bottle blows, siphon the rest into a secondary, put it in a warm place, and allow fermentation to finish.

In season (garden): fava beans, asparagus, lettuce, oranges (south).

In season (forage): birch sap, elderflower, dandelion (flowers), cleavers (leaves), hawthorn leaves (early spring) and blossom (late spring), nettles, oak leaf, blackberry tip/leaves, maple syrup, fiddleheads, male pine cones, hop shoot.

BEECH

Beech trees (genus *Fagus*) can be found across much of the planet from South Australia and Tasmania to Asia Minor, North America, and Europe. There are ten species of beech and they can grow to heights of up to 40m (130ft). Gray squirrels are a pest and will damage young beech trees. At one time the leaves of the beech were used as bedding instead of straw.

Foraging for beech

There are many different varieties of beech with varying characteristics, including fern-shaped leaves and leaves the color of copper. Common beech has leaves of around 10cm (4in) in length, pale gray and smooth bark, and grows generally in woodland but also in parks and housing developments.

Growing beech

Beech likes light, well-drained soils and they do well on chalk; avoid planting on clay or moisture-retentive soils. (See Tree Planting, p. 60, for more details.)

Beech Leaf Noyau

One of the people on my foraging walks told me of a friend who was always trying out homebrew recipes on him and his mates. Apparently this man could ruin the simplest ale. Even his sloe gin, despite his best efforts, somehow managed to taste tart and was almost undrinkable. So when a bottle of liqueur made with beech leaves was produced it was met with great reluctance and trepidation. As a testament to friendship everyone in the group took a sip at the same time, and all their worst fears just melted away. Even this man couldn't mess up what is perhaps one of the tastiest liqueurs the woods have to offer.

INGREDIENTS	EQUIPMENT
750ml/3 cups London gin	saucepan
½ cup of fresh, very young beech leaves	1-liter/1-quart sealable jar/bottle
225g/8oz sugar	
300ml/1 cup of water	muslin cloth
glass of brandy	jug (pitcher)

METHOD

Pluck the young beech leaves completely from the twigs, put in a jar, and cover with the gin. Put the jar into a dark cupboard for three weeks, shaking occasionally.

Heat the water, stirring in the sugar until it dissolves. Meanwhile, strain the liquor into the jug (and compost the leaves). Add the sugar solution and slug of brandy to the jug and stir. Pour into bottles and store for at least three months before drinking.

Other uses
Beech nuts, also known as beech mast, are great eaten raw.

BIRCH

I can remember the first time I went looking for birch trees (genus *Betula*) because I found loads that were clearly dying. I was quite distraught until I discovered that they are pioneering trees that will be the first to colonize an area and therefore need a lot of light. As soon as bigger trees move in, in this case pine, the light gets blocked out and the tree dies—it's just nature taking its course.

There are sixty species of birch and most have light bark with long lenticles (lines) running horizontally across it. The bark readily peels from the tree and makes great tinder for fires. Peeling the strips of bark away from the tree does not damage it; indeed the tree itself sheds some bark to allow more light to get to the trunk.

Foraging for birch sap

One of the first signs that spring has sprung is when small, neatly wrapped parcels of leaves start to appear on the trees. These buds indicate not only the start of spring but that the sap is rising, and sap can be tapped and drunk. The ambrosial birch sap need not be just a taste of early spring as it can be preserved as a wine.

Being a hater of dry soils, birch can be found by rivers and on the edges of wetlands. They can also be found in parks, by bicycle paths and railway tracks, and on woodland perimeters.

Any birch tree can be tapped, but make sure you tap an older tree of at least 25–30cm (10–12in) in diameter: any smaller and you risk damaging the tree before it has had a chance to grow. Drill a hole into the tree at a 30-degree angle facing downwards. The hole should just penetrate the bark and should be as thick as the piece of tube you will need to insert into the tree. Push the tubing right into the tree and put the other end in a bottle or secondary. Leave for a day or two, returning twice daily to check on progress. If the sap that comes out smells and looks a bit like dog pee then the tree has been infected with a fungus and the sap should be discarded.

It can be difficult to tap a birch tree if you live in a town or city.

My friend and fellow forager Fergus Drennan suggests that you climb the tree and tape or tie a large plastic bottle to a higher branch before tapping up there. The sap rises right up the tree so you should still get a good amount.

When you have finished tapping the tree, make sure you plug up the hole. There are several ways to do this, including shoving a piece of cork into the hole and covering it with wax so you can come back on alternate years, pick the wax off, pull out the cork, and tap again. Personally, when I plug a birch I find a small twig or branch underneath the tree, cut that to shape with a penknife, then hammer it home with a stone. If you don't plug a tree you leave it open to infection, which could kill it.

Birch sap does not keep very well and should be put into use as soon as possible. If refrigerated it will last for only a few days, but it can be frozen until needed.

Growing birch
Birch trees will thrive on shaded, cool, moist, free-draining soils, and as they need some sun on their leaves they make ideal trees for northeast-facing gardens. Shallow roots mean you should plant away from utilities. Preferred acidity level is pH 5.0–6.0. (See Tree Planting, p. 60, for more information.)

Birch Sap Wine
Birch sap wine is certainly a delicacy of the woods, so much so that it is available commercially in many countries. By altering the amount of sugar used in the fermentation process you can determine

how sweet or dry your wine turns out to be. This recipe will make a slightly dry wine.

INGREDIENTS	EQUIPMENT
4 liters/1 gallon birch sap	drill and tubing
250ml/1 cup white grape concentrate	large saucepan/cauldron
1kg/2.2lb sugar	fermentation bucket
2 tsp citric acid	4.5-liter/1-gallon secondary
½ tsp tannin	airlock and bung
packet of hock wine yeast	siphoning tube

METHOD ....

Bring the sap, concentrate, and sugar to a boil, remove from the heat, and add the citric acid, then stir until the sugar has fully dissolved. Allow to cool to room temperature then stir in the tannin and sprinkle the yeast on. Cover loosely and leave for ten days.

Siphon into a secondary and rack after about four weeks. Allow to ferment out before bottling and age for at least three months.

BROAD BEANS (FAVA BEANS)

Pythagoras, the Greek philosopher and mathematician of right-angled triangle fame, was reported to have had a fear of broad beans (*Vicia faba*). He thought the embryo-shaped beans contained the souls of people. Apparently he died during a pursuit by his enemies when at one point his only means of escape was through a field full of broad beans. He found it impossible to screw up the courage to run through them and was slaughtered.

Growing broad beans

Broad beans are very easy to grow. Plant at a thumb's depth in late autumn for an early spring crop, or in early spring for a summer crop. Space your beans 20cm (8in) apart and pinch off the top 8cm (3in) growth after the first bean has developed as this helps rid the plant of blackfly.

Broad bean seeds are very easy to collect and store (see p. 59), and digging the dead plants back into your soil will enhance its nitrogen levels.

Tip: rolling up some corrugated cardboard (to mimic a plant stem) and slotting it into a plastic bottle with the end cut off makes - an insect hotel, a nesting site for ladybugs that will eat blackfly. Dead-heading and leaving plant stems in the ground will do the same job.

Broad Bean Wine

Unlike other recipes in this book you can use up old beans that are past their best. Even ones that have gone a bit black will do the job.

INGREDIENTS	EQUIPMENT
2kg/4.5lb shelled broad beans	large saucepan/cauldron
100g/3.5oz golden raisins	4.5-liter/1-gallon secondary
1 lemon	airlock and bung
4.5 liters/1 gallon of water	muslin cloth
1.5kg/3.3lbs sugar	fermentation bucket
white wine yeast	siphoning tube

METHOD

Boil the beans for an hour before straining the liquid into a fermentation bucket. Chop or mince the golden raisins, then add them, the sugar, and the juice of the lemon. Stir until the sugar has fully dissolved. Add the yeast when cooled to room temperature. Cover and leave for about a week.

Strain into a secondary and affix airlock. Allow to ferment out, racking once. Bottle and age for one year before drinking.

BROOM

Broom (*Sarothamnus scoparius*) is thought in herbal medicine circles to "increase the power of the heart." In folklore it is magical, and those who ate it were thought to feel "euphoric and amorous," so it was used as an aphrodisiac. And if you are wondering, yes, it was once used to brush floors.

Broom is an evergreen perennial shrub native to western and central Europe. It can grow to around 5m (15ft) high. Outside Europe, in Australia, New Zealand, and the US, it is regarded as an invasive weed after being introduced in the nineteenth century. As its rapid growth hinders reforestation and it burns readily, its presence can be an aid to a forest fire.

Foraging for broom

Broom can be found on wasteland, on dry, sandy soils at low altitudes. It won't grow on chalk or limestone soils so don't expect to find it in areas where these soils predominate. Broom has been mistaken for the deadly laburnum tree, a close relative, but laburnum flowers hang down and are more tightly packed together.

It is rather time-consuming to collect the flowers for the wine recipe that's coming up, but this kind of foraging can be excellent stress relief. Listening to your favorite radio station or music through headphones and getting away from everyone and everything can amount to a meditative experience. Alternatively, convince your family or a pile of mates to join in to make the afternoon's picking fun.

Broom Flower Wine

This recipe was sent to me by Joy Mardon from Wales, a fellow forager who enjoys experimenting with the flavors of wild food. It makes for a very floral wine, as you might expect, with a slight honey aftertaste, which you might not expect.

INGREDIENTS

2 quarts of broom flowers

3 liters/3 quarts of water

1.5kg/2.2lb sugar

½ cup of cold black tea or 1 tsp grape tannin

1 Campden tablet (optional)

champagne yeast

1 tsp yeast nutrient

EQUIPMENT

large saucepan/cauldron

fermentation bucket

muslin cloth

4.5-liter/1-gallon secondary

airlock and bung

METHOD

Remove all the green bits from the broom flowers. Put into a pan with 1.5 liters/6 cups of water and allow to simmer for ten minutes.

Add a Campden tablet (if using), pour into a fermentation bucket, and leave for three days.

Strain through a muslin cloth (or jelly bag) into a secondary.

Mix the rest of the water with the sugar, bring to a boil, and stir until fully dissolved. Allow the sugar solution to cool to blood heat and add the champagne yeast and yeast nutrient. Pour into the secondary, along with the cold tea.

Allow to ferment out, racking if necessary. It should turn a lovely clear yellow color.

Will benefit from six months' aging before drinking.

CHERRIES

The four hundred species of cherry (genus *Prunus*) are native to the northern hemisphere from America to Asia. Trees that live for sixty or so years can reach heights of 20m (65ft) and more. They made it over to England when that lover of food King Henry VIII tasted them in Flanders and ordered them to be grown in his extensive gardens.

Foraging for cherries
Cherry trees are planted for their spring blossom, and the fruit can be an afterthought. This means that when traveling through towns and cities during late spring you will see roads around housing developments strewn with the splatterings of red, unharvested fruit. Trees can also be found in broadleaf woodlands, on gravel soils, in public parks, by bicycle paths, and close to railway lines.

There are many different varieties of cherry and not all are great to eat raw, but they can all be used to make the following recipes. Even the bitter bird cherry, a smaller red cherry that grows wild and can often be overlooked, can be used. Smaller wild cherries work very well in cherry brandy. The recipes below use a mixture of cherries as I find using more than one variety makes for a better taste.

The branches of a cherry tree can be quite high up, so if possible a ladder can be used. One year during cherry season when friends and their child came to stay we found putting the child on our shoulders to pick for us was by far the easiest method (although she refused to share!).

Growing cherries
Alternatively, if you have enough space they are a worthy tree in any garden, but do be warned: some varieties can grow to massive sizes so their roots could cause structural problems if planted too close to property. If you don't have space, consider dwarf varieties, which grow to more manageable heights—anything between 1m and 5m (3ft and 15ft).

Cherry trees don't grow well in wet areas so make sure you plant in a free-draining area. Test-dig a pit a week before planting and fill with water; if it drains away, you can go ahead with planting.

Birds are the biggest problem when it comes to growing cherries as they can strip a tree in no time. The use of netting can be problematic as the birds can get stuck. A sometimes effective alternative is to tie CDs around the tree to scare them away before they feast. You could also consider getting a cat, or encouraging a neighbor's cat into your garden.

Cherry Wine

At around 15%, and very quaffable, this wine really is one to get a party going.

INGREDIENTS

2kg/4.4lb cherries

1kg/2.2lb sugar

1 cup of red grape concentrate

½ cup of cold black tea or 1 tsp tannin

juice of 2 lemons *or* 6 tbsp lemon juice

1 tsp yeast nutrient

4.5 liters/1 gallon of water

1 Campden tablet (optional)

Burgundy red wine yeast

EQUIPMENT

2 fermentation buckets

large saucepan/cauldron

muslin/cheesecloth

4.5-liter/1-gallon secondary

airlock and bung

siphoning tube

METHOD

Put the cherries into a fermentation bucket and cover with 3 liters/3 quarts of hot water. Add the Campden tablet (if using).

After leaving for two days, boil the rest of the water up and add the sugar, stirring vigorously until fully dissolved.

Strain the cherries through a muslin/cheesecloth into another fermentation bucket and add all the other ingredients, making sure that the yeast and nutrient are not added until the water is hand-hot.

After a further ten days, decant into a secondary with airlock attached.

Rack after two months and do not bottle until it has completely finished fermenting, which could take up to a year. Cherry wine improves with age and is best left to condition for at least another year. The results will be worthwhile!

Cherry Brandy/Gin

This recipe is made in a similar way to damson and sloe gin, only as cherries can be much sweeter, less sugar is needed. The recipe can be adapted using different spirits and, of course, different cherries. Surprisingly, even the sourest cherries seem to make a fairly sweet and very delicious brandy.

INGREDIENTS
500g/1lb cherries
85g/3oz sugar
500ml/2 cups of brandy (or another spirit)
cinnamon stick

EQUIPMENT
large sealable jar
muslin/cheesecloth

METHOD

Clean and destalk the cherries. Put a layer of cherries into the jar and sprinkle over a layer of sugar. Continue until all the cherries and sugar have been used up, then pour over the brandy. Shake the jar two or three times a day for three days, then add the cinnamon stick.

After those three days, put your jar in a cool dark place and return to it to shake it occasionally over a three-month period.

Strain into bottles and leave in a cool dark place for a further two months before enjoying.

Cherry Cordial—Vissinada ——————————————

If you like sour drinks, Vissinada is an interesting beverage to make. Originating in Greece, it is a most refreshing drink to sip when the sun starts to get hotter—which coincidentally is roughly the same time that cherries are ripe.

INGREDIENTS

1kg/2.2lb sour cherries

1kg/2.2lb superfine sugar

300ml/10 fl oz of water

1 tsp lemon juice

EQUIPMENT

large saucepan

cherry pitter (optional, but very useful)

jam pots

METHOD ···

Pit the cherries, place a layer of them into a saucepan, then cover with sugar. Repeat until you have used all the cherries. Leave for three hours.

Pour the water into the saucepan and bring to a boil, skimming off any scum that forms. Simmer until the syrup thickens, adding the lemon juice just before you take it off the heat.

Allow to cool, and at this stage you have *vision gliko*, a Greek jelly that is traditionally eaten by the spoonful as a sweet. It can be placed into sterilized jam pots for use as a jam or as a drink. To make the drink, dilute with cold water to a ratio of 5:1 and add ice.

Other uses

Salted leaves are used in Japan as an ingredient of a sweet known as *sakuri mochi*, and the resin has been used as a kind of chewing gum.

CLEAVERS

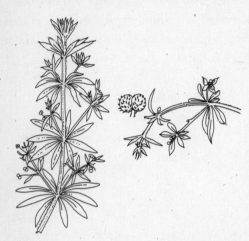

Cleavers (*Galium aparine*) are so common that they go by many different names in different parts of the country. I have heard them being called "sticky bud" in Wiltshire and "sticky willy" in Scotland, and in my home town, Northampton, we had the most imaginative name "stick weed."

If you are still unsure of what cleavers are, you may remember them from your school days. Think of the plant that was uprooted and thrown on the backs of unsuspecting friends and siblings, leaving tiny buds sticking all over their clothes. At least that's how I remember them!

The Celts believed that if you drank nothing but cleavers juice for sixty days your skin would become so beautiful that everyone would fall in love with you. I tried this one spring, but alas, the pub called and I could not last the full two months.

Cleavers are around for most of the year (see next section for a summer recipe) but early spring is the traditional time to make cleavers juice as it helps rid the body of all the winter excesses.

Foraging for cleavers

Cleavers can be found growing in areas where the soil has been disturbed, often on the edges of paths in public places, woodland and field perimeters, and on garden plots. They love full sun or partial shade so won't be found in areas where cover is dense. Cleavers will grow to a height of about 1.5m (5ft), often sprawling at the base of trees and smothering other plants.

Cleavers Juice 1

This recipe is more of a cleavers infusion and requires the smallest amount of effort for a great spring tonic.

INGREDIENTS

a good two handfuls of cleavers

1 liter/1 quart of water

EQUIPMENT

large pitcher

muslin/cheesecloth

METHOD

Put the cleavers into a pitcher and pour over the cold water. Leave overnight to infuse, giving the cleavers a little squeeze whenever you walk past them.

Strain through a muslin/cheesecloth into bottles and store in the fridge. It is ready to drink immediately and will stay fresh for a week. Take three or four full wine glasses a day.

Cleavers Juice 2

For a stronger spring tonic, try this method. It can be used by the health-conscious in place of grass drinks as a lymph cleanser. It is certainly an acquired taste, however, and can be mixed with other juices for a more appealing flavor.

INGREDIENTS	EQUIPMENT
a good two handfuls of cleavers	blender
1 liter/1 quart of water	muslin/cheesecloth

METHOD

Chop up the freshest, greenest parts of the plant and put in a blender. Add the water and blend until the cleavers are cut into tiny pieces. Strain and serve immediately for maximum benefit. It can be refrigerated and used throughout the day but you may need to shake before use as it will separate.

Other uses

When picked young—between November and April—cleavers can be used as a vegetable. However, they are often stringy and I'd suggest just using the tips. Outside of these months cleavers can be terribly bitter, although they can still be boiled to make a wild stock.

DANDELIONS

The word "dandelion" comes from the French *dent de lion* meaning "tooth of the lion," after the leaves, which look as if they are made up of jagged teeth. They are native to Europe, North America, and Asia. Dandelions (*Taraxacum officinale*) have been used as a liver tonic due to their diuretic qualities; in India they are even cultivated for this reason.

Foraging for dandelions

St. George's Day (April 23) is traditionally the time to go out and pick dandelion flowers, and certainly they are in abundance at this time. They flower all year round, but up to early summer it will be easier to pick in one go.

Have a real hunt around for neglected places as this is where dandelions love to grow. Check meadows, any grassy places such as playing fields and parks, wastegrounds, and grass verges. I'd be very surprised if you don't have plenty of dandelions growing somewhere close to your house.

Dandelion Wine

Picking dandelions in the spring may seem like a chore, but by the time it gets to autumn or winter that chore will have become a memory of a great day out, especially if you have a glass of dandelion wine in your hand. This is a classic country wine and one for which many people have developed their own recipe. I forget who gave me this version, but it's now the only one I use, for it makes a perfect dandelion wine.

INGREDIENTS

3 liters/3 quarts of dandelion flowers

2kg/4.5lb sugar

2 lemons

1 orange

4.5 liters/1 gallon of water

1 tsp yeast nutrient

1 Campden tablet (optional)

champagne yeast

EQUIPMENT

large saucepan/cauldron

fermentation bucket

4.5-liter/1-gallon secondary

airlock and bung

muslin/cheesecloth

siphoning tube

METHOD

Cut the green bits totally off the dandelion heads to avoid bitterness. Place the heads into a fermentation bucket, cover with boiling water, and loosely cover. Add the Campden tablet (if using).

Leave for two days to allow the flavors to infuse, then strain into a large saucepan and add the sugar and the peelings of the citrus fruit, making sure there is no white pith at all. Bring to a boil and simmer gently for ten minutes.

Pour into a clean and sterile fermentation bucket, adding the juice of the lemons and orange. When hand-hot, sprinkle in the yeast and yeast nutrient.

Cover loosely and leave for five to ten days or until fermentation calms down. Siphon into a secondary and allow to ferment out. Rack if necessary. Bottle when fermentation has ceased, and if possible age for one year.

Dandelion Champagne

It can be infuriating waiting for wines to be ready, and with most flower wines it is worth experimenting with a champagne first to make sure you like the taste. The complexity of wine is different from a simple champagne but it is enough to try one to get an idea of what you will be fermenting. Moreover, dandelion champagne makes for a thirst-quenching distraction while you wait for your wine to ferment.

INGREDIENTS

2 liters/2 quarts of dandelion flowers
9 liters/9 quarts of water
1kg/2.2lb sugar

EQUIPMENT

fermentation bucket
large saucepan/cauldron
muslin/cheesecloth

4 lemons (2 for juice, 2 sliced)

3 tbsp mild white wine vinegar

METHOD ···

Cut the green bits totally off the dandelion heads to avoid bitterness and place into a fermentation bucket. Boil up half the water, add the sugar, and stir until dissolved. Pour over the dandelion heads, adding the lemon juice, vinegar, and lemon slices. Cover with a cloth and leave for one to four days or until it starts to bubble a bit.

Strain through a muslin/cheesecloth into swing-top bottles and drink after about two weeks.

Dandelion and Gorse Wine (by Fergus Drennan) ——

I'm quite a purist when it comes to wine-making in the sense that I like things to be one thing or the other. After all, in this case, both dandelion wine and gorse wine would be good in their own right. Nevertheless, call it alchemy, fortuity, whatever you like, it just seems to be that in this instance the marriage of dandelion and gorse produces a wine greater than either plant could produce on its own.

INGREDIENTS

1.5 liters/6 cups of dandelion flowers

1.5 liters/6 cups of gorse flowers

1kg/2.2lb sugar

4.5 liters/4.5 quarts of spring water

1 Campden tablet (optional)

juice and grated zest of 2 lemons

2 tsp yeast nutrient

high alcohol tolerant yeast

EQUIPMENT

2 fermentation buckets

muslin/cheesecloth

4.5-liter/1-gallon secondary

airlock and bung

METHOD

Place the flowers in a fermentation bucket. Bring 3.5 liters/3.5 quarts of the water to a boil and pour over the flowers. Cover with a loose-fitting lid or cloth and allow to infuse for three days. It can be useful to stir in a crushed Campden tablet at this point (if using).

After steeping, strain through muslin into a second fermenting bin. Bring the last liter/quart of water to a boil and dissolve the sugar in it. Next, add to this the yeast and yeast nutrient, the lemon juice and zest, and while still hot pour in with the strained liquid. Give it a shake or stir and add the yeast. Leave loosely covered for five days in a warm place before transferring to a secondary. Leave to ferment out.

Other uses

Dandelion heads can be eaten raw, and a couple added to a salad are delicious. The leaves are best eaten in the spring as younger leaves are less bitter.

ELDERFLOWERS

As with elderberries (see Summer), before you pick anything from an elder (*Sambucus nigra*) you are supposed to ask the hag that lives in the tree for her permission. Indeed some druids will ask every tree its permission before picking from it. Apparently some can be moody bastards and will sometimes say no.

As folklore can be shorthand for remembering important infor-mation, I surmise that the hag in this tale represents death. The wood of the elder tree contains cyanide, which when burned within confined quarters, such as the one-roomed hovels many peasant

farmers would have lived in during the
Middle Ages, can fill the room with
noxious smoke, killing its occupants. I
suspect, then, that the hag in the elder
tree is always a bit moody when it
comes to asking her for firewood.
Although perhaps she is just as likely
to say, "Help yourself to the flowers,
just leave some to turn into berries."

Foraging for elderflowers
To help in the identification of the
elder tree, look for a jelly-like fungus
growing on it, known as "tree ear"
(once known as "Jew's ear").

There is a theory that if you pick elderflowers in the morning
they are fresh and lovely, but in the evening they smell of cat pee. I
have never found this to be true, but they can start to deteriorate
later in the season and will indeed smell unpleasant.

Once harvested, elderflowers should be lightly tapped to get rid of
insects and removed from the stem with a fork or even a dog comb.

See Elderberries (p. 168) for more details.

Growing elder
Elder love fertile, well-drained soil with a pH of 5.5–6.5 and full sun
to light shade. They grow from softwood or hardwood cuttings. They
are shallow-rooted so will need watering well in the first year. (See
Tree Planting p. 60 for information.)

Elderflower Champagne

Almost everyone in drink-making circles has their own elderflower champagne recipe, each differing only slightly. This recipe originated with Mark, one of the members of the Bristol Brewing Circle.

A slight variation on this method is made by John Lewis-Stempel in the *The Wild Life* (see Further Reading, p. 301). He adds a quarter of a cup of wild rose petals, replaces the sugar with honey, and uses cider vinegar for a 100 percent wild elderflower champagne.

INGREDIENTS

6 large elderflower heads

1kg/2.2lb sugar

8 liters/2 gallons of water

4 lemons (2 for juice, 2 sliced)

3 tbsp mild white wine vinegar

EQUIPMENT

fermentation bucket

large saucepan/cauldron

muslin/cheesecloth

METHOD

Shake the elderflowers to remove any insects. Put the sugar into a sterilized fermentation bucket. Boil up half the water and pour over the sugar, stirring continuously until it has dissolved. Add the elder-flowers, the juice of the lemons, the vinegar, and lemon slices. Cover with a cloth and leave for between one and four days, until it looks like it's starting to bubble a bit.

Strain through a muslin/cheesecloth into swing-top bottles and drink after about two weeks.

Caution: Elderflower champagne can be very volatile so shouldn't be stored in thin glass bottles. It should also not be stored in any place where it can do damage. It is advisable to keep the bottles cool before opening: I have known the swing-tops to go flying across the room.

Elderflower Cordial

This recipe calls for citric acid, and when I wandered into the chemist's to buy some I got a few funny looks. I relayed this tale to a friend and was told that citric acid is often used to mix street heroin—a fact that makes me feel nervous now whenever I need to buy some (citric acid, that is).

INGREDIENTS

20 elderflower heads

1.5kg/3.3lb sugar

1.2 liters/5 cups of boiling water

1 sliced lemon

2 tsp citric acid

EQUIPMENT

small fermentation bucket

muslin/cheesecloth

METHOD

Place all the ingredients in a small sterilized fermentation bucket. Pour over the boiling water and stir until you can no longer feel the crunch of undissolved sugar at the bottom of your bucket. Some scum may rise and this should be skimmed off. Cover with a dish towel or pillowcase. Stir now and then overnight, then strain through a piece of muslin/cheesecloth into sterile bottles and refrigerate. It is ready to drink immediately and should be diluted to taste. It makes an excellent mixer and goes particularly well with gin.

Elderflower Wine

Many country wine-makers only make a few wines every year, and elderflower is generally one of them. It is a delicately flavored wine that's great when drunk in the winter, as a reminder of warmer, brighter days.

INGREDIENTS

1 liter/1 quart of boiling water

3.5 liters/3.5 quarts of water

1.3kg/3lb white sugar

2 cups of elderflowers

Grated rind of one lemon

Juice of one lemon

1 Campden tablet (optional)

Gervin—No 5 White Label yeast

yeast nutrient

1 tsp grape tannin or ½ cup of cold black tea

EQUIPMENT

large saucepan/cauldron

fermentation bucket

muslin/cheesecloth or fine sieve

4.5-liter/1-gallon secondary

airlock and bung

siphoning tube

METHOD

Dissolve the sugar in the boiling water. Put flowers into fermentation bucket and mix with lemon rind. Pour over rest of the water and add Campden tablet if using. Allow to stand for 4 hours, stirring occasionally.

Strain through a fine sieve or muslin cloth. Stir in lemon juice, yeast, yeast nutrient, and tannin or tea. Keep at room temperature and away from direct sunlight to ferment. When you are sure all the bubbling has slowed, which should be after about 4–10 days, depending on how warm it is, siphon into a secondary.

Allow to ferment fully, which should take about three months, before bottling. Racking once during this time won't hurt, especially if there is a buildup of sediment. Don't rack more than twice unless you really need to; this could let too much air in causing your wine to become sherrylike.

Allow to age in the bottles for at least another three months before serving. Should be ready in time to have a taste of the summer on Christmas Day, raising a glass to the old hag who let you have her elderflowers all those many months ago.

GORSE

As the old country saying goes, "Gorse is in flower when kissing is in season"—a whimsical way of saying that gorse is in flower pretty much all year round. There are around twenty different species of gorse, such as *Ulex europaeus*, in Europe and in North Africa. They can grow to a height of 3m (10ft) but are often around 2m (6ft) or less.

Foraging for gorse

Gorse is that big prickly bush that can be found in abundance in wild places such as the Pacific Dunes, and is considered a highly invasive and exotic plant. It can also often be seen on the edges of golf courses, and in areas where there have been fires. Gloves are helpful when picking the coconut-smelling flowers as gorse can be very prickly.

Gorse Flower Cordial

Gorse flower cordial is often drizzled onto vanilla ice cream to give it a sort of coconut/almond flavor. It can also be drunk on its own or used as a mixer for drinks such as Malibu and white rum.

INGREDIENTS

500ml/2 cups of gorse flowers

1.5kg/3.3lb sugar

1.2 liters/6 cups of boiling water

1 sliced lemon

2 tsp citric acid

EQUIPMENT

fermentation bucket

muslin/cheesecloth

METHOD

Wash the flowers, then place all the ingredients into a fermentation bucket. Pour over the boiling water and stir until you can no longer feel the crunch of sugar at the bottom of your bucket. Cover loosely and leave overnight.

Strain through a piece of muslin/cheesecloth into sterile bottles and refrigerate. It is ready to drink immediately and should be diluted to taste at a ratio of 4:1. Best drunk within a fortnight.

Gorse Flower Wine

Of all the flower wines, gorse is often overlooked, which is a shame. It is one of my favorites.

INGREDIENTS

3 liters/3 quarts of gorse flowers

1.5kg/3.3lb sugar

EQUIPMENT

fermentation bucket

large saucepan/cauldron

4 liters/1 gallon of water

1 cup of white wine
    grape concentrate

2 oranges

1 tsp citric acid

½ cup of black tea or 1 tsp grape tannin

1 tsp yeast nutrient

1 Campden tablet (optional)

champagne yeast

4.5-liter/1-gallon secondary

airlock and bung

siphoning tube

METHOD ···

Put the flowers into a fermentation bucket, boil half the water, and add to the bucket. Stir in the sugar, grape concentrate, and juice of the oranges. Take the white pith off the orange peel and add the peel and citric acid. If using a Campden tablet, add it now, then leave for twenty-four hours.

Add the rest of the cold water and allow to cool until it reaches room temperature, then add the yeast, nutrient, and tea. Leave to ferment for four days before straining into a secondary. Rack once after a month and more if needed. Allow to ferment out.

This wine will benefit from at least two months' aging.

First Flower Champagne

There aren't many flowers around in the early spring except for a few obstinate ones that seem to hang on in there whatever is thrown at them. During this time, which can still feel like winter, a much longer walk will be required to find enough to make a decent-sized batch of anything. This is a good thing. It's too easy to forget the outdoors when the rain is lashing against the windows and stay inside, even on the weekends, instead of braving the weather.

INGREDIENTS

500ml/2 cups of mixed gorse/dandelion/
   white dead nettle/red clover flowers

250g/9oz sugar

2 liters/1 quart of water

juice of 1 lemon

slices of 1 lemon

1 tbsp mild white wine vinegar

EQUIPMENT

large saucepan/cauldron

fermentation bucket

muslin/cheesecloth

METHOD ··

Wash all the flowers and place into the fermentation bucket. Boil up half the water, add the sugar, and stir until dissolved. Pour over the flowers, adding the lemon juice, vinegar, and lemon slices. Cover with a cloth and leave for one to four days, or until it starts to bubble a bit.

Strain through a muslin/cheesecloth into swing-top bottles and drink after about two weeks.

HORSERADISH

Horseradish (*Armoracia rusticana*) is native to Europe and has been naturalized to North America and Britain. It is in the same family as mustard and wasabi, which accounts for its real kick of a flavor. White flowers can be seen in the spring, and its leaves can grow up to 1m (3ft) tall. The leaves are not generally used; instead it is prized for its root, which can grow to as long as 1.5m (5ft).

Foraging for horseradish

On the edge of fields, close to disused railway lines and on waste-ground you will see the long feathery leaves of horseradish growing for much of the year. In the summer, mark a spot where leaves are growing and return in the autumn or spring when horseradish is at its best. If you don't mark it, the leaves will have died down and the roots will be difficult to locate.

By law you will need the landowner's permission to dig up horseradish root. However, on a conservation note, as horseradish grows from the tiniest of slivers left in the earth, you don't need to worry too much about the impact harvesting will have on future generations. I regularly forage from a patch that has grown from a few plants to a 20m^2 (215ft^2) coverage over a few years.

Growing horseradish

Horseradish is frighteningly easy to grow. Cut pieces about 15cm (6in) long off another root and put them in the ground at a depth of 5cm (2in). Feed in summer if looking unwell.

Horseradish is invasive and almost impossible to get rid of. Generally, once it's in, it's in, so be certain you want some before planting it, and consider container growing.

Horseradish Vodka—Khrenovukha

I was first given this traditional recipe by a Russian friend of mine, Sasha Kotcho-Williams. Like her and many other Russians I now swear by it whenever I get a cold. The powerful horseradish jumps right up your nose and waters your eyes with one swift kick, giving your sinuses no option other than to clear within moments.

Variations on this recipe include adding chilies, cloves, or peppercorns—for those who think horseradish doesn't have enough of a kick. If drinking for fun rather than medicinally, food pairings include salted fish, rye bread, and smoked bacon.

INGREDIENTS

1 liter/1 quart of good vodka

1 large fresh horseradish root

5 tsp of honey

EQUIPMENT

bottle or clean sealable jar

small glass

METHOD

Peel the horseradish root then slice it carefully with a very sharp knife into long thin slivers of about 10cm (4in); you should end up with twelve to fifteen of them. Place them in your thoroughly cleaned bottle. Pour a little vodka into a small glass, stir in the honey until it dissolves, then pour this over the horseradish slivers. Pour the rest of the vodka into the bottle up to the neck, covering the horseradish.

Leave in a dark place to infuse for three or four days, after which time pour it through a colander or sieve, discarding the horseradish and returning the flavored vodka to a clean bottle. Use within three to four months.

JAPANESE KNOTWEED

When I first heard of Japanese knotweed (*Fallopia japonica*) I will admit to being in awe of the plant. When it comes to weeds, this plant is the daddy. In fact, if Japanese knotweed was a Top Trump card you'd always want it in your hand. To get rid of it organically you would need to dig down 5m (15ft) and burn the soil. It can reproduce from a piece the size of a cork touching the ground, it can grow up to 20cm (8in) a day, and it can push through concrete and tarmac. Thought to have been brought over in the nineteenth century to stabilize

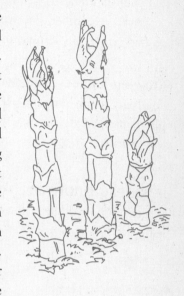

newly constructed railway embankments, it has really taken over. Why not do your bit to weaken its hold and enjoy a beer or a glass of wine at its expense?

Foraging for Japanese knotweed

Unfortunately, knotweed pops up all over the place—riverbanks, railway lines, coastlines, woodlands, wasteground. As it can grow very quickly you need to go looking for it in early spring before it gets tough and woody. It pops up out of the ground like purple asparagus spears. It's the top 20cm (8in) you need to pick as these are the most tender.

It is worth pointing out that some very noxious chemicals are sometimes used to get rid of knotweed so be certain before picking that your patch hasn't been sprayed.

Also, remember, knotweed is a controlled substance so if you are harvesting, any leftovers will need to be burned.

Growing Japanese knotweed

Due to its highly invasive nature, it is not advised that you cultivate this plant. Once it sets root, there is no getting rid of it. You have been warned!

Japanese Knotweed Ale ———————————

This is a rather odd beer that takes on the flavor of knotweed without being overpowered by it.

INGREDIENTS

1kg/2.2lb dark malt extract

55g/2oz Japanese knotweed

750g/1.5lb sugar or pale dried malt extract

13 liters/13 quarts of water

ale yeast

sugar for finishing

EQUIPMENT

large saucepan/cauldron or two big pans

muslin/cheesecloth

fermentation bucket

siphoning tube

hydrometer (optional)

thermometer (optional)

METHOD

Bring 7 liters/7 quarts of water to a boil then throw in the knotweed and keep boiling for thirty minutes, adding the malt extract and sugar in the last ten minutes.

Strain into the fermentation bucket. Pour over 6 liters/6 quarts of cold water and allow to cool. When cooled to room temperature, add the yeast.

Seal the bucket and leave in a warm place for a week, or until it has fermented.

Place a level teaspoon of sugar into each empty beer bottle and siphon the liquid into the bottles, making sure that you don't siphon in any of the sediment. Cap the bottles.

Leave the bottles for ten days, then they are ready to be opened. Knotweed beer does not keep for very long and should be drunk as soon as possible. You may want to add hops, but I think this ruins the flavor.

Japanese Knotweed Wine

See Rhubarb Wine on p. 257. Simply replace the rhubarb with knotweed and follow the same method.

Dandelion and Knotweed Mead

If you have patience, then I'd strongly suggest trying some knotweed mead. Mead is one of our oldest brewed drinks. By adding knotweed and dandelion you'll be giving it an extra hint of a floral flavor that injects a spring morning onto the taste buds.

INGREDIENTS

3.3kg/7.3lb Japanese knotweed
   (frozen and thawed)
250ml/1 cup dandelion flowers
1kg/2.2 lb honey

EQUIPMENT

saucepan
fermentation bucket
muslin/cheesecloth
secondary

4 liters/1 gallon water

activated champagne yeast starter

1tsp yeast nutrient

airlock and bung

METHOD ··

Bring the water almost to a boil and stir in the honey. Put the knotweed and dandelions into a fermentation bucket and pour over the honey mixture. Allow to cool, then add the yeast and nutrient.

After five to ten days, or when vigorous fermentation has ceased, siphon into a secondary. Rack after about two months and leave to ferment out.

Mead will need at least a year to age and about thirty minutes to breathe before drinking. The best things come to those who wait.

LIME

There are around thirty species of lime tree (genus *Tilia*), all of them native to the northern hemisphere. They can grow up to 40m (130ft) tall and are wonderful, majestic trees. There's a ten-thousand-year-old lime in Westonbirt arboretum, the UK's national arboretum. It has lived for so long due to repeated coppicing. This has resulted in the tree actually becoming a circle of trees, and standing in the middle of the ring gives one an awesome respect for the amount of time modern man has been around.

Foraging for lime

Often lime trees are planted in avenues leading to stately homes, and lining promenades in Victorian parks. They can also be found in ancient woodlands and are often part of planting schemes in newer woodlands.

Golden Lime Sap Wine (by Fergus Drennan) ————

Many trees can be tapped with various amounts of success; lime, along with birch, will give the most consistent results. However, given that *Tilia* species are wonderfully generous as far as wild food goes—gorgeous leaves for salads or wraps in the spring, and ambrosial blossoms for tisanes, wines, and cordials in early summer—it's well worth celebrating and extending the tree's fabulous resources by giving this a go.

Remember to get permission before tapping, or at the very least look official. I once tapped a whole line of trees in a town street wearing a yellow fluorescent jacket and safety hat. I climbed up a ladder and strapped on 2-liter plastic bottles with tape, and when questioned I said I was doing a PhD in fungal infections of native trees.

I jest, of course . . .

INGREDIENTS

4 liters/1 gallon of lime sap

1kg/2.2lb sugar

juice of 1 lemon

1 tsp yeast nutrient

1 packet high alcohol yeast

EQUIPMENT

drill and tubing

two 4.5-liter/1-gallon secondaries

large saucepan/cauldron

airlock and bung

funnel

To obtain the sap, follow the instructions given on p. 103 for tapping birch sap. Then make a yeast starter culture as directed on p. 33.

Put all the sap and sugar into a large pan and bring to a boil, stirring to dissolve the sugar. Add the juice of the lemon and the yeast nutrient.

Divide it equally between the two secondaries using the sterilized plastic funnel. Allow to reach room temperature before adding the yeast starter culture and fit bungs and airlocks. Leave in a warm place for five days before transferring all the sap into just one of the secondaries. Ferment until no bubbles appear in the airlock (one to three months). Before bottling it in early summer it can be good to stuff in a few large handfuls of lime blossom and leave to infuse for a week. Drink young.

If you get excited about 100 percent wild wines, as I do, you could experiment down that route. Boil 35 liters (35 quarts) of sap down to 4 liters/1 gallon and once cooled to room temperature add a homemade high alcohol tolerant yeast starter.

When fermented out, you can keep adding small quantities of tree sap syrup to see if it will ferment further. Fergus's note: *I've only tried this method with birch sap as it's far easier to collect in quantity.*

Relaxing Bedtime Tea

Light in the summer can be like courgettes (zucchini): you think you're never going to get any, then suddenly, boom, there's more than you can possibly need. It can therefore be useful to have some relaxing wild tea on hand to help you drift off to sleep despite the huge spotlight shining on you moments after your head touches the pillow.

While walking around any area with natural hedgerow during springtime you will see hawthorn in blossom, which can be picked and dried. Lime flowers a little later, usually during midsummer; lime flower can also be picked and dried. Lemon balm can be found from spring to autumn and will die down during the winter months. It too can be dried for later use.

INGREDIENTS	EQUIPMENT
1 tsp lime blossom	kettle
1 tsp hawthorn blossom	teapot
1 tsp lemon balm	strainer
250ml/7 fl. oz of water	mug

METHOD

Boil the water in the kettle. Place the herbs into a teapot, pour over hot water and leave to infuse for at least five minutes, and up to fifteen minutes. Pour into a mug and relax.

NETTLES

Nettles (family *Urticaceae*) are a common sight and can be found on most wasteland and at woodland edges all year round. There are many different strengths of nettle sting, from the fen nettle found in the east of the UK, which hardly stings at all, to a nettle found in California whose sting can linger for up to three days. The

Romans found our nettles feeble and decided to import a species with a stronger sting. They were a strange lot and did this in order to whip themselves with it to keep warm in our colder climate. So if you ever get stung and it seems worse than usual you can join in with the rest of us foragers and shout, "Bloody Romans!"

Foraging for nettles

Nettles should not be foraged from land that is contaminated so try to acquaint yourself with a bit of local history before picking. They often grow in places that have been inhabited by man, and I have found many growing around old Roman settlements. They are phosphate lovers and will happily grow on the sites of old toilets. They also like disturbed soil.

Old nettles should be avoided; only the top leaves should be harvested. There are two reasons for this: first, the young top leaves are the tastiest; second, nettles are the habitat for at least five of our native butterflies. When harvesting nettles it is advisable to wear thick gardening or even welding gloves to avoid being stung. It is possible to pick them without being stung, but this takes quite a bit of (painful) practice.

Here are two nettle ale recipes from my friend Stonehead. Apart from having an ancient stone circle, Stonehead also has plenty of nettles—unsurprising, as we now know, as nettles often grow in areas where humans, through composting and manure, have raised the nitrogen levels in the soil.

Nettle Ale 1

Those used to real ale might have trouble with this recipe, even though it is a deliciously refreshing drink which is rapidly becoming a staple drink in the UK.

INGREDIENTS

22 liters/5.5 gallons of water

2kg/4.5lb (4 carrier bags full) of
   nettle tips

juice of 2 lemons

juice of 2 oranges

3kg/6.5lb sugar

100g/3.5oz cream of tartar

large dandelion root *or* large ginger root (optional)

ale yeast

EQUIPMENT

large saucepan/cauldron

fermentation bucket

muslin/cheesecloth

siphoning tube

METHOD

Boil all the water. Place clean nettles into a fermentation bucket and pour the boiling water over them. Add washed and bruised roots if using. Allow to infuse, cool, then strain back into the cauldron/pan. Add the lemon and orange juice, sugar, and cream of tartar. Heat gently and stir until the sugar has dissolved—do not boil. Pour back into the fermentation bucket and leave to cool to room temperature before pitching the yeast. Cover tightly with muslin cloth and leave in a warm place for three to seven days, or when fully fermented.

Siphon into bottles and leave to condition for a week before drinking. Serve cold.

Nettle Ale 2

Like all good homebrewers, Stonehead has a recipe that he brews up before a party. This is his simple, stronger nettle ale. He uses brewer's yeast, but I've had much better results with ale yeast.

INGREDIENTS

5kg/11lb (10 carrier bags full) of
   young nettles
20 liters/5 gallons of water
10 lemons (juice them,
   then cut off the rind)
640g/1.4lb sugar
140g/5oz cream of tartar
ale yeast

EQUIPMENT

large saucepan/cauldron
fermentation bucket
airlock
muslin/cheesecloth
siphoning tube

METHOD

Rinse the nettles, drain, and boil in the water for fifteen minutes.

Strain the liquor into a fermentation bucket containing the lemon juice, lemon rind (no pith), sugars, and cream of tartar. Stir vigorously and allow to cool to blood temperature.

Sprinkle the yeast over the top, cover the vat loosely with a cloth, and leave for twenty-four hours. Replace the cloth with an airlock and leave to ferment for a further four to six days.

Strain, and either bottle or keg. If using a keg, it's worth adding another half a pound of sugar to help get the pressure up.

Leave for at least seven days before drinking. Serve chilled.

Nettle ale made in this way went down a treat last year with about twenty people who consumed the best part of five gallons at a barbecue.

Nettle Wine

Nettles are a great wild food. Don't worry about getting stung, as cooking wilts the hairs and will neutralize the sting. Keep it simple: a fresh spring nettle soup with sour cream and a few wild garlic leaves can be an absolute delight. The wine, on the other hand, is the opposite: it can lack something when drunk on its own. This can be virtuous, as it works very well when used as a base for a wine cocktail. For a wild cocktail, mix with a little elderflower champagne, a few drops of rosewater, and a splash of ginger beer. I can't think of a better way to mark the start of the foraging season.

INGREDIENTS

2 liters/2 quarts carrier bag of nettles

3.3kg/7lb sugar

2 liters/2 quarts of water

1 orange

1 lemon

120ml/½ cup of cold black tea

1 tsp wine nutrient

white wine yeast

EQUIPMENT

large saucepan/cauldron

fermentation bucket

gallon secondary

airlock and bung

siphoning tube

muslin/cheesecloth

large plastic spoon

METHOD

Wash the nettles and place inside a fermentation bucket with the sugar, water, tea, nutrient, and the juice and rind of the citrus fruits. Allow to cool to room temperature, then add the white wine yeast. Stand the bucket for five days in an area that is consistently warm (no more than 70°F). After about five days, strain into a secondary, attaching an airlock and bung.

Rack once during fermentation. Bottle when fermentation has ceased; this should be in about three months, depending how warm you keep it.

Hair of the Dog Tea

Hangover cures are probably as old as hangovers. The Romans used to put twenty bulbs of garlic into a gallon of wine. The Greek dramatist Aristophanes had a different idea and said in a poem, "Take the hair, it's well written, of the dog by which you're bitten. Work off one wine by his brother, and one labor with another"—which is where the phrase "hair of the dog" comes from. This tea can come as a godsend after too much alcohol has been consumed, and I remain eternally grateful to my herbalist friend Max Drake who shared it with me.

In case you haven't heard of meadowsweet, it's a tall plant that grows typically in damp meadows. It's the creamy-white fragrant flowers you're after.

INGREDIENTS	EQUIPMENT
thumb-sized piece of bruised ginger root	kettle
1 tsp meadowsweet	teapot

1 tsp rosemary

1 tsp nettle leaves

3 green cardamom pods

500ml/2 cups of hot water

tea strainer

mug

METHOD

Boil the kettle. Put all the ingredients into a teapot and cover with hot water. Allow to infuse for five minutes. While you're waiting, hold head and say, "Never, ever again."

Pour and sip. This will make a few cups, and you can keep topping up the teapot and drinking all day, or until you start to feel a bit more human. Drink plenty of water as well.

PINE

Anecdotal evidence suggests that in the winter of 1534–5 Jacques Cartier, the captain of a pioneering French vessel, found himself stranded by 1.8m (6ft) thick sheets of ice on the St. Lawrence River in Canada. Supplies soon dwindled, and scurvy broke out. Of the 110-man crew barely ten were able to move as they were so sick. Luckily, local knowledge pointed out a resource full of vitamin C that surrounded them—pine needles. A simple decoction was made and distributed among the crew, and most were brought back from the brink of death.

Foraging for pine

Pine (genus *Pinus*) is often grown on plantations, which is why pine woodland is commonplace. Due to the size pine trees can grow to they are sometimes found planted close to busy highways, intended as a barrier.

Scots pine is native to the UK, northern Europe, and as far south as Portugal. It can sometimes be found growing wild on heath and moorland.

When picking needles, go for the greenest, newest needles possible. Young trees should be left alone. If foraging in a woodland, look around for fallen branches as this saves you from taking anything from the tree.

Pine Needle Cordial

As pine needles are available all year round this drink has quickly become a staple in our house. The taste on its own is unique, and may be one of those acquired tastes, although the resinous flavor enhances the juniper in gin and therefore makes this an ideal mixer.

As with many recipes, once shared they are developed. 125ml/½ cup of edible flowers such as Himalayan balsam, elderflower, or dandelion can be added to the mix for color and added flavor. Award-winning chef and friend Leona Williams (of St. Werburghs city farm café) adds a thumb-sized piece of ginger along with edible flowers, which works amazingly well.

INGREDIENTS

50g/1.7oz pine needles

2 tsp citric acid

225g/8oz sugar

500ml/2 cups of boiling water

EQUIPMENT

saucepan

large bowl

METHOD ···

Put the pine needles into the bowl with the citric acid and sugar. Pour over boiling water, cover with a dish towel, and leave overnight. Decant into sterilized bottles.

Other uses

Hot water poured over pine needles then left for at least five minutes can make an excellent tea. Also, if you ever find yourself stuck in the wild with no access to boiling water, pine needles can be chewed (then spat out) to obtain the vitamin C.

ROSE (PETALS)

There are around 150 different species of rose (genus *Rosa*), and roses have been cultivated for thousands of years. They are mostly native to Asia but some are native to Europe, North America, and Africa. Roses were used cosmetically and medicinally by the Greeks, Romans, ancient Chinese, and Persians. The Chinese still use roses to treat the spleen and liver.

Foraging for rose petals

Collect petals in late spring, selecting ones that have just opened or are fully opened but fresh-looking. Collect only the petals, not the central flower—that way rosehips will still be produced later on (see Rosehips, p. 258, for more details).

Japanese Rose Petal Vodka (by Fergus Drennan) ——

To make this delightful drink, the alcoholic equivalent of Turkish Delight, is simplicity itself. The blossoms of any pesticide-free fragrant rose, wild or cultivated, can be used. I usually go for *Rosa rugosa* (Japanese rose) for the superior color and aroma, but the dog or field rose works just as well flavor-wise. In the latter case I usually stuff a few (ten to fifteen) corn poppy blossoms in the bottle to intensify the color.

Some *Rosa rugosa* varieties have completely white rather than pink blossoms. It can be fun to use these as that way there is no clue whatsoever to the marvelous flavor that awaits people when they are handed the final product. *Rosa rugosa* can be found most often as a garden plant or in public places such as parks, supermarket parking lots, and sports arenas. It also grows wild on shingle beaches, especially in southern England.

INGREDIENTS

1 liter/1 quart of rose petals

750ml/3 cups of vodka/gin or tequila

sugar (to taste): approx 1–1½ tbsp/cup

EQUIPMENT

2 large sealable jars

muslin/cheesecloth

METHOD ·······

Tip the blossoms onto a tray and leave for fifteen minutes to give any beetles a final chance to leg it. Gently fill a jar, pushing the blossoms down a little but not overpacking. Pour in the spirit to fill, shake, allow to stand for half an hour, then push down the blossoms with a wooden spoon handle (or similar) to release any air. Fill to the very top, cap, and leave for a day or so, two days max.

Strain through muslin/cheesecloth into the second jar, squeezing firmly to make sure you get all the spirit out. Add the desired amount of sugar, stirring to dissolve. This tipple is now ready to drink neat, over ice, as a mix, or even as a flavoring for both sweet and savory dishes.

SUMMER

Blackberry wine

Blackberry cordial

Blackberry varenye

Blackcurrants: Crème de cassis

Blackcurrants et al: Berry kompot with herbs

Carrot whisky

Chili vodka

Cleavers coffee

Courgette and golden raisin wine

Crab apple wine

Comforting crab apple liqueur

Elderberry port

Elderberry cordial

Elderberry liqueur

Elderberry and blackberry wine

Lavender cordial

Lavender mead

Mint: Crème de menthe

Mint cordial

Mint et al: Windy tea

Mugwort porter

Mulberry liqueur

Rape: Cruciferous champagne

Rosebay willowherb champagne

Sumac lemonade

Walnuts: Nocino

IT CAN BE IMPOSSIBLE to go out for a forage at this time of year without someone saying, "What are you doing? What's that? Isn't that poisonous?" Summer seems to be the only season when some people think the outdoors exists.

I love getting up at five a.m. on at least a few occasions at this time of year, because that's when summer is nothing short of magical. What's more, you will only see the occasional jogger, dog walker, or fisherman, which takes the audience participation out of foraging.

Weeds grow almost before your very eyes at this time of year, especially after a rainstorm, so identify and eat the ones you can while weeding your fruit and vegetable plot. But the harvest is starting and it will be easy to fill a bag with produce from a single visit to an average-sized plot.

Water can be an issue, especially if you have a container garden. Containers can be moved out of the sun and into the shade on especially hot days.

Wine-makers can struggle to prevent their fermenting wines from reaching high temperatures that could cause the yeast to die off or ferment too quickly. Secondaries and fermentation buckets can be insulated from the heat by putting sheets over them. If there simply isn't a cool place in your house, you could keep your fermenting booze in a bowl of water so that their containers cool down. Certainly keep your drinks away from direct sunlight, especially red wines, as the sun can ruin their color.

In season (garden): plums, blackcurrants, redcurrants, cherries, raspberries, strawberries, carrots, gooseberries, runner beans, lettuce, peas, potatoes, sweet corn (maize), tomatoes, turnips.

In season (wild): lime flowers, elderberries, gooseberries, black-berries, early apples, wild strawberries, hops, sorrel, fat hen, red clover flowers, yarrow (flower), ground ivy, dandelion.

BLACKBERRIES

Blackberries (*Rubus fruticosus*) are another foragers' favorite and can be found throughout the northern hemisphere and in South America. Many of the older books and my childhood memories of the 1980s insist that blackberries are an autumn fruit rarely seen before the end of August. These days, if you get out in the autumn to pick blackberries you may be disappointed as the majority of the fruit seems to have gone by this point. But you will still find some hanging on in there: climate change seems to have extended the blackberry season to the end of autumn, even into winter.

For most, the blackberry is the first (and often only) food that will be foraged. I think blackberries work well as a barometer for how popular foraging is becoming. Over the last five years I've seen more and more people out and about picking blackberries.

It is interesting to note that blackberries used to be a garden plant while raspberries were seen as wild. Over the last five hundred or so years this has changed rather dramatically.

Foraging for blackberries

Picking them is not without its hazards, and plastic bags are a no-no due to the thorns: one snag of your bag and a day's picking can end up falling among the thorns. It is these thorns that give blackberries one of their country names, "lawyers": once they trap you it's very difficult to get loose!

Blackberries (or brambles) tend to take over wasteground if left unchecked; they can also be found on the edges of parks, in wooded thickets, by railway lines and bicycle paths, at field edges, and as undergrowth in forests.

Growing blackberries

The biggest bonus of growing blackberries in your garden (apart from having them very close at hand) is that you can grow one of the many thornless varieties, such as Black Diamond, Nightfall, Apache, Chester, or Triple Crown.

Plant canes in the autumn about 1.5m (5ft) apart in well-draining soil and in full sun or partial shade. As blackberries can easily take over you could try taming yours by training it with wires; you could even consider growing it in a large pot. You won't be seeing much fruit in the first year as blackberries grow on two-year-old growth. Once a cane has produced it is worth pruning it back.

Blackberry Wine

A country favorite, and certainly a good blackberry wine can be a great thirst quencher on a hot day. This recipe is based on one by Mike Griffiths from north Nottinghamshire.

INGREDIENTS

2kg/4.4 lb blackberries

1 cup of strong black tea

1.5kg/3.3lb sugar

4 liters/4 quarts of water

juice of 1 lemon

1 tsp pectolase

red wine yeast

1 tsp yeast nutrient

EQUIPMENT

large saucepan/cauldron

fermentation bucket

4.5-liter/1-gallon secondary

airlock and bung

muslin/cheesecloth

siphoning tube

potato masher

METHOD

To extract more juice from the fruit it helps if you keep them in the freezer overnight then allow them to thaw before using. Make sure the berries are clean and place them into a fermentation bucket. Crush with your clean hands or a sterilized stainless-steel or plastic potato masher. Boil 1 liter/1 quart of water, pour over the fruit, add the sugar, and stir until the sugar has dissolved. Add the rest of the cold water then stir in the remaining ingredients. Cover, then leave to stand in a warm place for three days.

Strain into a secondary and attach the airlock. Rack after a month and allow to ferment out. Blackberry wine can sometimes be quite drinkable as soon as it has fully fermented.

Blackberry Cordial

Blackberries freeze very well so this cordial can even be made from that rouge bag of berries you find at the back of the freezer one cold winter's morning.

INGREDIENTS

1.5kg/3.3lb blackberries

1.5 liters/1.5 quarts of water

5 cloves

1 tsp lemon juice

100ml/3.5 fl. oz brandy

400g/14oz sugar

EQUIPMENT

2 medium saucepans

spoon

potato masher

muslin/cheesecloth

METHOD ....

Wash the blackberries and freeze overnight. Thaw, put in a saucepan, and cover with the water. Bring to a boil and mash them to help break up the skins. Set aside and when cool enough to handle, strain into the second pan along with the cloves, lemon juice, and brandy.

Bring to a boil, stirring in the sugar. Allow to boil for a further twenty minutes. Cool and bottle. It will remain at its best in the fridge for about two weeks, but will be fine for much longer than that.

Blackberry Varenye

This recipe was given to me by Sasha Kotcho-Williams. It's a traditional Russian recipe for, well, runny jam—halfway between a jam and a syrup. You can make it out of almost anything, but fruit and berries are the most popular.

The result is versatile—put it on your toast, dribble it over ice cream, stir it through yogurt or porridge, or be traditional and stir a spoonful or two into your (non-milky) tea. Having a fruit flavor in your tea can be an odd experience at first, but after a few cups I am sure you'll be hooked.

Varenye made from raspberries, blackberries, and red- and black-currants is considered especially healthy and is often given to ill people.

INGREDIENTS

1kg/2.2lb blackberries (or raspberries, or
  currants)
100g/3.5oz blackberry leaves (substitute
  as above if desired)
700g/1.5lb sugar (you can add more
  to taste, but the more you add the
  thicker your varenye will be)
500ml/2 cups of water
3 tbsp lemon juice

EQUIPMENT

saucepan
jam jars

METHOD ··

Bring the water to a boil, steep the leaves in it for ten minutes, then discard the leaves and dissolve the sugar in the water. Add the fruit and lemon juice and boil for about ten minutes. Pour into sterilized jars and seal.

Yields five to six small jars that will keep for at least a year.

BLACKCURRANTS

Blackcurrant shrubs (*Ribes nigrum*) are native to northern Europe and northern Asia. Growing up to 2m (6ft) tall they grow dark purple, almost black edible berries about 1cm (0.5in) in diameter. Studies have concluded that consuming blackcurrants can help reduce the effects of heart disease, diabetes, and Alzheimer's disease, which has earned them that tabloids-favorite title of superfood.

Foraging for blackcurrants

It is sometimes difficult to beat the birds to the blackcurrants when they're in season during late summer. They can be found in the wild in woodlands close to streams and are often hidden amid the undergrowth in public parks. There are other black berries that could be confused with blackcurrants, such as laurel berries (which are poisonous), so compare with your local greengrocer's berries Remember, never pick and eat anything you are not 100 percent sure of.

Growing blackcurrants

One-year-old blackcurrant bushes can be bought during the winter months to be planted in soil enriched with compost, and they need a fertile and moist soil in a spot that gets plenty of sun. Space bushes 1.5m (5ft) apart and clear the area of weeds. Prune in the third year during the autumn by cutting back one third of the oldest branches as close as you can to ground level, and repeat for subsequent years. A well-cared-for bush will yield 5kg/10lb of fruit for twenty years or more.

Crème de Cassis

We joke that my friend Fiona only drinks two units of alcohol a year as she simply "doesn't like the stuff," which I find very odd. Those two units are normally consumed at her aunty and uncle's house in the foothills of the Pyrenees during the summer where she drinks their homemade crème de cassis.

INGREDIENTS

1kg/2.2lb blackcurrants

750ml/6 cups of eau de vie or vodka

150ml/5 fl. oz of water

300g/11oz sugar

EQUIPMENT

large sealable jar

muslin/cheesecloth

small saucepan

blender or potato masher

METHOD

Wash the blackcurrants and place into a large jar. Pour over the eau de vie or vodka and leave for five months.

Put into the blender or mash with a potato masher and then strain. The object is to get as much juice out as possible.

Heat the water until hot enough to dissolve the sugar then stir in the sugar until you have a syrup. Allow to cool before mixing with the liquor. Decant into bottles, seal tightly, and keep in a cool dark place for a further three months before drinking.

Berry Kompot with Herbs

This is one of the many recipes given to me by my Russian friend Sasha. Eastern European kompots differ from the French compote and can be diluted to make a cordial or added to tea instead of sugar, as with Varenye (see p. 154).

INGREDIENTS

500g/1lb blackcurrants

300g/10oz redcurrants

300g/10oz raspberries

500g/1lb sugar

2 liters/2 quarts of water

EQUIPMENT

3-liter/3-quart jar (or several smaller jars)

fine sieve or colander with muslin/

cheesecloth

saucepan

potato masher or rolling pin

1 lemon

1 large bunch of lemon balm or mint

some herbs (almost any will do, but use less of the following: rosemary,
    tarragon, thyme, sage, lime blossom)

METHOD ···

Put the blackcurrants in a saucepan and mash with a potato masher
or the end of a rolling pin. Boil the water, pour it over the fruit, stir
in the sugar, and boil for a few minutes.

   Pour through a fine sieve, or a colander lined with muslin.
Return the liquid to the saucepan (discarding the seeds) and bring
almost to a boil, then add the lemon (quartered), the redcurrants
(removed from the stalks), the raspberries, and herbs (leaves only).
Bring to a boil, then pour into the sterilized jar(s).

   Wait at least three days before serving. Will keep for a year or
longer.

CARROTS

Carrots are a member of the same family (Umbelliferae) as hemlock,
parsley, and cumin. They are thought to originate in Afghanistan and
used to be a variety of colors but never orange. It wasn't until the
sixteenth century, when Dutch growers crossbred yellow carrots
with red carrots in honor of William of Orange, that our orange
carrot (*Daucus carota*) was first born—or at least that's the most
popular of the many theories.

   China munches its way through over a third of the world's
carrots. Here in the UK we are massive carrot lovers too, eating a

staggering 677,144 metric tons of them every year. Carrots have always been popular and arrived before the *Mayflower*.

Growing carrots

In the UK, northern Europe, and parts of North America you can risk a planting of carrots under a cloche in late winter for an early crop, though sowing in early spring is more usual. Carrots take two and a half to three and a half months to grow to full size and can be planted continuously in the South and from late winter to early fall in the north. In a similar way to potatoes, carrots are split into main crop and earlies. The earlies are usually small and stubby-rooted; the main crops are the long, slender carrots familiar to shoppers. If you don't have a garden, carrots can easily be grown in a bucket either indoors or out.

Carrot Whisky

This recipe was given to me by Jeremy Daniel Meadows from New Zealand. Although it is certainly not a whisky, it does pack a punch. Jeremy insists that using two types of yeast will help add to the strength. I'm not so sure, but it seems to work.

INGREDIENTS

4.5 liters/1 gallon of carrot juice

4.5 liters/1 gallon of water

2kg/4.4lb brown sugar

1.5kg/3.3lb white sugar

500g/1lb chopped golden raisins

500g/1lb barley

thumb-sized piece of peeled ginger root

1 Campden tablet (optional)

EQUIPMENT

large saucepan/cauldron

fermentation bucket

two 4.5-liter/1-gallon secondaries

two airlocks and bungs

siphoning tube

1 tsp citric acid

1 tsp tartaric acid

3 tsp yeast nutrient

2 vitamin C pills

1 tsp of pectolase

high strength wine yeast

white wine yeast

METHOD ···

Bring 2 liters/2 quarts of the water to a boil, add the sugars, golden raisins, acids, and nutrient and simmer for fifteen minutes. Pour into a fermentation bucket and add the carrot juice and a further liter/quart of water. If using, add the Campden tablet too. Leave for twenty-four hours.

Crush the vitamin pills and add them to the must along with the grated ginger and pectolase, and pitch the yeasts.

Rinse the barley in warm water and keep insulated overnight. Add the rest of the water and pour into the fermentation bucket. Leave for two days, stirring occasionally, then strain into two secondaries. Rack after two weeks.

After three weeks, dissolve 200g/8 oz sugar into 250ml/1 cup of water and add that to the secondaries. After a further two weeks add 400g/1lb of sugar dissolved in 250ml/1 cup of water. Allow to ferment out, racking once more if necessary.

Bottle and keep for as long as possible before trying. At least six months, preferably years, by which time the smell of carrots should have disappeared and it will taste more like a mixture of dark rum, sherry, and bourbon.

CHILIES

Related to tomatoes, potatoes, deadly nightshade and tobacco, peppers (genus *Capsicum*) have traveled the world from the Americas, where they originated. Some argue that they are among the first cultivated foods as ancient man would have needed something to disguise the at best bland and at worst rancid food he'd have eaten.

Growing chilies

Chilies are easily grown from seed. They are self-pollinating so can be grown indoors. Sow in 20cm (8in) pots at a temperature of 21°C (70°F) to guarantee germination. They can be planted in late winter to ensure a good size is reached by the fruiting period. Peppers will redden as they ripen (although some varieties will ripen to different colors).

Chili Vodka

Chili vodka is one of those "man" drinks where the word "man" can be transposed to mean "a little stupid." The effects of a sip of chili vodka—depending on its strength, of course—can last for a whole evening. It causes the same burning sensation as eating a raw chili. A chili vodka made with sixty chilies infused for three months is used for initiation purposes by our homebrewing circle in Bristol. As yet no one has drunk more than a mouthful, and no one has gone back for seconds. I guess this means none of us is a real man.

INGREDIENTS	EQUIPMENT
20 chilies (the variety is your choice—all are different strengths)	sealable jar
vodka	

METHOD ···

Wash the chilies and put into a jar. Top up with vodka and leave for between three and twenty days, depending on the strength of flavor required. The truly hardcore (or manly) might even leave the chilies in the bottle for up to three months for a mouth-burning sensation like no other.

CLEAVERS

For information, see the cleavers juice recipes under Spring (p. 114).

Cleavers Coffee

The sticky buds appear by late summer and are the only ingredient in this interesting "coffee." A strange name for it, I know. It tastes nothing like coffee. It is, however, a very refreshing drink all of its own and worth the effort if only to see what can be made with an everyday weed.

INGREDIENTS	EQUIPMENT
cleaver buds	roasting pan
	coffee grinder or mortar and pestle

METHOD ···

Gather as many of the seeds (or sticky buds) as you can; at least one tablespoonful will be needed per cup of coffee. Some suggest sending your children out into places full of cleavers then picking the buds off them afterward. Otherwise you can lightly grip the cleavers at the bottom of the plant and gently move your fingers up the stem to remove the buds.

When you have gathered enough, gently roast them in an oven on a low heat—120°C/250°F/gas mark half—for one hour or until they have gone crispy. If collected on a sunny day they will benefit from sun-drying first.

Allow to cool, then grind as you would coffee beans, with either a coffee grinder on a fine setting, a mortar and pestle, or the nut grinder attachment on a food processor.

Use as you would regular filter coffee.

COURGETTES/ZUCCHINI

The courgette or zucchini is a member of the squash family, making it a close relative of pumpkins and gourds. The word "zucchini" comes from the Italian *zucchino,* which means "small squash" or "marrow," so basically it's an immature marrow (*Cucurbita pepo*).

Growing courgettes

Courgettes are easily grown from seed. Place at a depth of 2cm (1in) into small pots filled with seed compost and put on the windowsill in the springtime. Don't let the pots dry out, and allow to grow until two true leaves have formed. The two leaves that first appear are not true leaves but grow to give energy to the seedling; it is the leaves that grow after these that are known as the true leaves.

Plant out only after all danger of frost has passed, in nutrient-rich soil. Kill all slugs that come anywhere close to your seedlings— they seem to love courgette plants. Feed when fruits appear and keep watered in dry weather.

Courgette and Golden Raisin Wine _____

Every year there is a cry across community gardens and vegetable patches around the world: "What on earth am I going to do with all these courgettes?" Packed lunch boxes have courgettes sitting inside them as a healthy alternative to chocolate bars; thinly disguised, they lurk on the plate at every meal across the summer months; I've even heard of people making courgette ice cream. Courgettes certainly are one of those vegetables synonymous with the word "glut." Luckily, us wine-makers can make use of them and turn them into a fairly good dry white wine. As a wine on its own there's not a huge amount of taste, hence the addition of bananas and golden raisins. You could also experiment with some green beans in the mix!

INGREDIENTS	EQUIPMENT
3kg/6.5lb fresh courgettes	small saucepan
1kg/2lb sugar	fermentation bucket
2 overripe bananas	4.5-liter/1-gallon secondary
500g/1lb golden raisins	airlock and bung
4 liters/4 quarts of water	mincer (or sharp knife)
1 tsp citric acid	siphoning tube

a thumb-sized piece of bruised ginger root

1 tsp yeast nutrient

1 Campden tablet (optional)

champagne yeast

METHOD ··

Chop the courgettes into 3cm (1in) pieces and put into the freezer overnight to soften. Allow to thaw, and meanwhile bring 500ml/ 2 cups of water to a boil and stir in the sugar. Mince the golden raisins (or chop finely) and add these to the water too. Set aside. Mash the banana and mix it with all the other ingredients (except the yeast) in the fermentation bucket. Cover and allow to cool to hand-hot. If using a Campden tablet, add it now. Leave overnight.

Add the yeast and leave for four days loosely covered before straining the liquid into a secondary and attaching an airlock and bung. Rack after a month and then again if needed. Allow to ferment out before bottling.

This wine will benefit from at least three months' aging.

CRAB APPLES

Crab apples (*Malus sylvestris*) are the wild brothers or ancestors of our cultivated apples. Contrary to popular belief they are not all sharp and acidic; some are even good to eat straight off the tree. They are widespread throughout Europe, Asia, and North America, and the trees are anything between 4m and 12m (12ft and 40ft) tall.

Foraging for crab apples

I am sure you've seen a tree full of crab apples as you've gone about your business. Year after year that fruit sits on the trees unharvested. They mostly grow in parks and on roadsides but can sometimes be found in hedgerows and in woodlands.

Growing crab apples

See Apples (p. 197).

Crab Apple Wine

It is almost impossible to say what a crab apple wine will taste or even look like as there are so many varieties of crab apple all with different flavors and colors. What I can say is this: most will create a decent, fairly dry wine.

INGREDIENTS

2.5kg/5.5lb crab apples

500g/1lb raisins

1.5kg/3.3lb sugar

4 liters/4 quarts of water

1 tsp citric acid

1 tsp pectolase

1 tsp yeast nutrient

1 Campden tablet (optional)

champagne yeast

EQUIPMENT

fermentation bucket

muslin/cheesecloth

4.5-liter/1-gallon secondary

airlock and bung

siphoning tube

METHOD ··

Wash the crab apples and take out the stalks. Then crush them and place into the fermentation bucket. Top up the bin with 3 liters/ 3 quarts of cold water and add the pectolase, the citric acid, and the Campden tablet (if using). Leave loosely covered for twenty-four hours.

Boil the remaining water, dissolve the sugar in it, and add this, the raisins, the nutrient, and the yeast to the fermentation bucket. Leave to ferment for one week.

Rack at least once and leave to ferment out before bottling. This wine will benefit from at least six months' aging.

Comforting Crab Apple Liqueur ─────────────────

This simple recipe is apparently popular in Denmark where they drink it with rich meats.

INGREDIENTS

20 crab apples

1 liter/1 quart of vodka

EQUIPMENT

large sealable jar

muslin cloth

METHOD ··

Cut your crab apples in half and place them into the jar. Fill with vodka (keep the vodka bottle) and put in a cool dark place for three months. Return to the jar every now and then just to give it a jolly good shake.

Strain back into the vodka bottle and return to the cool dark place for a further two months before drinking.

ELDERBERRIES

Elder (*Sambucus nigra*) grows throughout Europe, North Africa, Southwest Asia, North America, and Canada. Elderberries and alcohol go hand in hand. The berries are known as the "Englishman's grape."

Foraging for elderberries

Elder is rather prolific and can readily set seed inside walls, often stripping the mortar of all its moisture and crumbling it. It tends to grow as a rather big weed at roadsides, in parks, wastegrounds, and woodlands, in fact pretty much anywhere it is given space.

Cut the lower bracts and leave the ones higher up for the birds to eat.

See Elderflowers (p. 120) for more details on foraging and growing elder.

Elderberry Port

Elderberry port has been described as one of the finest homemade wines there is. It is one of those recipes for which many people will have their own slight variation—perhaps with more elderberries, or no blackberries or sloes. The following recipe is my favorite. I have seen some replace the oranges with bananas to give the overall wine greater body.

INGREDIENTS	EQUIPMENT
1kg/2.2lb elderberries	large saucepan/cauldron
500g/1lb blackberries	fermentation bucket
500g/1lb oranges	4.5-liter/1-gallon secondary

140g/5oz sloes

3.5 liters/3.5 quarts of water

1.5kg/3.3lb sugar

1 Campden tablet (optional)

port style or red wine yeast

water to top up

airlock and bung

siphoning tube

muslin/cheesecloth

large funnel

large plastic spoon

METHOD

While weighing the fruit, put the water on to boil. Peel the oranges, ensuring that as much pith as possible has been taken off them. Put the fruit and sugar into a sterilized fermentation bucket and cover with the water. Stir until the sugar dissolves.

Allow to cool, then strain the must through a muslin/cheese-cloth into a secondary. As a lot of fruit is used the large funnel may get quite heavy and it would be helpful to have an extra pair of hands at this stage. Add the Campden tablet (if using) and leave for twenty-four hours.

Add the yeast to the secondary and leave to ferment violently. After a few days, when it has calmed down, top up with cold water. Rack after a month and then again as required, and allow to ferment out.

You may notice that the fruit is still viable and can be used again by following this process. You may wish to add a further 500g/1lb of elderberries to ensure a full-bodied port.

Elderberry Cordial

Elderberry cordial, even when diluted, keeps that rich, dark, deep, red wine color that is so distinctive of the fruit. It is great to make a batch of the stuff ready to help you through the winter months as the high vitamin C and antioxidant content can help keep coughs, colds, and flu at bay.

INGREDIENTS

600g/20oz elderberries

600g/20oz honey

12 cloves (optional)

800ml/3 cups of boiling water

EQUIPMENT

saucepan

large bowl

muslin/cheesecloth

METHOD

Place the elderberries into a saucepan and cover with the boiling water. Allow to simmer gently for about fifteen minutes, stirring occasionally. Strain the elderberries through the muslin/cheesecloth into the bowl, allowing as much liquid as possible to be extracted. Return the strained liquid to the saucepan and add the honey. Boil for about ten minutes, stirring occasionally to prevent the honey burning.

At this point you can also add the cloves. They are traditionally used and will help preserve the cordial beyond the usual two-week shelf life of homemade cordials. However, they impart a strong flavor, and many prefer this cordial without them.

Decant into sterilized bottles. It will keep for at least two weeks, or longer if put into plastic bottles and frozen (or if using cloves).

Elderberry Liqueur

As elderberries are full of antioxidants and high in vitamin C, elderberry liqueur is often kept in the medicine cabinet and taken out during the flu season (though it may seem like a travesty to imbibe elderberry liqueur solely as a medicine: it is so moreish that since developing this drink I have found it very difficult to make anything else using elderberries).

INGREDIENTS

800ml/3 cups pints of elderberries
750ml/26 fl. oz bottle of vodka
50g/2oz sugar
the rind of ½ a lemon

EQUIPMENT

1 large sealable jar
muslin cheesecloth

METHOD ··

Put the elderberries into a large jar and pour all but the last 20ml/0.5 fl. oz of vodka over them. Drink that last 20ml/0.5 fl. oz and keep the bottle.

Add the lemon rind (with as little pith as humanly possible). Seal, then shake the jar and put into a dark cupboard for three months.

Pour the sugar into the vodka bottle—though you may wish to "upgrade" to a swing-top bottle for aesthetic reasons—and strain the liquor over the top of it. Shake vigorously and return to the cupboard for at least two months, shaking again every time you remember it is there (at least once a day for the first week, then less).

After this time it is perfectly drinkable, but if you can manage to restrain yourself, it will improve with age.

Elderberry and Blackberry Wine ⸺⸺⸺⸺

Two of the most popular country wines are elderberry and blackberry. No surprise, then, that they are also often considered two of the best country wines. They can even sometimes be found for sale in top-end delicatessens. Of course the subjective nature of taste means that not everyone agrees with this, and you can couple this with the fact that all fruits taste differently year after year. Just because you made an excellent elderberry wine last year does not mean you will do so every year.

A solution is at hand, and that is to blend with another wine. This can be done before or after your wine has brewed. Elderberry wine can be superb, or it can be very tanniny. Blackberry wine can be superb, or it can be a little sickly. Luckily, both berries are around at the same time and their faults tend to cancel each other out.

This recipe is inspired by Mike Griffiths.

INGREDIENTS

2kg/4.5lb blackberries and elderberries
   (equal quantities)

1.5kg/3.3lb sugar

125ml/½ cup of very strong black tea

4 liters/4 quarts of water

juice of 1 lemon

1 tsp pectolase

1 Campden tablet (optional)

1 tsp yeast nutrient

red wine yeast

EQUIPMENT

large saucepan

fermentation bucket

4.5-liter/1-gallon secondary

airlock and bung

siphoning tube

muslin/cheesecloth

METHOD

Freeze the berries overnight, then allow to thaw. Put the berries into a fermentation bucket and squeeze out as much juice as you can. Add the sugar, pour over 1 liter/1 quart of boiling water, and stir until the sugar has fully dissolved. Add the rest of the water and all the other ingredients, including the Campden tablet if using, cover, and leave to stand for three to four days in a warm place (three days if only using blackberries, four if only using elderberries).

If you dispense with the blackberries and just make pure elderberry wine, don't add any tea; conversely, for every 500g/1lb of elderberries that are replaced with blackberries, add a quarter of the cup of tea. So, for example, a fifty-fifty mix (1kg/2lb elderberries and 1kg/2lb blackberries, as this recipe assumes) would need 125ml/ ½ cup of tea.

Strain into a secondary, rack after one month, and allow to ferment out. The more elderberry you use, the more the wine will benefit from being left to condition in the bottle.

LAVENDER

The smell of lavender (*Lavandula angustifolia*) has been popular since the Romans used it in their bathwater—the name "lavender" derives from the Latin *lavare*, meaning "to wash." It is still used today in the form of lavender oil, often indulged in by old ladies in vast amounts. In this form some (including me) can react against it, developing a dry mouth, sore eyes, and a running nose. Perhaps these old ladies know this, and are acting maliciously: if I'm on a long bus journey they always seem to sit in front of me.

Foraging for lavender
Lavender is native in the Mediterranean and parts of Africa and India. I have never come across wild lavender, but you might find a

garden escapee. I still count it as a wild plant, because if you walk around most suburban areas you will see at least one out-of-control specimen and I'm certain the owner wouldn't miss a few flowers, especially from the most feral of the plants. The bees might, however, so try not to over-pick from one source.

Growing lavender

Grow from cuttings. Take a cutting of 7cm (3in) and pull off the bottom leaves. Dust with hormone rooting powder, plant in a compost/coir/grit mix, and do not allow to dry out.

When a little bigger, plant out in well-drained, neutral-to-alkaline soil in full sun. Prune to encourage new growth and protect during harsh winters.

Lavender Cordial

This is an age-old recipe, and most sources agree that it makes for a great summer drink. It is also very easy to do.

INGREDIENTS

1 tbsp lavender flowers

500ml/2 cups of water

100g/3.5oz sugar

EQUIPMENT

2 saucepans

muslin/cheesecloth

METHOD

Put the sugar into the saucepan and cover with the water, stirring until it has dissolved. Add the lavender flowers and cover, bring to the boil, then take off the heat for a time to allow the lavender flavor to infuse. About thirty minutes will do.

Strain the liquid through a muslin/cheesecloth into another saucepan and bring back to a boil. Keep boiling, stirring continuously until it has reduced to a thick, syrupy consistency.

Take off the heat, allow to cool, then decant into sterilized bottles.

Caution: Avoid lavender if nursing or pregnant.

Lavender Mead

It's easy to sound like the back of a wine bottle when talking about lavender mead as the delicate floral overtones of this beverage will convince you that there's a summer's day in your glass. You'll almost be able to hear the bees buzzing around, pollinating the tiny lavender flowers.

This recipe is from Alex Hughes, a member of the Bristol Brewing Circle.

INGREDIENTS

1.5kg/3.3lb runny, delicately flavored honey

125ml/½ cup of dried lavender flowers

1.5 liters/1.5 quarts of boiling water

sweet mead yeast

1 tsp yeast nutrient

EQUIPMENT

fermentation bucket

4.5-liter/1-gallon secondary

solid bung

airlock and bung

siphoning tube

METHOD

Place the jars of honey into a bowl of hot water and leave for a few minutes. This loosens the honey in the jar and makes it easier to pour. Once loosened the honey should be poured into a fermentation bucket, covered with boiling water, and stirred.

Place the lavender in the bottom of a secondary and pour over the honey mixture. Top up with cold water to one gallon. Sprinkle over the yeast and yeast nutrient, attach a solid rubber, bung, and shake the secondary. Remove bung and add airlock.

After two months, rack, removing the lavender. Rack again after about six months. Ferment out and bottle. Mead will vastly improve if left in the bottle for at least one year.

MINT

Mint (genus *Mentha*) has been prized since ancient times. In Athens, different plants were used to perfume different parts of the body; mint was especially used on the arms. A native of Europe, mint has naturalized to most corners of the world. Some mints can grow to around 1m (3ft) tall and can spread far and wide.

Foraging for mint
Mint can be found in the wild at the edge of woodlands, on waste-ground, and as a garden escapee. I found a great patch in an area that used to house a formal garden.

Growing mint
Before even thinking of planting mint, be aware that it is known as a garden "thug." It can rapidly colonize an area, popping up where you least expect or want it. The easiest way to control it is to grow it in a container, or bury a bucket with a hole cut out of the bottom and plant it in that.

Mint can be grown from seed but it is far easier to grow from a cutting. Take 10cm (4in) of growth from a mature plant, pull off the bottom third of leaves, and place in water on a bright sunlit window sill. Change the water every three days and await visible roots. As soon as you can see some, plant the cutting in a small pot with good compost. Don't allow to dry out.

Alternatively, dig up 10cm (4in) of root in the spring and plant it where you wish mint to grow.

Crème de Menthe

Crème de menthe is a classic drink often taken after a meal as a digestive.

INGREDIENTS

50g/1.7oz fresh mint

500ml/2 cups of water

300g/10oz sugar

1 liter/1 quart of vodka

EQUIPMENT

saucepan

large sealable jar

muslin/cheesecloth

METHOD

Put the leaves in a jar and cover with the vodka. Leave for two days.

Boil the water and sugar and stir until fully dissolved. Strain the vodka and compost the mint leaves. Mix the two liquids together and store in an airtight jar in a cool dark place. Leave for three months before drinking.

Mint Cordial

Mint cordial is an excellent mixer with gin and can be used in cocktails to replace mint when it is out of season.

INGREDIENTS

220g/8oz fresh or dried mint

1kg/2.2lb sugar

500ml/2 cups of water

handful of fresh mint

EQUIPMENT

saucepan

muslin/cheesecloth

METHOD

Put all the ingredients into a pan, bring to a boil, then simmer gently for fifteen minutes. Take off the heat, cover, and allow to cool. Strain and decant into sterilized bottles, refrigerate, and use within one month (or put into plastic bottles and freeze).

Windy Tea

Beer drinkers and people who live with beer drinkers will be well aware of the problems that can arise the day after a few too many have been sampled. This tea helps rid oneself of that problem, and also helps dispel uncomfortable trapped wind.

INGREDIENTS

1 tsp mint

1 tsp fennel

1 tsp nettles

250ml/1 cup of water

EQUIPMENT

kettle

teapot

strainer

mug

METHOD

Pick the top four leaves from nettles in the spring (wearing gloves) and dry. Pick the mint at any time and try to use fresh. The fennel can be picked either for its leaves all year round or for its seeds in the autumn. In order to harvest fennel seeds, put a paper bag over the seed heads just before they are about to drop, fasten the bag, and allow the seeds to drop into it.

Put the herbs into a teapot and cover with the boiling water. Leave to infuse for five minutes before straining into a mug.

MUGWORT

Mugwort (*Artemisia vulgaris*) is supposed to make you dream lucidly. Many who practice witch-craft will smoke or drink a mugwort infusion before sleeping. I'm not sure how true this is, but as mugwort contains thujone, the same chemical that can be found in absinthe, which is supposed to cause hallucinations, perhaps this is how the link arose.

Mugwort grows to a maximum height of 2m (6ft), is native to Europe, Asia, and North Africa, and has now been naturalized in North America.

Foraging for mugwort

Mugwort grows on roadsides, on field edges, on wasteground, and on river banks. Once one plant has been found, a search will often reveal many more. I tend to harvest about a third of one plant late in the summer when it has come into flower, leaving the rest to live on and spread for the following years.

When using mugwort in place of hops it is best dried. To do this, simply hang the plant upside down for a week in an area that has a flow of air and is away from sunlight. I like to hang my herbs on my banister.

Mugwort Porter

The basic porter part of this recipe is by the master brewer of the Bristol Brewing Circle, Ali Kotcho-Williams. His porter used 53g/2oz of UK fuggles hops at the start of the boil and 21g/1oz during the final ten minutes.

INGREDIENTS	EQUIPMENT
4.23kg/10lb UK pale ale malt	large saucepan/cauldron
665g/1.5lb UK brown malt	mash tun
555g/11lb extra dark crystal malt	boiler *or* another large saucepan
110g/3oz chocolate malt	mashing/sparge bag (optional)
71g/2oz dried mugwort	fermentation bucket
25 liters/5 gallons of water	airlock
Muntons gold ale yeast	siphoning tube

METHOD

Mash the grains at 66°C (151°F) for one hour in half the water, drain into a fermentation bucket, then sparge the grains using the other half of the water. Mix the sparge water with the wort, add the mugwort, and boil for an hour.

Cool as quickly as possible, ideally with a wort chiller (see p. 24). Otherwise, place the fermentation bucket onto cool tiles, move it outside or put it in the coldest room of the house, or in iced water. When the wort has reached around 21°C (70°F), pitch the yeast.

Fit the lid and airlock and leave to ferment for four to fourteen days.

Siphon into beer bottles with a teaspoon of sugar in them, or a beer barrel with four tablespoons of sugar.

MULBERRIES

Of all the wild fruit on offer, mulberries (genus *Morus*) are always a joy to find, especially as you can't buy them in stores.

King James, of Bible fame, thought it would be a great idea to plant a load of mulberry trees as the leaves are food for silkworms. He thought he would manufacture his own silk, make a fortune, and not have to trade with China. What he hadn't done was his home-work. It's only white mulberry leaves that silkworms eat, not the black variety he planted.

Foraging for mulberries

Mulberries are not common but can be found planted in ornamental gardens, occasionally in municipal parks, and rarely as a wayside tree. If you do find one make a mental note of it so that you can return to it year after year. The easiest way to harvest mulberries is to put a sheet around the tree and shake it like hell. And, if out picking mulberries, don't forget to eat as many as you can!

Growing mulberries

Mulberry trees are slow-growing, which means it takes ages before they bear fruit, sometimes more than ten years. They can be propagated by seed or from hardwood cuttings (see p. 60) taken from two-to-four-year-old trees in the autumn.

Seeds should be taken from the fruit, cleaned of all the flesh then put into seed compost and kept in a warm greenhouse or on a window sill until a woody stem appears. At this point they can be put outside, and after two years they can be planted in the garden. They will need plenty of light and a well-drained, warm, deeply loamed soil.

Mulberry Liqueur

In my opinion, mulberries tend to start to lose their flavor as soon as they are picked, which is probably why you don't see them in the shops. To maintain their flavor beyond the month or so you might find them growing in late summer and get a great drink, they should be preserved as soon as they are picked—placed directly into brandy or a spirit of your choosing.

INGREDIENTS

800ml/3 cups of mulberries
750ml/3 cups of brandy
250ml/1 cup of water
300g/10oz sugar

EQUIPMENT

1 large sealable jar
muslin/cheesecloth

METHOD ··

Put the mulberries into a large jar and pour all but the last 20ml/ 0.5 fl. oz of brandy over them. Drink the last 20ml/0.5 fl. oz of brandy and keep the bottle. Seal the jar.

Heat the water in a saucepan and stir in the sugar until it has fully dissolved. Add this to the jar. Seal then shake the jar and put it into a dark cupboard for three months. After three months, strain the liqueur and eat the mulberries. Bottle the liquid and put it back in the dark cupboard. It can be drunk right away, but waiting for at least three months will improve the flavor.

RAPE/CANOLA

Rape (*Brassica napus*) can be seen across the United States and Canada during late spring, its bright yellow flowers vividly brightening up the landscape. Staring out of a train window at fields of the stuff always reminds me of my home town, Northampton, and one of our family jokes. Whenever my parents took us out on a trip we would inevitably pass a rape field—something for which Northamptonshire is famed. The smell would act as an early warning and have us all on our toes, scanning the horizon. The first person to see the field would shout, "Rape, rape!" and the whole family would snicker.

Foraging for rape

Rape is often an escapee from a farmer's field and can be found on the edges of farming areas or downstream from a farm. It can spread like wildfire, especially on wasteground. It has bright yellow flowers that appear from late spring to late summer.

Cruciferous Champagne ———————————————

The word "cruciferous" helps describe the flowers of rape and all plants in its family, the cabbage family: they all have four petals and are therefore cross- or crucifix-like. Mustard, charlock, even winter cress can be used in place of rape flowers in this recipe.

Cruciferous champagne has the sort of refreshing taste that characterizes elderflower champagne (see p. 122) while adopting some of the fiery nature of ginger beer.

INGREDIENTS

1.5 liters/1.5 quarts of yellow cruciferous flowers

750g/1.5lb sugar

3 liters/3 quarts of water

juice and rind of a lemon

2 tbsp cider vinegar

EQUIPMENT

fermentation bucket

muslin/cheesecloth

METHOD ....

Pick the flowers and wash to remove any insects. Put all the ingredients (not the water) into a sterilized fermentation bucket, bucket, or big mixing bowl. Boil the water, allow to cool, then pour into the fermentation bucket. Leave for one week or until it starts to fizz. Strain into sterilized swing-top bottles.

It will keep for as long as you need it to, and as with all country champagnes you will need to keep an eye on the bottle as they can be prone to explosions, especially in hot weather. It is therefore good practice to keep them in the fridge to slow down the yeast production (the reason for the fizz)!

Other uses

The flowers of all brassicas can be used in salads. The wild mustard flowers can be particularly fiery, which is often enough to liven up the most boring salad.

Leaves from all wild brassicas are also an excellent substitute for vine leaves.

ROSEBAY WILLOWHERB/FIREWEED

The alternative name for rosebay willowherb (*Epilobium angustifolium*) is fireweed, thought to have arisen from its tendency to populate wartime bombsites. This certainly makes sense for another local name, London weed. Its purple flowers must have brought a splash of color to a bleak time of rationing and war. Some say the "fireweed" label comes from the fact that it populated railway lines very quickly as the steam trains roared up and down the country carrying the seed with them. Both may very well be true, as plant names often have more than one source.

Foraging for rosebay willowherb

This plant can be pollinated by wind. Get the train into a breezy city like Edinburgh just before the Festival and you will see splashes of purple flowers all over the city. It loves disturbed soils and often populates river banks, railways, anywhere it can make itself at home. As bees seem to love it I only forage a few flowers from each plant, leaving at least half for them.

Rosebay Willowherb Champagne ─────────

INGREDIENTS

125ml/½ cup of dried rosebay
   willowherb flowers

6 liters/6 quarts of water

1kg/2.2lb sugar

3 tbsp cider vinegar

2 tsp citric acid

2 tbsp lemon juice

EQUIPMENT

large saucepan

fermentation bucket

dish towel

large plastic spoon

muslin/cheesecloth

METHOD ···

Pour the sugar into a large saucepan and cover with 2 liters/2 quarts of cold water. Bring to a boil and stir in the sugar. Put all the other ingredients into a fermentation bucket or a large mixing bowl and cover with the water. Add a further 4 liters/4 quarts of cold water and cover with a dish towel. Leave to stand for three days, stirring when you remember. By this point the flowers should have lost all their color.

Transfer into thick, sterilized swing-top or champagne bottles with screw-down corks. It will be ready to drink after ten to fourteen days but will keep for much longer.

As with all "champagne" drinks, the bottles are liable to explode and should be kept in a place where this won't be a big problem if it does occur. Alternatively they can be kept cool in a refrigerator.

Other uses

Rosebay willowherb leaves can be eaten when young and can be added to salads. The leaves can also be dried and used as a tea, which is said to be popular in some parts of Russia. Less widely known is the fact that dried leaves when smoked have a stupefying effect. "Stupefying" is an interesting way of describing the not-too-unpleasant but fairly brief sensation that arises from putting the leaves into rolling paper.

The roots, too, can be eaten but are not the choicest. If you have the time, the inner pith of the stem is slightly sweet, if a little fiddly to get to.

SUMAC

As the name suggests, the staghorn sumac has branches that resemble a stag's antlers, and unlike many trees they are sort of hairy. I fell in love with the sumac as soon as I saw one, and so, it would seem, have many gardeners. The staghorn sumac is native to the northeastern states in the US and southeastern Canada.

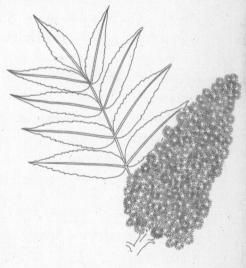

Foraging for sumac
When harvesting, ensure that you pick staghorn sumac (*Rhus typhina*), not any of its poisonous relatives.

Sumac is predominantly an urban tree and can be seen in almost every suburban corner of every town and city. In that respect it is like a present-day monkey puzzle tree or pampas grass: many folk choose to have it in their front gardens to show off to the world their exotic tastes. Check wasteground that backs onto gardens too.

Growing sumac

Sumac will grow to around 5m (15ft) tall and will tolerate poor soil. Although it likes full sun it will grow in partial shade. They also send suckers out and will rapidly take over an area if not kept in check. Seeds can be planted straight into the ground but it is far easier to replant a sucker from an established tree.

Sumac Lemonade ──────────────

One of the first wild soft drinks I made was from the berries or "droops" of a staghorn sumac. I had seen the tree the previous summer and knew that its bright red fruit clusters had to have some sort of use.

INGREDIENTS

5 to 10 droops of sumac (depending on
   age and size)

125ml/½ cup of boiling water

1 liter/1 quart of cold water

5 tsp honey

EQUIPMENT

large jug or bowl

muslin/cheesecloth

potato masher (optional)

METHOD ···

Place the droops into the cold water and leave for a couple of hours to infuse. If you happen to be passing, give them a little squeeze to help impart the flavor. But do be aware that droops can be a little itchy. Some will use a potato masher to do this job.

Dissolve the honey in the hot water, stirring vigorously to ensure that it is fully mixed in. Allow this to cool a little, then add to the mixture.

Strain and serve. It can be used as a mixer just as you would use lemonade.

Other uses

Sumac droops can be grated to create the Middle Eastern spice known as sumac, or sometimes summaq. This lemony powder can be added to hummus.

It is also known to have been smoked (along with other herbs) by indigenous Americans.

WALNUTS

Walnut trees (genus *Juglans*) can grow up to a massive 40m (130ft) tall and there are twenty-one different species. They spread from Japan in the east to South America in the west.

Walnut wood was once highly prized for furniture-making, before tropical woods took over. Perhaps if the fashion once again turned to natively grown walnut wood the amount of illegal logging would reduce.

Foraging for walnuts

Various different types of walnut can be found in wild areas across the country. Be careful when harvesting black walnuts, as your hands will be dyed black and it will take days to scrub them back to normal!

Growing walnuts

Walnut trees can be successfully grown from seed. Collect fully ripe walnuts and put them in your fridge for two months. Remove the outer skin but leave the hard nut in the middle. Plant straight out where it is to grow at a depth of 3cm (1in) using a mix of sand, soil, and grit. Cover with a wire mesh at first if there are squirrels in the vicinity. Do not allow to dry out. The ideal soil should be well-drained, and trees need to be planted around 20m (65ft) apart so they can grow to full height.

Nocino ──────────────────────────

This recipe for Nocino was given to me by Gilly Wright, who rightfully states that it should have a health warning attached as it is so moreish.

Nocino is an Italian liqueur made from green underdeveloped walnuts. It is thought to be a digestive aid and was once popular among monks in northern Italy. Tradition states that you must use an odd number of walnuts when making Nocino.

Green walnuts must be picked early in the season so that they are easily cut with a knife.

Be warned, Nocino is hangover-inducing and may well reduce your brain to the size of a walnut.

INGREDIENTS

EQUIPMENT

29 green walnuts

large glass jar

2 cinnamon sticks

muslin/cheesecloth

5 whole cloves

slotted spoon

zest of 1 lemon

500g/1lb sugar

1 liter/1 quart of pure alcohol, vodka, or grappa

optional spices to taste: mace, star anise, and vanilla pod

METHOD ··

Rinse and pat dry the walnuts. Cut into quarters. Put the walnuts, spices, zest, sugar and booze into a large glass container. Cover and shake to mix well. Store for six weeks, shaking daily.

Remove the walnuts and solids with a slotted metal spoon. Strain into swing-top bottles and store in a cool dark place.

Nocino starts off bitter, but mellows with age, so most Italians leave it for a year before opening it.

AUTUMN

Roasted acorn warmer/acorn coffee

Acorns: Giliø kava

Apples: Sort of cider

Spiced apple wine

Apples: Cyser

Beet and gooseberry wine (Goozbeit)

Dandelion and burdock cordial

Boozy dandelion and burdock

Wild dandelion and burdock ale

Damson wine

Damson gin/rum/vodka

Damson cordial

Five-plum wine

Dandelion coffee/dandelion warmth

White grape wine

Grape and elderberry wine

Hazelnut milk

Heather mead

Himalayan balsam et al: Autumn
   flower champagne

Simple hop beer

Hops: Easy grain beer

Hop wine

Pear wine

Pumpkin beer

Perfumed quince and persimmon wine

Quince kompot with lemon and wine

Ratafia of quinces

Sweet corn: Herby corn stalk—free ale

Yarrow ale

Yarrow et al: Cold and flu tea

THE PARKS AND countryside seem to empty and life takes on a more gentle state. Mix this with the autumnal colors that paint our great land and you have arrived at my favorite time of year.

Above and beyond any other season, autumn can be one of the busiest times. It is when most people will be out and about collecting wild foods; it is also harvest time on the vegetable patch. Many people may be struggling to know what to do with their excess produce, which also means the canny among us can have some extra donations from friends to turn into booze.

Beginners should hang on through this period as by the second year (and forever more) the burden of work is made lighter by your own supply of wines, which should have nicely aged from the previous year.

Don't worry too much if you don't have time to make drinks out of everything. Most homes have a freezer these days and many fruits and vegetables actually benefit from a couple of nights in the freezer, so just fill it up and wait for a quieter moment.

After such a big harvest your vegetable patch will need attention. Clear away anything that might carry disease into the next season, such as old potato shoots, brassica roots, and, of course, any diseased materials. But don't tidy too much. Plenty of spaces for small mammals and beneficial insects will aid your war on pests when it resumes the following year.

In season (garden): apples, beans, peas, radishes, corn, turnips, blackberries, grapes, pears, raspberries, beets, carrots, marrows, pumpkins, rosemary, sage, thyme, parsnips, mulberries, passion fruit.

In season (wild): apples, crab apples, blackberries, damsons, sloes, hawthorn, yarrow, hazelnuts, rosehips, dandelion (root), burdock (root), ground ivy, nettles, rowan berries, mulberries, medlars, passion fruit.

ACORNS

"When the oak is felled the whole forest echoes with its fall, but a hundred acorns are sown in silence by an unnoticed breeze" (Thomas Carlyle).

The mighty oak has for centuries been seen as a symbol of strength and has been wrapped up in myth and legend. In ancient Greece the rustling of oak leaves was thought to show the will of Zeus. The ancient oak in Sherwood forest is thought to have been planted on the final resting place of Robin Hood. Perhaps these trees have been revered by man for so long as they transcend generations, serving as a link to our ancestors.

Foraging for acorns

There are between five hundred and six hundred species of oak, all of which grow from and carry acorns in a goblet- or egg-cup-shaped cup. They can be found planted in churchyards, parks, and sometimes standing majestically in the middle of fields—a lone relic of a time when much of this country was covered in trees.

Roasted Acorn Warmer/Acorn Coffee ————

This recipe is from John Lewis-Stempel's *The Wild Life*. He suggests that, although tasting nothing like coffee, it is a pleasant drink which just like dandelion coffee is reminiscent of barley cup. I agree with him, and like most wild "coffee" drinks it should be rebranded as "warmer" (or "warmth") so as not to disappoint the ardent coffee drinker (see Dandelion Coffee, p. 215).

INGREDIENTS

40 acorns

EQUIPMENT

coffee grinder

baking sheet

METHOD ···

Shell the acorns, boil for ten minutes, drain, then leave to dry in a ventilated spot. After a day or two, by which time the acorns will have dried out, roast them in the center of the oven on a low heat—120°C/250°F/gas mark half—for fifteen minutes. Grind in a coffee grinder and treat as normal filter coffee.

Giliø Kava

This traditional drink is a variation on the above and is often served in cafés and bars in Lithuania instead of coffee.

INGREDIENTS

40 acorns

500ml/2 cups of milk or cream

a little milk or cream, sugar, honey,
   or molasses to taste

EQUIPMENT

saucepan

coffee grinder

muslin/cheesecloth

METHOD ···

Dry the acorns at room temperature for three days, longer if conditions are damp. Shell and place in a saucepan, cover with milk or cream, and gently simmer for one hour (or until soft). Strain the acorns through muslin and pat dry. Scorch the acorns in a hot, dry saucepan. Grind the acorns and store in an airtight container.

Place four teaspoons of ground acorn powder into 500ml or 2 cups of boiling water, keep boiling for three minutes, then strain into cups. Add cream or milk and sugar to taste, as you would with normal coffee, or honey or molasses.

Other uses

Acorns can be made into a flour, which when mixed with wheat flour can lend a nutty taste to muffins and other cakes.

APPLES

Believe it or not, apples (genus *Malus*) are related to roses. Originating in western Asia, these perennials are hugely diverse, numbering some seven thousand different varieties.

The apple is frequently associated with the biblical story of Adam and Eve despite there being nothing to suggest that an apple featured in the book of Genesis. One scholarly suggestion is that it was a pomegranate.

Foraging for apples

Apples are thought to be the first cultivated tree fruit and can now be found on every continent (apart from Antarctica). Often the fruit is left to rot on trees in people's gardens as they simply can't cope with the amount; a friendly knock might be all it takes to get a few bags, especially if you offer a bottle of wine or cider in return. They grow wild by train lines and roads, in abandoned orchards and gardens, and occasionally in parks. Crab apples can be found on the edges of woodlands and on roadsides (see Crab Apples, p. 165).

Growing apples

An apple will not grow true to form if grown from seed, therefore they are always grown from branches grafted on to rootstock. Grafted trees can be bought from garden centers and specialized nurseries. Trees ideally need soil with a pH of 6.5 in full sun and with protection from strong winds. (See Tree Planting, p. 60.)

Sort of Cider

My first glass of Sort of Cider was given to me in a little village just outside Cirencester whose pub, only open for two days a week, consisted of a table full of locals and two pumps. When the couple I was staying with told the locals how this cider was made it was met with polite derision. That is not to say it isn't a great drink, because it is, but as the locals at this tiny pub muttered to themselves, "It's not cider." Maybe not, but it's a perfect introduction for those not sure about getting or making a cider press who want to make a great alcoholic apple drink. (For more information, see Cider-making, p. 69.)

INGREDIENTS

1kg/2.2lb apples

500g/1lb sugar

4 liters/1 gallon of water

thumb-sized piece of bruised ginger root

½ tsp cloves

pinch of nutmeg

champagne yeast

EQUIPMENT

cheese grater

fermentation bucket

muslin/cheesecloth

4.5-liter/1-gallon secondary

airlock and bung

siphoning tube

METHOD

Wash the apples and grate into a fermentation bucket. Top up with the water and add the yeast. Leave lightly covered for five to ten days.

Strain through a muslin/cheesecloth into a secondary, add the sugar and spices, and shake vigorously. Leave for another ten days before siphoning into screw-top or swing-top bottles.

Sort of Cider may still be volatile so check by loosening the bottles daily. It should be drunk as soon as it's made.

Spiced Apple Wine

Alex Hughes, the brains behind this recipe, finally got fed up with the annual travesty of walking around most towns and cities with a temperate climate and witnessing apples left hanging and rotting on trees. So he held an apple amnesty at his place of work. His motives were not purely altruistic, it has to be said, as his marriage to former drinking partner and best friend Gemma was looming. He hardly had any money and had 120 guests to get drunk, but he did have a home-made apple press. Thus the recipe for spiced apple wine was born.

INGREDIENTS

4.5 liters/1 gallon of apple juice *or*
   15kg/33lb apples (or less, depending
   on the efficiency of your press)
500g/1lb golden raisins
1kg/1lb sugar
1 cinnamon stick or a handful of
   cassia bark
3 to 4 cloves
Sauternes wine yeast

EQUIPMENT

apple press (if using apples)
fermentation bucket
4.5-liter/1-gallon secondary
muslin bag
airlock and bung
spoon
siphoning tube

METHOD

Press the apples (if using) and extract the juice.

Put the sugar and golden raisins into a fermentation bucket and pour over the apple juice. Place the cinnamon stick/cassia bark and cloves into a muslin bag and lower into the mix. Add the yeast and leave, only returning to stir once a day with an appropriate-sized spoon. Keep this up for three days.

Leave for six weeks, then strain into a secondary and attach an airlock and bung. After four months, rack, then leave for a further four to six months.

Around ten months after pressing your apples, it should be ready for bottling. It should also be time to start looking for apples and begin the whole process again.

Cyser

One of the main reasons people continue to homebrew is the thousands of different flavors you can produce from similar ingredients. This recipe makes a sort of flat, sweetish cider that tastes like a mead and has a bit of a kick to it. You can reduce the amount of honey in order to have a slightly less alcoholic drink. If not, make sure your friends know it's not cider they're drinking or there'll be some very sore heads in the morning.

INGREDIENTS

4.5 liters/1 gallon of apple juice *or*
   15kg/33lb apples (or less, depending
   on the efficiency of your press)
1kg/2.2lb flower honey
2 to 10 cloves (depending on preference)
cinnamon stick
Sauternes wine yeast
1 tsp yeast nutrient

EQUIPMENT

apple press (if using apples)
fermentation bucket
large saucepan/cauldron
muslin/cheesecloth
siphoning tube

METHOD

Crush and press apples (if using). Place the juice into a large saucepan and heat until lukewarm, being careful not to boil. Meanwhile, place the jar of honey into a bowl of hot water, which should make it easier to pour. Add the spices, stir in all the honey, and keep stirring until fully dissolved.

   An alternative and more traditional method of mixing the ingredients together is to shake the honey and apple juice vigorously for some time.

   Filter into a fermentation bucket, and when cooled to blood-heat add the yeast and yeast nutrient. Leave to ferment for three to ten days in a warm place before transferring into a secondary.

Rack every few months if becoming cloudy. Bottle when the cyser clears. It will benefit from being allowed to age for at least a year.

BEETS

Romans were the first to cultivate *Beta vulgaris* for its root; before then it was the leaves that were prized as food. The Romans didn't eat the root, they grew it for medicinal reasons. There is little evidence to suggest it was eaten until the sixteenth century and even then the roots were very probably spindly affairs. So, relatively speaking, the beet is a new food.

Growing beets

I have found beets one of the easiest plants to grow.

For best results, plant the seeds after the first frost. Beets can also be grown in a window box all year round; simply bring your window box inside when there is a chance of frost. I would suggest buying a smaller variety of beet if you plan to grow them in a container. Detroit Dark Red is a good one to try. If you are growing outside for the first time I would suggest getting a Boltardy variety, simply because they are easier to grow.

It is often suggested that the "seeds" should be sown thinly. I disagree, and sow them close together. This isn't just down to my rebellious nature, but also a matter of preference. I enjoy eating beet leaves in salads and the young shoots are deliciously sweet. They can be constantly thinned as you need them throughout the growing period. I do, however, sow them in rows about 38cm (15in) apart.

By the way, I put "seeds" in quotes as each seed is in fact a seed pod containing many seeds.

Beets will grow in most soil conditions, for example they have worked on my clay soil and in my compost-filled window box. However, ideally the pH level should be between 6.5 and 7.5.

Water in dry weather and ideally keep the surrounding soil weed-free. All varieties should take anything from two to four months to grow.

Beet and Gooseberry Wine—Goozbeit ⸺

Mention beet wine to experienced home wine-makers and you will often get the same reaction: a scrunched-up face and the words "It's a bit earthy." Beet wine is certainly not an award winner and sits with some of the older recipes as a curiosity. Just because you can make wine out of a vegetable does not mean that you should.

Spurred on by its reputation, Jon Baldwin from Minnesota decided to step up to the plate and try to improve this disgrace of the country wine world. After some experimentation he invented Goozbeit, and under rigorous tests at his local homebrew club (jack-ofallbrews.org) the overwhelming response was that the earthiness had disappeared as a result of the addition of gooseberries, making this a much more palatable, even tasty brew.

INGREDIENTS

22-liter/5-gallon bucket of beets
    (cleaned and sliced thin)
22 liters/5 gallons water
1.5kg/3.3lb light dried malt extract

EQUIPMENT

large saucepan/cauldron
fermentation bucket
muslin/cheesecloth
slotted spoon

3kg/6.5lb sugar

6kg/13lb gooseberries

⅛ tsp Vegemite
   (nutrient for yeast)

dry wine yeast

blender

siphoning tube

large secondary or five 4.5-liter/1-gallon
   secondaries

airlock and bung

hydrometer

METHOD

Put the beets in a saucepan, cover with water, and cook until tender. Strain out the liquid and return to the pan. Keep the beets aside for eating, feeding to a pig, or even turning into a beet cake.

Add the dried malt extract slowly, and once dissolved add the sugar, stirring gently until completely dissolved. Heat up to just below boiling point, add the gooseberries to the beet must, and simmer for twenty minutes.

At this point the gooseberries need to be carefully fished out and processed in a blender, or crushed in a jelly bag. They will be hot so use a slotted spoon. The resulting puree must then be returned to the must and the yeast spread added. The liquid is then brought up to simmer point again.

Leave to cool to room temperature and strain into a fermentation bucket. Yield should be about 22 liters (5 gallons). Take a gravity measurement using the hydrometer; it should be about 1095. Add the yeast and leave it alone for about two weeks at room temperature.

Take another gravity measurement; it should be about 1015. Siphon into secondaries and attach airlock and bung. Bottle, then leave for six months to two years before enjoying.

BURDOCK

Burdock (*Arctium*) is a biennial, meaning that its lifecycle takes two years. During the first year the plant will store energy in its root, then in the second year this energy is used to shoot the plant up and grow seed. Burdock root would thus have been a major source of carbohydrate (energy) for our ancestors.

Foraging for burdock
Burdock can be found on waste-ground, disturbed ground, field edges, and occasionally in public parks.

It is easier to spot in its second year as its distinctive reddish, thistle-like burrs can be seen from a distance. But by this time the root is too woody and therefore no longer viable. So, once you have located the second-year plants, look around at ground level for the big rhubarb-like leaves of the first-year plant. This is what you need to dig up.

When digging up burdock (as with any root), make sure you get the landowner's permission. I don't always go for the biggest plant, with leaves the size of elephants' ears, as these can be rather woody and the root can be very deep. Instead I go for plants with leaves the size of a child's bike wheel.

Dig at a 45-degree angle around the root so that you can see what you are unearthing, and when you have finished, backfill the hole. So that you are not taking too much away from nature, take some seed from the burrs of a second-year burdock and plant them in the space you have left. Also, to be on the safe side, don't dig up burdock if you see only one or two plants nearby as you may destroy future generations' enjoyment of dandelion and burdock!

Growing burdock

Whenever I have grown burdock I have found it to be erratic, often growing from seed planted a year or two previously. The seed will benefit from stratification, a mimicking of winter conditions, so a month in the fridge before planting will help.

Burdock likes nutrient-rich soil and should be planted in full sun or partial shade. Seeds should be planted in the spring at a distance of 75cm (2ft) apart.

Dandelion and Burdock Cordial

Dandelion and burdock is for many people a taste of childhood. I remember becoming a fan one summer and refusing to drink anything else. Its popularity in the past can be put down to its liver-purifying properties. It'll certainly come in useful if you intend to try all the recipes in this book.

INGREDIENTS	EQUIPMENT
2 tsp ground burdock root	large saucepan/cauldron
2 tsp ground dandelion root	muslin/cheesecloth
1.5 liters/1.5 quarts of water	mortar and pestle *or* coffee/nut grinder
3cm (1in) ginger root	

2 star anise

juice of 1 lemon

600g/20oz superfine sugar

METHOD

Dry the burdock and dandelion roots, following the same procedure as for Dandelion Coffee (see p. 215), and grind to a fine powder. Bring the water to a boil and add the powders, star anise, ginger root, and lemon juice. Simmer for twenty minutes, then add the sugar, stirring continuously until fully dissolved.

Allow to cool, then strain into bottles through four thicknesses of muslin/cheesecloth. Serve four parts water to one part cordial.

Boozy Dandelion and Burdock

"Boozy" is something of an understatement, actually. When I made this recipe it fermented to around 9% vol.

INGREDIENTS

3 large burdock roots

3 dandelion roots

500g/1lb sugar

30ml/1 fl. oz black treacle

juice of 1 lemon

ale yeast

4.5 liters/1 gallon of water

EQUIPMENT

spade

large saucepan/cauldron

fermentation bucket

muslin/cheesecloth

METHOD ··

Dig up the roots and chop off any green topmost growth. Scrub them clean then chop into bite-sized chunks. Boil in half the water for half an hour then stir in the sugar, treacle, and lemon juice. Strain into a fermentation bucket, add the rest of the water, and cool to room temperature. Add the yeast. Leave for ten days, stirring daily. Bottle, and allow to condition for at least a week.

Wild Dandelion and Burdock Ale ————————————

Inspired by a similar recipe from *The Wild Life* by John Lewis-Stempel, this ale is perhaps closer to a traditional country drink and is made using wild yeast. It resembles root beer, with the bonus of being alcoholic.

INGREDIENTS

110g/4oz chopped burdock root

110g/4oz chopped dandelion leaves

450g/1lb chopped nettle leaves

a handful of birch twigs

4.5 liters/1 gallon of water

550g/11oz honey

2 tbsp dry cider

skins of five crab apples

EQUIPMENT

large saucepan/cauldron

muslin/cheesecloth

fermentation bucket

siphoning tube

METHOD ··

Put the leaves, twigs, and burdock root into a large saucepan and add half the water. Bring to a boil and simmer for thirty minutes. Stir in the honey until it dissolves. Strain into a fermentation bucket and add the rest of the water, the cider and the crab apple skins. (At this point you could also add an ale yeast to improve your results.)

Leave in a warm place to ferment for about five days. Siphon into bottles primed with honey (use 1 teaspoon of honey per 1 pint/500ml bottle) and leave for a week before drinking. Drink within a week or two of making.

Other uses
Washed, peeled, parboiled then roasted, burdock makes an excellent addition to a meal instead of potatoes. It is widely eaten in Japan, where it is known as *gobo*.

DAMSONS

The name "damson" derives from "plum of Damascus," as they were first cultivated in that ancient Syrian city. They were brought to Europe by the Romans and trees can often be found close to ancient Roman camps.

Foraging for damsons
One year, around harvesttime, I decided to have a wander. It was late summer and I had reaped most of what I'd sown; it was time to reap what I hadn't sown. I was expecting to return with just a bag full of haws and, if I was lucky, an apple or two from a wizened, neglected apple tree.

What I found was tree after tree full of damsons (*Prunus domestica*, subsp. *insititia*) when the previous year there had been none. I soon realized that the size of this find meant one small carrier bag would not be enough. The succulent purple fruit felt like a gift from the gods, and I sprinted home on my bike to get my pannier bags, which were duly filled.

Damsons can be found in similar spots to their close cousins the sloe: hedgerows, field edges, roadsides, and close to railway lines. They are much bigger than sloes, more rounded, a bluish-purple in color, and much sweeter. If you still need to be sure, cut one open to see if it contains the distinctive pit of the plum family.

Damson Wine

Damson wine is a traditional country wine and there are many recipes for it. Some refuse to use raisins, preferring grape concentrate; others prefer to leave it out altogether. Personally, I think it benefits from using one or the other to add more body.

INGREDIENTS
2kg/4.5lb damsons
225g/8oz raisins
1kg/2.2lb sugar
4 liters/4 quarts of water
1 tsp yeast nutrient
1 tsp pectolase
1 Campden tablet (optional)
Burgundy wine yeast

EQUIPMENT
large saucepan/cauldron
fermentation bucket
potato masher
muslin/cheesecloth
4.5-liter/1-gallon secondary
airlock and bung

METHOD

Ensure that all the bits of leaf and other matter have been removed from the damsons, then wash them and put in a fermentation bucket.

Cut up the raisins and put them in the bucket too. Mash them up a bit with a potato masher, then cover with 3 liters/3 quarts of boiling water. Allow to cool, then add the pectolase and Campden tablet (if using).

Leave for one day. The must will have turned to a thicker blackcurrant color. Boil the remaining liter/1 quart of water, dissolve the sugar in it, and add this to the must. Now add the yeast and nutrient and stir well. Lightly cover and leave at room temperature for ten days.

The wine must now be slowly strained into a secondary. Don't be tempted to push the fruit as this will make the resulting wine hazy. Top up with boiled and cooled water if you need to.

Leave the secondary in a warm room and wait for about a month. Then taste it—you may wish to add a few teaspoons of sugar. Allow to ferment out, rack if hazy, then bottle and allow to age for at least a year before drinking.

Damson Gin/Rum/Vodka

Damson gin is the connoisseur's choice of flavored gin. I like to think of sloe gin as VHS and damson gin as Betamax. My damson gin sits in a cut-glass decanter in pride of place in my living room and in my opinion is on par with any serious whisky (although I am sure many whisky drinkers will disagree).

Damsons are quite sweet so liqueurs made with them need less sugar than sloe liqueurs, and the overall flavor is richer and thicker. They are worthy of experimentation with your favorite spirit; so far I have made damson gin, rum, and vodka. It's a waste to use expensive spirits as the flavorsome damsons transform any liquid they are put in. The addition of the sprig of ladies' bedstraw (*Galium verum*), even in such a small amount, can make for a unique-tasting drink that will get your guests wondering.

INGREDIENTS
750ml/3 cups of gin
250g/9oz sugar
500g/1lb damsons
1 sprig of ladies' bedstraw (optional)

EQUIPMENT
large sealable jar
muslin/cheesecloth

METHOD

Wash the damsons and put in the freezer for a couple of days. Then put them into a sealable jar, secondary, or any other container that you can seal and which has a neck big enough to get the damsons in and out. Pour in the sugar, add the bedstraw if you wish, then cover with the spirit of your choice. Shake vigorously.

Continue to shake as often as you remember over the next three to four months. Don't worry if you end up leaving it a little longer than this: I have, and it still works fine. Strain through a muslin/cheesecloth into the bottles and leave to rest for as long as you can. If using cheap rum it is highly recommended that you leave for at least another six months as it just won't taste any good before this time.

Damson Cordial

This cordial keeps that deep red of the damson until you add water and it transforms into a pink drink. It works perfectly as a summer beverage with both hot and cold water.

INGREDIENTS

1kg/2.2lb damsons

1.25kg/2.5lb sugar

1.25 liters/1.25 quarts of water

EQUIPMENT

large saucepan

muslin/cheesecloth

METHOD

Put the damsons into a large pan and simmer for about an hour until their skins are falling off. Strain through a muslin/cheesecloth. Return to the pan with the sugar and bring to the boil. Skim off any scum that rises to the top and simmer for about three or four minutes.

Allow to cool, then decant into bottles.

Five-plum Wine

Over the year different plums will come into season: the first is the cherry plum, followed by cultivated plums, then greengages, damsons, and finally sloes. Using your freezer you can collect a selection of these and make a complex wine with an excellent bouquet.

You can mix together whatever plums you have, as long as the weight adds up to 10kg/20lb; they should all spend some time in the freezer to soften. The following recipe makes 20 liters/4.5 gallons of wine; to make a smaller batch simply divide all the ingredient quantities by your desired factor.

INGREDIENTS

500g/1lb greengages

1kg/2.2lb cherry plums

1kg/2.2lb cultivated plums

1.5kg/3.3lb sloes

EQUIPMENT

large saucepan/cauldron

fermentation bucket

potato masher

muslin/cheesecloth

6kg/13lb damsons

2 ripe bananas

250g/9oz raisins

250ml/1 cup of grape concentrate

20 liters/9 gallons of water

6kg/13lb sugar

5 tsp pectolase

5 tsp yeast nutrient

all-purpose wine yeast

large secondary *or* 5 smaller ones

airlock(s) and bung(s)

siphoning tube

METHOD

Freeze all the plums and allow to thaw. Peel the bananas. Boil half of the water and stir in the sugar. Add all the ingredients to the fermentation bucket and leave for ten days in a warm place, occasionally returning to mash the fruit with a sterilized masher.

After those ten days, strain into a series of secondaries or one big one. Attach airlock and rack after a month. Allow to ferment out, racking on occasion if required. Age for at least three months.

DANDELIONS

Bob Flowerdew, the organic gardener from BBC Radio 4's *Gardeners' Question Time*, once conducted an experiment with a dandelion root (*Taraxacum officinale*). He nailed it to his shed door and left it there for a year. All manner of weather hit this root; pelting rain, scorching sun and freezing temperatures did their worst. He then buried it to see if it would grow, and sure enough it did. All of which helps to explain why it can be so difficult to get rid of dandelions once they have decided to live on your land. I just ate all my roots or turned them into drinks, and now there are none. I even dig up ones from neighboring plots at times and they don't seem to mind.

Foraging for dandelion roots

Dandelion roots are best unearthed in the autumn as at this time of year the plant is storing up its energy to get it through the long winter months and the roots are at their fattest. They can also be dug up during spring, when the plant is storing energy ready to flower. You can dig up the roots at any other time, but they will not be as fat and therefore you will need to dig up more in order to get a good harvest. Look out for big basal rosettes (big leaves) as these signify big roots. They grow just beneath the basal leaves and are generally a dirty yellow color.

You will need the landowner's permission to dig up a dandelion, but most treat them as a weed and will probably think you are a little odd to ask!

Dandelion Coffee/Dandelion Warmth ───────────

When we hear the word "coffee" we have an idea of what to expect. We think of the caffeine hit that goes hand in hand with the coffee bean; we think of the rich aroma that wafts across train stations in the morning. Dandelion coffee is simply not like that. It does have its own smell, but not one that is rich in association. It has its own flavor, too, though one that comes without a kick of caffeine. As a result, dandelion coffee is often shunned by ardent coffee drinkers, which is a real shame.

I think it needs to be renamed to encourage people to give it a go, so that they don't compare it with their favorite drink but savor it and value it as a drink in its own right. That way it might get a fair hearing (tasting). "Dandelion Warmth" fits the bill for me, summing up the warm flavor and smell that erupts from your mug.

INGREDIENTS

dandelion roots

wood avens root (optional)

EQUIPMENT

spade

baking sheet

coffee grinder

METHOD ··········

Once dug up, wash the roots, then dry in the sun for four hours (if there is no sun they will just need longer in the oven). Place on a baking sheet and make sure none are touching. Bake on a low heat—120°C/250°F/gas mark half—for a couple of hours until they turn light brown. Chop into pieces no bigger than your thumbnail. Allow to cool, and store in an airtight container. They will keep for about a year but I'd recommend using them before then.

You then have two options: either use like coffee beans, grinding finely and then filtering; or (the lazy way) take a big handful, place in the bottom of a teapot, pour over hot water, and leave to brew for about five minutes. You'll need to experiment a little with quantities to get your desired flavor/strength. I also like to add a touch of grated wood avens root (herb bennet) as I think this greatly enhances the flavor.

GRAPES

Grapes (genus *Vitis*) originated in eastern Anatolia, one of the provinces of modern-day Turkey, and now around nineteen million acres of our planet are taken up by grapes, most of them used in the production of wine. There are around sixty-five different species of grape and most grow in the northern hemisphere. Grapes are a climbing plant and will reach up to 20m (65ft) in height.

Foraging for grapes
There are areas where grapes have gone wild from back gardens. You should really ask permission before picking them.

Growing grapes
Hardwood cuttings (see p. 60) can be taken in late autumn or winter. You should check that the wood is still green in the center to ensure its viability. Make a cut above a bud and one 5cm (2in) below. Dust with rooting powder and insert into deep trays. They should be kept frost-free and a bottom heat of 21°C (70°F) should be maintained, meaning you can use a heated fermentation mat (see p. 25) to keep them warm. Pot individually in the spring before planting out the following spring.

Softwood cuttings can also be taken from late spring to summer and should be around 8cm (3in) tall, although more importantly containing at least three nodes. Take off leaf growth by one half, apply rooting powder and harden off before planting out in the spring.

Grapes should be planted in a south-facing warm spot in cooler climes and can be grown in a greenhouse or polytunnel. They will need support such as a fence, but do be aware that they can really spread out. Plant in the late autumn to early spring. Place the root-ball in a hole 15cm by 15cm (6in by 6in) and backfill with well-rotted manure or good-quality compost.

Do not allow to dry out.

White Grape Wine

The old world wine-making regions may not add any yeast when making grape wine, instead relying on the wild yeasts of the region. It's a combination of this yeast, the variety of grape, and the growing conditions that makes for such an abundant variety of wines. Competing with sometimes thousands of years of experience and yeast cultivation is certainly an uphill struggle, but that's not to say that many small producers can't make superb wines. You can too.

Wine-making can be as simple as crushing grapes and fermenting the juice. Often, though, there are too many other yeasts in the air to compete with and you need to kill these off and add your own or face waiting a long time for something disappointing.

INGREDIENTS	EQUIPMENT
5kg/11lb white grapes	potato masher
500g/1lb sugar	acid test kit
250ml/1 cup of water	hydrometer and hydrometer jar
1 tsp tartaric acid	2 fermentation buckets
1 Campden tablet (optional)	4.5-liter/1-gallon secondary
white wine yeast	airlock and bung
	siphoning tube

METHOD ....

Check that the grapes are fully ripe and discard any that are moldy. Remove the stalks and rinse under the tap to wash off any insects. Mash the grapes gently with a potato masher in a fermentation bucket, making sure you don't crush the seeds. Stir in a crushed Campden tablet (if using) and leave for a day.

Check that the acidity level is between 3 and 3.4 pH and add the tartaric acid if too alkaline (or potassium carbonate if too acidic).

Then pour some of the grape juice into a hydrometer jar and take a reading. It should read 1090; if it is lower, add a sugar solution made from boiling the water and stirring in the sugar. This should be done a bit at a time, taking hydrometer readings as you go.

Strain the juice into another fermentation bucket, add the yeast, and leave for one week. After this time strain into a secondary and attach an airlock and bung.

Rack after one month, and again if necessary. Allow to ferment out.

This wine will improve greatly with age, for as long as you can leave it.

Grape and Elderberry Wine ———————————

Often recipes get developed due to what is available, and the following is no exception. Having found a wild source for grapes in Bristol I realized I only had enough grapes to make half a gallon, or just three bottles. Grapes and elderberries are ready at the same time of year, and knowing that the elderberry is often referred to as the "Englishman's grape" it seemed daft not to make a wine that combined the two. The result was a wine full of character that could certainly be passed off as a great vintage.

INGREDIENTS

1kg/2.2lb grapes

1kg/2.2lb elderberries

1 ripe banana

1.5kg/3.3lb sugar

4 liters/1 gallon of water

1 tsp yeast nutrient

1 Campden tablet (optional)

Bordeaux-style red wine yeast

EQUIPMENT

large saucepan/cauldron

fermentation bucket

4.5-liter/1-gallon secondary

airlock and bung

muslin/cheesecloth

siphoning tube

METHOD

Place the elderberries and grapes into the fermentation bucket and add the mashed banana. Boil the water and mix in the sugar. Pour over the fruit and allow to cool to room temperature. Add the Campden tablet (if using) and leave for twenty-four hours.

Add the yeast and nutrient and leave for ten days in a warm place.

Strain into a secondary and attach an airlock. Rack after one month, and again if required. Allow to ferment out before bottling.

This wine will be magnificent after a year's aging.

HAZELNUTS

On my foraging walks I often find plenty of hazel trees (genus *Corylus*) but rarely any hazelnuts. The problem is simple: squirrels!

The gray squirrel, to be more exact. The little blighters nick food and kill trees, and in Central Park they have even been known to become crackheads! Mind you, if you have ever sat on a park bench and had one sit next to you it is hard to stay angry at them.

That's not to say that you can't find huge hauls of hazelnuts; it's just that if there's a big population of squirrels in an area it's best to move on and find somewhere else.

Foraging for hazelnuts

Hazel can be found in woods, at woodland edges, and sometimes as an understorey in forests, and beneath oaks in broadleaf woodlands. Woodland renewal schemes often plant hazel.

Hazelnut Milk

It was my brother, gardening writer Dave Hamilton, who first showed me how to make nut milk and I remember being amazed as I watched a handful of nuts being transformed into this thick, creamy beverage. It has been hypothesized that hazelnut milk was enjoyed by our hunter-gatherer ancestors over nine thousand years ago. It is rich in protein and flavorsome so during a time when both qualities were scarce, this is certainly probable.

INGREDIENTS

200g/7oz hazelnuts

500ml/2 cups of water

honey to taste

EQUIPMENT

blender

sieve

METHOD

Shell the hazelnuts, then soak overnight.

Drain them, then put into a blender with the water and whizz them up. Strain through a sieve.

The result should be a rich and creamy milk. If you want to use the milk in oatmeal, on your granola, in a dessert, or you're simply not too fond of the taste, then a spoonful of honey may be most welcome.

Other uses

Hazelnuts are delicious roasted. Put on a baking sheet and pop into an oven at 180°C/350°F/gas mark 4 for twenty minutes. Allow to cool. They can then be crushed and added as a topping to cakes and desserts, or try them on their own. Roasting really does transform them and needs to be tried to be believed.

HEATHER

An evergreen shrub that grows no taller than 60cm (2ft). Curiously the Bach flower remedy that uses heather (*Calluna vulgaris*—family Ericaceae) is for people obsessed with themselves who dislike being alone. The flowers are used in normal herbal medicine as an anti-septic, diuretic, and anti-rheumatic, which is certainly less curious.

Foraging for heather

Heather likes to grow on acidic soils, often on moorland and marshy ground where it can dominate. It is best picked when in flower as these are the most flavorsome parts.

Heather Mead

The earthy, peaty flavors that characterize the best whiskys are evident in this mead. The following recipe is from Alex Hughes, a member of the Bristol Brewing Circle, and this is the drink I repeatedly returned to while helping him make room in his shed (for more bottles). It can be adapted by using any flowers, not just heather or lavender (for Lavender Mead, see p. 175).

INGREDIENTS

1.5kg/3.3lb runny, delicately flavored honey

125ml/½ cup of dried heather flowers

1.5 liters/6 cups of boiling water

sweet mead yeast

1 tsp yeast nutrient

EQUIPMENT

fermentation bucket

4.5-liter/1-gallon secondary

solid rubber bung

airlock and bung

siphoning tube

METHOD

Place the jars of honey into a bowl of hot water and leave for a few minutes. This loosens the honey in the jar and makes it easier to pour. Once loosened, the honey should be poured into a fermentation bucket, covered with boiling water, and stirred.

Place the heather in the bottom of a secondary and pour over the honey mixture. Top up with cold water to one gallon. Pitch the yeast and yeast nutrient, attach the solid rubber bung, and shake the secondary. Remove the bung and add the airlock.

After two months, rack, removing the heather. Rack again after about six months. Ferment out and bottle. Mead will vastly improve if left in the bottle for at least one year.

HIMALAYAN BALSAM

Himalayan balsam (*Impatiens glandulifera*) was introduced to UK gardens in 1839 and soon spread across much of Europe, New Zealand, the United States, and Canada. It can reproduce by firing seeds a distance of up to 7m (23ft), and as there can be anything up to eight hundred of them per plant it doesn't keep to its garden home for very long. This makes it an invasive plant. It may look very beautiful in a valley at the base of a snow-capped mountain, but over here it can choke out our native plants, and as it's rich in nectar our bees will favor it above our own plants, a fact that doubles its biodiversity-reducing impact. By eating the seeds or using the flowers you can help keep Himalayan balsam at bay.

Foraging for Himalayan balsam

Himalayan balsam can often be found on river banks as the seeds are readily sent downstream. If you find just one or two plants, hunt further downstream and I almost guarantee you will find more. It can also be found at woodland edges and on wasteland.

When foraging for Himalayan balsam, don't be afraid to cut down as many plants as you can find. You will be helping our native wild flowers by getting rid of this beast.

Fireweed, Bramble Tip, and Policeman's Helmet Wine

I love working with other home wine makers to come up with new wines. Recently I teamed up with Nottinghamshire's Mike Griffiths, who has been making wine since before I was born. Combining a variety of edible flowers into Mike's bramble tip wine helps transform it from a white wine into more of a rosé. I've chosen to use Himalayan balsam flowers and fireweed, both readily available at this time of year and both often be found growing along riverbanks or in waste ground. Luckily this is also often the habitat for brambles (blackberry vines).

The great joy of using Himalayan balsam flowers is not only that they impart a lovely reddish-pink tinge to any wine or even cordial or jam you are making, but that you are helping biodiversity by using them. Himalayan balsam, an invasive interloper, can produce up to 700 seeds per plant. It also fires these seeds up to 7 meters away from the plant once it's gone to seed, so it is very difficult to eradicate. It is slowly spreading across all the states, having made its home in most of the northern states. It grows tall enough to smother our native flower species while also being irresistible to bees, and is therefore favored above all other flowers—a double blow to biodiversity. By eating the flowers or using them in wines, the plant never has a chance to seed and therefore we can help to eradicate it.

INGREDIENTS

2 liters/2 quarts of bramble tips
   (just dropped into the bucket and not
   particularly pressed down; the tip is the
   end 4 or 5 inches of a young bramble)
juice of 1 medium lemon
1 cup of Himalayan balsam flowers
1 cup fireweed flowers
500g/1lb golden raisins
1kg/2lb sugar

EQUIPMENT

large saucepan/cauldron
large spoon
fermentation bucket
siphoning tube
secondary
airlock and bung

1 tsp yeast nutrient

1 tsp general purpose wine yeast

3.5 liters/3.5 quarts of water

METHOD

Chop or mince the golden raisins and add them to a big pan with the bramble tips. Add the water and bring to a boil, then cover and add the sugar and stir until dissolved; simmer for an hour. Replace the cover and allow to cool. Strain into a fermentation bucket over the flowers and stir in the lemon juice, yeast nutrient, and yeast.

Cover the bucket loosely and leave to ferment in a warm place until any foaming has died back. Syphon into a secondary, top up with cold water, put under an airlock, then sit back and wait.

When the fermentation has finished and the wine is clear (after roughly three months), rack off into a clean secondary (there'll probably be a decent deposit from the golden raisins), top up again, and transfer to the coolest place you have in the house. Bottle after another 3 months and leave to stand for 6 months more.

Autumn Flower Champagne

Himalayan balsam flowers add real color to this most flavorsome champagne, making it blush a bright pink.

INGREDIENTS	EQUIPMENT
3 liters/3 quarts of water	kettle
1kg/2.3lb sugar	fermentation bucket/food-grade bucket
1 liter/1 quart of balsam flowers	muslin/cheesecloth
500ml/2 cups of clover flowers	saucepan

3 tbsp cider vinegar

2 tsp citric acid

2 tsp lemon juice

METHOD ···

Wash the flowers to ensure they are bug-free. Place in a fermentation bucket with the other ingredients apart from the sugar and water. Cover with half the water and give it a stir. Meanwhile, bring the rest of the water to the boil and stir in the sugar. Add that to the rest of the mix.

Leave with the lid loosely on or a dish towel over the top, occasionally returning in order to give it a stir. After two to four days it should have started to fizz. When it does, strain into bottles. Put the bottles straight into the fridge, or release the gas from them daily as they can be prone to exploding.

Other uses

Himalayan balsam flowers can be used to add color to jams and other foods. The seeds can also be eaten either raw or cooked. My brother Dave makes a lovely burger by blending the seeds with wild mushrooms and moulding into shape with his hands before grilling until browned. To pick the seeds, wrap a paper bag around the plant and let them fire into this rather than risk sending seeds all over the place.

HOPS

Hop bines (*Humulus lupulus*) can be found in the wild creeping up trees and telegraph poles; the name originates in the Anglo-Saxon word *hoppan*, meaning "to climb."

The hop is always thought of as the key ingredient in beer-making. That is true, but there used always to be a distinction between an ale and a beer: a beer was the word used to describe a hopped beer while an ale traditionally would be an unhopped beer. Over time this distinction has been forgotten.

Two of the King Henrys, VI and VII, hated hops, the former calling them "an unwholesome weed." Both banned their use in beer-making.

Foraging for hops

The downside of foraging for hops is that it can be difficult to ascertain exactly which variety they are, and therefore what type of flavor they will impart. This isn't a great worry as after a while you will learn the characteristics of the hops you forage and use them appropriately.

To harvest, do the same as with grown hops: either cut down a bine and take the whole thing home or pick the hops off one at a time. In the wild, hops normally wrap themselves around a tree, giving the hop-picker a perfect place to sit and pick. Do remember that hops have a soporific effect and can make you drowsy so climb down from a tree if your eyelids are getting heavy.

Growing hops

Before planting your hops, assess the site: they need plenty of sunlight, lots of room to grow, and a well-drained soil. Commercially they are grown up poles reaching to around 5m (15ft) so they can therefore be grown up the south side of a house, up carefully erected poles or wires. I have had a great harvest by training my hops to grow a bit horizontally as well as vertically. They basically just need room so that the bines don't choke each other.

Hops can be grown from seed but it is far easier to grow them from softwood cuttings, which become available from specialized suppliers during the spring. Plant directly where they are to grow in fertile soil, watering them well in. Root stems can also be dug up from more established plants and the same procedure followed.

Continue to water well in dry weather and prune last year's growth to ground level during the dormant winter period.

Drying hops

When the female cones have fully grown your hops are ready to dry. Some choose to dry their hops in a food dehydrator or oven, keeping a low heat not exceeding 60°C (140°F). To save energy, and in my opinion obtain similar results, hops can be dried naturally. I spread mine up the banister in my hallway, which is away from bright lights, has a flow of air, and is insect-free. Perhaps not everyone lives with a tolerant person, though. Any room can be used to dry hops just so long as it's not too bright. Direct sunlight will affect the levels of the yellow lupulin needed to make your beer bitter, and thus sort of defeats the object of drying them.

Once dried, hops can be frozen and used when needed. I like to freeze mine in 25g/1oz bags so that at a glance I know how much I have.

Simple Hop Beer

This is a great recipe for the novice beer-maker. In fact, if I want to quickly make a beer up with the minimum amount of fuss I turn to this recipe. Beer-makers who regularly use kits are normally shocked by it as essentially it's the same as a kit beer only you are in charge of the ingredients.

INGREDIENTS

13 liters/13 quarts of water

1kg/2.2lb malt extract

55g/2oz dried hops

750g/1.5lb sugar or pale dried
   malt extract

ale yeast

EQUIPMENT

large saucepan/cauldron

muslin/cheesecloth

fermentation bucket

siphoning tube

hydrometer (optional)

thermometer (optional)

METHOD ···

Bring half the water to a boil, pour in the malt extract and sugar, and boil for thirty minutes. Throw in the hops and boil for a further thirty minutes. (The hops can be wrapped in a little square of thick muslin cloth as this will make it easier to fish them out. A kind of giant tea bag.)

Strain the liquor into the fermentation bucket. The hops should be added to the compost heap as they are highly beneficial.

Pour over the rest of the cold water and allow to cool. When the temperature is about 18°C (65°F), sprinkle on your yeast. The gravity (if using a hydrometer) should be roughly 1030.

Seal the bin and leave for a week or until it has fermented (when you have a consistent hydrometer reading over a few days).

Place a level teaspoon of sugar into each empty beer bottle and siphon the liquid into the bottles, ensuring you don't siphon in any of the sediment. Cap them.

Leave the bottles for ten days, then they are ready to drink. The beer should be about 4.5%.

Easy Grain Beer

The BBC (the Bristol Brewing Circle) first gathered on a cold and wet early spring evening. It consisted of five members who barely knew each other, having met through bulletins on the Internet. They all turned up at a mutually agreed place by bike and left a few hours later slightly more inebriated than when they'd arrived.

That evening we made this recipe, our first attempt at using grains instead of malt extract in the beer-making process. The result was a slightly hoppy and malty light ale.

INGREDIENTS

20 liters/20 quarts of water (hard if
   possible)
65g/2.5oz Goldings hops
2.25kg/5lb pale malt
225g/8oz crushed crystal malt
ale yeast

EQUIPMENT

large saucepan/cauldron
mash tun
boiler *or* another large saucepan
mashing/sparge bag (optional)
fermentation bucket
muslin/cheesecloth
thermometer
siphoning tube

METHOD

Put the pale malt and crushed crystal malt (grains) into a sparging bag and lower into the mash tun or saucepan. (Although not essential, a sparging bag stops grains from clogging up the tap on the brew boiler and makes it much easier to clean. If not using a sparging bag, just put the grains into the boiler.) Cover with 10 liters/10 quarts of water, allow the temperature to rise to 65–66°C (149–151°F), then keep it there for one hour.

If using a cooler mash tun, heat 10 liters/10 quarts of strike water to 72°C (162°F), pour this into the cooler, and stir in the grains. Take a temperature reading and make sure the 65–66°C (149–151°F) level is maintained for an hour.

The next stage is sparging (see p. 86), and this is one way of doing it. Filter off the liquid into a large sterilized container. Heat a further 10 liters/10 quarts of water to 77°C (171°F), pour this over the grains, drain, and repeat.

Pour all the mash (unmade beer) back into the large pan or boiler. Place the hops in a square of muslin cloth and tie up the corners— again, this saves mess. Dangle this into the boiler and boil for one hour. Stir occasionally. After another hour, filter into a fermentation bucket.

Cool as quickly as possible, ideally with a wort chiller (see p. 24). Otherwise, place the fermentation bucket onto cool tiles, move it outside, or put it in the coldest room of the house, or even in iced water. When the wort has reached around 21°C (70°F), add the yeast.

Fit the lid and airlock and leave to ferment for four to fourteen days, or until the hydrometer gives a stable reading over a few days.

Siphon into beer bottles with a teaspoon of sugar in them, or a beer barrel with four tablespoons of sugar.

Hop Wine

It may seem a waste to make a wine with hops rather than the usual beer, but hop wine is very quaffable and tastes less alcoholic than it

is. What is most interesting is that although having the characteristics of a wine it also has those of an Indian Pale Ale. My girlfriend,
who does not like beer, will drink hop wine, which is quite a victory
after eight years of trying to get her to appreciate the hop!

INGREDIENTS

75g/3oz hops

300g/11oz green (undried) hops

25g/1oz bruised ginger root

juice of 1 lemon and juice of
   1 orange

or 2 tsp citric acid

225g/8oz chopped raisins

1.5kg/3.3lb sugar

4.5 liters/1 gallon of water

1 tsp yeast nutrient

1 Campden tablet (optional)

Sauternes wine yeast

EQUIPMENT

large saucepan/cauldron

muslin/cheesecloth

fermentation bucket

4.5-liter/1-gallon secondary

airlock and bung

siphoning tube

METHOD

Boil the hops and ginger in the water for an hour. Put the raisins,
sugar, orange and lemon juice or citric acid into a sterilized fermentation bucket and strain over the liquid. Add the Campden tablet (if
using) and leave for twenty-four hours.

Leave to cool, and sprinkle over yeast and nutrient. Allow to
ferment for five days, then strain into a secondary. Rack once, and
allow to ferment out.

Age for six months.

PEARS

Pears are a pretty old fruit and have been enjoyed since prehistoric times and cultivated for at least the last four thousand years. Pear wood is highly prized as it is a stable wood. It's used to make bread boards and musical instruments.

In parts of Europe a pear tree (*Pyrus communis* and related species) would be planted at a wedding: its longevity and fruitfulness were thought to give strength to the marriage. With each subsequent girl child who was born another pear tree would be planted, for each boy an apple tree. If everyone adopted this practice we would soon have an abundance of apples and pears to turn into lovely booze.

Foraging for pears

Unfortunately pears don't seem to be as common as apples in the wild, though that's not to say you won't find any. They often grow close to railway lines, in public parks, and in former gardens. Many people who grow pears don't know what to do with them all, so if you see a laden tree don't be afraid to knock on the door and ask the owner if they would be happy to spare some pears. Why not offer them some wine in return?

Growing pears

Similar to apples (see p. 197).

Pear Wine ————————————————

Pear wine has to be one of my most favored country wines. Indeed, at the embryonic stages of my wine-making career I was ready to give up as I'd not been pleased with my handful of results. It was pear wine that really introduced my taste buds to what a good country wine can taste like. It also introduced me to the world of matching food with wine—a practice I had thought an affectation of the posh. The flavor of a mouthful of Stilton and a sip of pear wine exploded then melted in my mouth—a sensation that changed my mind and my opinion forever.

INGREDIENTS

2kg/4.4lb pears

1kg/2.2lb sugar

1 tsp pectolase

4 liters/1 gallon of water

1 tsp yeast nutrient

1 Campden tablet (optional)

champagne yeast

EQUIPMENT

large saucepan/cauldron

muslin/cheesecloth

fermentation bucket

siphoning tube

METHOD

Chop up the pears (no need to peel or core them; save the juice) and put into a saucepan. Fill with the water and slowly bring to a boil, then simmer gently for exactly twenty minutes.

Strain the liquid through a muslin cloth and onto the sugar in a fermentation bucket. Stir a little to help it dissolve. Add the Campden tablet (if using) and leave for twenty-four hours.

Cool to room temperature and add the yeast, nutrient, and pectolase.

Rack after one month, and again if required. Allow to ferment out. Will benefit from six months' aging.

PUMPKINS

If you grow your own vegetables there will come a point when you will excitedly want to grow something new, something a little different. One of the most fun vegetables people plump for is the pumpkin (*Cucurbita pepo, C. mixta, C. maxima* or *C. moschata*).

The word "pumpkin" derives from the Greek *pepon*, which means "large melon." It is uncertain where pumpkins originated, but the smart money is on the Americas.

Growing pumpkins

Pumpkins can be sown in late spring, in pots indoors, roughly a month before the last frosts. Plant in a good peat-free sowing compost with a small handful of vermiculite mixed in. Use a newspaper pot as pumpkins are not great fans of being transplanted. Plant two seeds per pot and thin out the weakest.

Harden off before planting out.

Pumpkin Beer

These days, around Halloween time pumpkins can be seen on people's doorsteps; they've become a kind of fashion accessory. They sit there as symbols of the wholesome house beyond the threshold. The day after Halloween comes the question "What on earth do I do with these pumpkins that weigh more than my child?" It's worth mentioning that if you are overrun with squashes you can use them instead of or as well as pumpkins.

INGREDIENTS

2kg/4.5lb pumpkin (or squash)

1kg/2.2lb malt extract

55g/2oz dried hops

750g/1.5lb sugar or pale dried malt extract

13 liters/13 quarts of water

ale yeast

EQUIPMENT

large saucepan/cauldron

muslin/cheesecloth

fermentation bucket

siphoning tube

hydrometer (optional)

METHOD

Chop your pumpkin up into fist-sized chunks, remove all the seeds, then roast for twenty minutes at 200°C/390°F/gas mark 6 or until the pieces have started to crisp. Allow to cool, then scoop the pulp out.

Bring 7 liters/7 quarts of water to a boil, then throw in the pulp and keep boiling for thirty minutes. At this point some people like to add hops. I personally don't see the need, but they do help to preserve the beer if used.

Pour the malt extract and sugar into the fermentation bucket and stir them together so they are fully mixed.

Strain the pumpkin liquid into the fermentation bucket. Stir the wort to make sure that the sugar has dissolved.

Pour over the remaining 6 liters/6 quarts of cold water and allow wort to cool. When cooled to room temperature, pitch your yeast. The gravity (if using a hydrometer) should be roughly 1030.

Seal the bin and leave for a week, or until it has fermented.

Place a level teaspoon of sugar into each empty bottle and siphon in the liquid, making sure that you don't siphon in any of the sediment.

Leave the bottles for ten days, then they are ready to drink. The beer should be about 4.5%.

QUINCES

Native to the land between the Caspian and Black Seas, quince trees (*Cydonia oblonga*) are often cultivated by gardeners in many places including the UK, New Zealand, Japan, and North America. Trees can grow to 8m (26ft) tall and the fruit itself is bright yellow and pear-like. Quinces are another one of the fruits Eve was suspected of eating in the Bible.

Growing quinces

Quince trees like to be in soil with a neutral pH and sheltered from the wind. They can self-pollinate so you only need to plant one tree. They are frost-tolerant—in fact they need a bit of cold—and they shouldn't be allowed to dry out. Mulch if necessary.

Perfumed Quince and Persimmon Wine ──────

This recipe incorporating quinces comes from Jeremy Daniel Meadows from New Zealand. He reports that it's a wine for which he has never had any negative feedback.

INGREDIENTS

2 quinces

800g/1.5lb ripe persimmons
   (aka sharon fruit)

565g/1lb can of seedless lychees

1.2kg/2.2lb sugar

250ml/1 cup of rose cordial

EQUIPMENT

2 large saucepans

muslin/cheesecloth

fermentation bucket

4.5-liter/1-gallon secondary

airlock and bung

siphoning tube

2 liters/2 quarts of water

2 liters/2 quarts of apple juice

1 tsp citric acid

¼ tsp tartaric acid

¼ tsp malic acid

1 Campden tablet (optional)

red start cuvee yeast

METHOD

Finely slice the quinces, chop up the persimmons, and boil in half the water for ten minutes. In a separate pan boil the sugar, cordial, and apple juice in the other half of the water.

Allow both pans to cool to room temperature, then pour into a fermentation bucket. Add the Campden tablet (if using), then leave for twenty-four hours.

Now add the acids, the yeast, and the lychees. Leave for one week before straining into a secondary.

Rack after one month, and again if necessary. Allow to ferment out.

This wine will benefit from at least three months' aging.

Quince Kompot with Lemon and Wine

This recipe comes from my Russian friend Sasha. It works as both a preserve and a drink. Like the other kompots in this book, it can be diluted to make a cordial or added to tea instead of sugar.

INGREDIENTS

6 ripe quinces

3 lemons

1kg/2.2lb sugar

500ml/2 cups of dry white wine

2 vanilla pods

2 liters/2 quarts of water

EQUIPMENT

large jar

saucepan

sieve

METHOD

Put the water in a saucepan along with the wine and the juice of one lemon. Wipe the fuzz off the quinces with a cloth and cut them in quarters. Remove the core and pits, then slice them thinly into the saucepan. When all the quinces have been added, put in two quartered lemons and bring slowly to a boil over a gentle heat.

Simmer for about twenty minutes, until the quinces have just softened. Strain the fruit and place in the jar. Return the cooking liquor to the pan and add the sugar and the vanilla pods. Bring to a boil and keep it there for ten minutes. Pour the syrup over the fruit and seal the jar.

Wait at least one day before eating/drinking.

Ratafia of Quinces

Traditionally, ratafia is a sweet liqueur or cordial that is flavored with almonds, cherries, or peach kernels, which can make ratafia a little toxic. This recipe is an adaptation of an eighteenth-century recipe by Vincent la Chapelle from *The Modern Cook*.

INGREDIENTS	EQUIPMENT
2 quinces	small saucepan
750ml/3 cups of brandy	cheese grater
150ml/5 fl. oz of water	large jar
300g/11oz sugar	muslin/cheesecloth
cinnamon stick	
10 cloves	

METHOD

Grate the quinces and place into the jar. Boil the water with the spices and stir in the sugar until fully dissolved. Allow to cool, then pour onto the quinces, adding the brandy. Shake vigorously. After three months strain into bottles and leave for a further three months before drinking.

SWEET CORN (MAIZE)

Sweet corn, or maize (*Zea mays*), is a grass that is thought to originate in South America. It is the third most grown cereal crop after wheat and rice.

The Maya worshipped maize, probably because it was their staple crop. They believed that man was created from maize. Unlike in most modern Western religions, the maize god was female.

Growing sweet corn

Sweet corn is a very easy plant to grow, given the right conditions. It can be planted straight out in early summer, after all danger of frost has passed, or indoors in late spring, to get a head start. If transplanting, allow to grow to about 15cm (6in) before planting out.

Sweet corn likes fertile soil with plenty of well-rotted manure. Sow in blocks of at least nine rather than in the traditional rows as this aids pollination. I like to underplant it with chamomile or nitrogen-fixing clover to maximize the use of space and keep down all other weeds. Seeds should be sown about one human foot apart.

Support plants in high winds and water well in dry weather. Keep the mature cobs from the biggest, healthiest-looking plants as one cob can often supply you with enough seed for yourself and many friends for the next year.

Herby Corn Stalk—Free Ale

This recipe is for all those who like to have something for nothing. It essentially costs nothing as all the ingredients can be either foraged or grown. One of the biggest costs encountered in home-brewing foraged and homegrown ingredients is of course sugar. Unfortunately, sugar is one of the most essential ingredients in brewing.

Corn stalks have to be pretty green and fresh for them to still have enough sugar in them, therefore as soon as you harvest your corn cobs you should also harvest your corn stalks. Different varieties of corn will have different levels of sugar in their stalks so if this recipe is disappointingly low in alcohol try a different variety next year. The four lowest nodes have the highest concentrations of sugar.

INGREDIENTS

6 corn stalks

6 liters/1.5 gallons of water

4 long sprigs of rosemary

handful of thyme sprigs

packet of ale yeast *or* some dregs from
   your last brew to be 100 percent free

EQUIPMENT

1 mallet

tough plastic bag

2 large saucepans

muslin/cheesecloth

4.5-liter/1-gallon secondary

airlock and bung

METHOD

The first part of this recipe is like no other and is in my opinion great fun as it involves bashing things. Parents, it's a great way of getting your kids to join in with an otherwise adult hobby. Cut the corn stalks into pieces, put them a few at a time into a tough plastic bag, and bash them to a pulp. Save any liquid in a saucepan.

Add the pulped corn stalks to the water and boil for an hour. Cool, and strain into another saucepan with the original liquid saved. Return to a boil and reduce to 4.5 liters/1 gallon, adding the rosemary and thyme (or any herb of your choice) toward the end of the boil.

Strain and decant into a sterilized secondary and pitch the yeast, or a small amount of dregs from your last brew. If using dregs, make sure they are no more than a fortnight old and that you have kept them in the fridge.

Leave for ten days or until fully fermented, then bottle.

Don't expect to throw the party of the century with this beer. It's certainly not the strongest.

YARROW

It is thought that wherever there is yarrow growing the land is blessed. It is known as a sacred herb by many, including the Chinese (it's in the *I Ching*) and the Celts, who used it to help them dream of a future partner.

The first part of its Latin name, *Achillea millefolium*, comes from the Greek warrior Achilles as yarrow was taken into battle by the ancient Greeks. When placed on a sword cut, yarrow helped the blood to coagulate and to seal up the wound. When I first read this I thought it utter nonsense. Then I cut myself, deeply, with a knife while working at the Eden Project, just prior to delivering a talk on foraging. I grabbed some yarrow, and I can tell you, its healing properties are astonishing.

Foraging for yarrow

A trip to most public parks or grassy areas on all but the coldest days of the year will normally result in the discovery of yarrow. A couple of words of warning for this one though, for the novice forager could mistake yarrow for a deadlier plant. Once, during one of my guided foraging walks, an inexperienced forager held up a plant to my face. It had been pulled up by the root, despite the fact that I had informed the group not to pull up any roots for conservation reasons. She asked me if it was yarrow. A quick inspection of the plant confirmed my suspicions: it was actually hemlock.

Thinking that no one would make the mistake again, a few years later I got an e-mail from a slightly more experienced forager to whom I had given some yarrow ale at one of my brewing classes. The e-mail had some photos attached of the yarrow he had collected. This "yarrow" also had an uncanny resemblance to hemlock and I advised him not to use it.

The *millefolium* part of yarrow's Latin name means "thousand leaves." Take a good look at the dark-green feathery leaf of a yarrow plant and you'll see how it got its name. This is the most noticeable difference between yarrow and other similar-looking plants.

Growing yarrow

Sow seeds in the autumn in pots in a greenhouse, or indoors before planting out in the spring. It is drought tolerant, survives in most soils, and even comes back after continual cutting if it spreads into the lawn. Many gardeners will know it as an invasive weed that can spread by rhizome or seeds.

Yarrow Ale

Long before hops were used as a bittering agent people were making ale using yarrow.

This recipe makes 100 pints and it has become a bit of a party ale, simply because I always brew it in this quantity. It is of course possible to make half or a quarter this amount simply by halving or quartering the quantities given here.

INGREDIENTS

3.5kg/7.7lb barley malt extract

2.5kg/5.5lb sugar

1.75kg/3.5lb fresh yarrow

56 liters/100 pints of water

a small jar of honey

ale yeast

EQUIPMENT

large saucepan/cauldron

large fermentation bucket

muslin/cheesecloth

siphoning tube

METHOD ⋯⋯⋯⋯⋯⋯⋯⋯⋯⋯⋯⋯⋯⋯⋯⋯⋯⋯⋯⋯⋯⋯⋯

Boil the yarrow leaves in water for thirty minutes (you may need to do this in batches, or use more than one pan).

Place the malt extract and the sugar in a large sterilized fermentation bucket, dustbin, or (the option I take) water butt.

Using a muslin cloth or very fine big sieve, strain the liquid over the malt extract and sugar, stirring to make sure that all of it dissolves in the liquid. Top up to make 56 liters/100 pints and allow to cool to room temperature.

Cover with a clean dish towel, old shirt, or whatever you can get your hands on. Secure this with some string and make sure your mates don't think it's a chair and sit on it (as happened once at one of my parties).

Leave for about a week to ten days, or longer if in a cooler place or you're making it in the winter. Then siphon the brew into a keg or barrel into which you have poured the whole jar of honey first. If making a smaller brew you can siphon into bottles primed with 1 teaspoon of honey per 1 pint/500ml.

Leave to mature for a further week to ten days.

Cold and Flu Tea ——————————————————

I find that if the early stages of a cold or flu are treated with the appropriate herbs then the length of time it lasts for can be lessened dramatically. This tea is one I swear by whenever I'm feeling run down.

Yarrow is widely used to help reduce fevers. Pollen from yarrow has been found in a cave dwelling and dated to over sixty thousand years old. Some historians believe this is evidence that humans have been using the plant as an herbal remedy for many millennia.

INGREDIENTS	EQUIPMENT
1 tsp yarrow	kettle
1 tsp peppermint	teapot
1 tsp elderflower	strainer
250ml/1 cup of water	mug

METHOD

Boil the kettle, put the herbs in a teapot, and pour hot water over. Allow to infuse for at least five minutes before straining into a mug.

WINTER

Bay and rosemary ale	Rosemary (infused) wine
Parsnip sherry and wine	Rosemary et al: Morning tea
Rhubarb vodka	Sea buckthorn gin
Rhubarb wine	Sloe wine
Rosehip wine	Sloe gin
Dried rosehip kompot	Rumtopf
Rosemary ale	Holy water!
Rosemary and yarrow ale	Prison booze

COMING IN FROM the cold and curling up on your favorite armchair in front of a roaring fire (or hot radiator) with a glass of your favorite tipple is what winter was invented for. Tradition has it that at this time of year ales should be brewed to be a little stronger, meaning red noses all round, not just from the cold.

It is sometimes difficult to maintain ideal homebrewing conditions during cold weather; try as you might to keep an even temperature while fermenting it is not always possible. This can mean sluggish yeast, but don't be too worried if fermentation slows or even stops: it will no doubt start again as the weather warms up. I keep a spare duvet cover on hand to cover my fermentation bucket during the winter, and this regulates the temperature well enough.

Trees can be planted if the ground is not too frozen, and pruning can also get underway. But if snow has fallen and the ground is frozen there isn't much to do in the garden, and there isn't much point going out foraging either—which makes this a great time for those DIY projects much favored by the homebrewer such as making a cider press or mash tun, keeping equipment spotless, or maybe just seeing your way through your stores!

In season (garden): apples, beets, rosemary, sage, thyme, parsnips, rhubarb, quinces, broccoli, cabbage, celery, turnips.

In season (wild): apples, crab apples, yarrow, rosehips, ground ivy, nettles, cleavers, bay, gorse, quinces, pine (needles).

BAY

Found throughout the world, bay was much revered by the Romans, hence its Latin name, *Laurus nobilis*, which means "noble (or renowned) laurel." According to the seventeenth-century herbalist and exponent of free healthcare Nicholas Culpeper, "The Bark of the root drunk with wine, provokes urine, breaks the stone, [and] opens obstructions of the liver and spleen." These claims are not backed up by modern practices, although it is thought to be a gastric tonic and a mild sedative, and is even used for its anti-dandruff properties.

Foraging for bay

Bay trees can be found growing across towns and cities in parks and in people's front gardens. They are often used as hedging and can sometimes be seen outside hotels sculpted into lollipop shapes.

Bay leaves are available all year round and can easily be mistaken for other types of laurel leaves, which should not be used. To aid identification, take what you think is a bay leaf, crush it in your hand, and smell it. If it smells just like the ones you use when making soups or curries, then it's a bay leaf.

Growing bay

Bay trees can grow to a height of 20m (65ft), so before planting think very carefully about positioning. They can be grown from seed, and germination, which is erratic, will take place at some point within six months if kept at 21°C (70°F). Growing from cuttings can also be difficult. In short, it is easier to buy a tree that is already growing. It is also advisable to grow it in a container as you can bring it indoors when it gets too hot or too cold. Allow the compost to dry out in winter months and don't overwater. Selective pruning will keep it from going too mental.

Bay enjoys medium fertile soil and should be mulched in the

spring to retain moisture. Lightly prune in the summer if necessary; it will even take a hacking in the summer if it gets too big. Protect from harsh frost and scorching heat.

Bay and Rosemary Ale

Of all the malt extract brews I have made, this ale has to be one of the finest. I was asked to supply a local herbalist with a barrel for a party to celebrate the opening of his shop and the general verdict was that it was made with ginger due to the heat created by the bay.

It is said that bay can have a slightly narcotic effect, therefore this ale generally helps parties go with a bit of swing.

INGREDIENTS

1kg/2.2lb malt extract

10 large rosemary sprigs

20 bay leaves

500g/1lb sugar

250g/9oz golden syrup (or honey)

packet of ale yeast

13 liters/13 quarts of water

2 tbsp golden syrup or honey for priming

EQUIPMENT

large saucepan/cauldron

fermentation bucket

muslin/cheesecloth

hydrometer (optional)

siphoning tube

METHOD ....

Bring 7 liters/7 quarts of water a boil and add the malt extract, then strip the rosemary and bay leaves into the water and keep boiling for thirty minutes. Remove from the heat and stir in the sugar until fully dissolved.

Strain the liquid into a fermentation bucket. Pour over 6 liters/

6 quarts of cold water, make sure room temperature has been reached, then pitch the yeast. The gravity (if using a hydrometer) should be roughly 1030. Leave for four to fourteen days to ferment.

Siphon into a keg using two tablespoons of golden syrup as a primer, or if using bottles then one teaspoon per bottle. Sugar can also be used.

Other uses
Bay makes an excellent insect repellent and can be used to deter moths from clothing and weevils from flour. Along with parsley and thyme it is also one of the essential herbs for a bouquet garni.

PARSNIPS

Parsnips (*Pastinaca sativa*) are thought to originate in the Mediterranean, but as the wild parsnip has a thin woody stem it took years of cultivation to get the fat roots we know today. Some evidence points toward the Romans, but we can't really be sure as they used the same word for carrots (idiots).

Growing parsnips
Plant out in late winter to early spring and sow at 15cm (6in) intervals. Make sure the ground has been prepared, that all stones and anything else in the ground that could cause splitting have been removed. Parsnips don't like nutrient-rich soil so don't plant in an area that has had compost or well-rotted manure added that season. Keep watered in dry weather and free of weeds.

Parsnip Sherry and Wine

It is best to use parsnips that have been touched by a frost as frost helps bring out the natural sugars. If using grocer-bought, aim to buy them during the colder winter months.

A small word of warning for this wine: it will loosen you up in more ways than one!

INGREDIENTS

1.8kg/4lb parsnips

1.3kg/3lb sugar

4 liters/4 quarts of water

1kg/2.2lb raisins

1 lemon

1 tsp pectolase

1 tsp yeast nutrient

1 Campden tablet (optional)

white wine yeast

EQUIPMENT

large saucepan/cauldron

fermentation bucket

muslin/cheesecloth

smaller saucepan

4.5-liter/1-gallon secondary

airlock and bung

siphoning tube

METHOD

First you will need to make the raisin juice. Wash the raisins in very hot water, allow to cool, then chop up. Put in a saucepan, cover with 1 liter/1 quart of water and simmer for five minutes. Push through a muslin cloth, set the juice aside, and compost the raisins.

Next, move on to the parsnips. Give them a good old wash and a bit of a scrub to get all the dirt off, but don't peel them. Place in a large pan and boil in the rest of the water. Cook until you can put a fork in them but not so they fall apart.

Meanwhile, put the sugar, the raisin juice, the juice and the rind of the lemon into a smaller pan and simmer for forty-five minutes, stirring occasionally.

Strain the parsnip liquid through a muslin cloth into a fermentation bucket (the parsnips can then be made into mashed parsnips, composted, or fed to your pigs). Also add the raisin juice and, when hand-hot, the yeast nutrient, pectolase, and Campden tablet. If using a Campden tablet, leave for twenty-four hours before moving to the next step.

Pitch the yeast, leave for ten days, then strain into a secondary.

To make sherry: plug up the secondary with cotton balls, leave for six months, rack if necessary. Siphon into sherry bottles and plug with sherry cork stoppers.

To make wine: attach an airlock and bung to the secondary, rack after one month (and again if necessary), and allow to ferment out before siphoning into bottles.

This wine/sherry will improve with at least six months' aging.

RHUBARB

There is generally some argument when it comes to the definition of rhubarb, whether it's fruit or vegetable. Botanically speaking, rhubarb (genus *Rheum*) is considered to be a vegetable. However, the waters were muddied in 1947 when a court in New York declared it to be a fruit. The reason had much more to do with the reduction in duty paid on imported fruit as opposed to imported vegetables than with any botanical or culinary consideration.

Growing rhubarb

Although rhubarb can be grown from seed it is far easier to grow from division. Beg or buy a rhubarb crown in late autumn from a plant that is three to four years old. Plant 10cm (4in) diameter pieces in soil enriched with well-rotted manure or compost at a distance apart of about 30cm (12in). Do not harvest in the first year and water well in hot weather.

Rhubarb can be forced by placing an upside-down bucket over the top of the plant; this will bring on your plant by as much as eight weeks. Don't force a plant two years in a row as that will damage it.

Rhubarb Vodka

Emma Ball from the Eden Project loves rhubarb, and every year she makes this drink, which is spectacular, in both color and flavor. Drink it as a chilled aperitif or use it as a mixer in summer cocktails.

INGREDIENTS

450g/1lb rhubarb
750ml/3 cups of vodka
225g/8oz sugar

EQUIPMENT

1-liter/1-quart glass jar
muslin/cheesecloth

METHOD

Gather your rhubarb stems, removing the poisonous leaves and any discolored parts. Chop into 3cm (1in) pieces and put into a very large jar. Add the sugar and vodka and seal. Shake well and leave for at least three to four weeks.

Strain into a bottle through muslin/cheesecloth and place in a cool dark place for three months. The discarded rhubarb can be eaten, and works well in a boozy rhubarb fool.

Rhubarb Wine

Mollie Harris, in her book *A Drop o' Wine*, suggests not picking young rhubarb nor the older hard and tough stalks; late spring to early summer is the time to pick. You should also use normal, non-forced rhubarb. If buying instead of growing, avoid overly pink rhubarb.

INGREDIENTS

2kg/4.5lb rhubarb

2 ripe bananas

250g/9oz raisins

800g/1.5lb sugar

2.5 liters/2.5 quarts of water

½ cup of cold strong tea or
   1 tsp grape tannin

4 tbsp orange juice

1 Campden tablet (optional)

1 tsp pectolase

1 tsp yeast nutrient

Chablis wine yeast

EQUIPMENT

fermentation bucket

muslin/cheesecloth

4.5-liter/1-gallon secondary

airlock and bung

siphoning tube

METHOD

Cut the rhubarb into 5cm (2in) chunks and put into the freezer overnight. Allow to defrost the next day, then repeat the procedure. This will help break down the rhubarb and you'll therefore be able to extract more juice from it.

Chop the raisins and mash the banana. Place in a fermentation bucket with the rhubarb and cover with the cold water, saving 300ml/1 cup for later. Stir in the pectolase, cover loosely, and leave for twenty-four hours. If using a Campden tablet, do so now.

Pour in the tea, yeast, nutrient, and orange juice. Leave in a warm place for four days.

Strain into a secondary. Meanwhile bring the remaining 300ml/1 cup of water to a boil, add the sugar, and stir until dissolved. Allow to cool then add to the secondary, attach an airlock and bung, and leave to ferment out. It will benefit from racking twice.

Leave in the secondary for one year before bottling, then drink after three months.

ROSEHIPS

During World War Two the citizens of Britain were asked to go out into the countryside and pick rosehips to help the war effort. These were generally gathered from wild roses such as the dog rose (*Rosa canina*). Vitamin C was needed, and rosehips have twenty times more than oranges. Different groups would compete with each other, and this helped increase the stock of rosehips.

Foraging for rosehips

Rosehips can often be found on trail edges, the edges of forests, and on shores across the country. Alternatively they can be found in hedgerows, in municipal parks, and on wasteground. Be careful when picking rosehips as the thorns can often break the skin, not to mention plastic bags. It is best to collect them in a plastic ice cream tub.

Rosehip Wine ────────────────────────────────

This is a classic country recipe, another that has attracted many slight variations. This recipe calls for more rosehips than most, which is of course a matter of preference, but I think it makes all the difference.

INGREDIENTS	EQUIPMENT
1.5kg/3.3lb fresh rosehips *or* 375g/12oz dried rosehips	large saucepan/cauldron
	fermentation bucket
1.25kg/3lb sugar	muslin/cheesecloth
1 tsp citric acid	string
4 liters/1 gallon of water	4.5-liter/1-gallon secondary
1 tsp pectolase	airlock and bung
1 tsp yeast nutrient	a couple of heavy bricks
Campden tablet (optional)	siphoning tube
general purpose yeast	

METHOD ···

Pick and wash the rosehips, and if not already frost-softened put in the freezer overnight and allow to thaw. Coarsely chop or blend, place in the center of a muslin cloth, knot it up so there are no gaps, and tie the string around the knot so that it looks like a massive conker. Place the rosehips into the fermentation bucket and make sure the string is poking out.

Boil the water and add the sugar, stirring until it has fully dissolved. Pour the sugar solution over the rosehips, then add the nutrient, citric acid, and pectolase. Add the Campden tablet (if using) and leave for twenty-four hours.

When cooled, pitch the yeast.

Pull the rosehips out of the must and tie the end of the string around the bricks so that the cloth bundle is suspended just out and the juice drips into the fermentation bucket. This helps to get the very last bits of rosehip juice into the must. Remove the bag when fully drained and compost the hips. (You can of course use anything heavy, not just bricks; even a door handle, unless the door is in constant use.)

Pour into a secondary and leave in a dark place. Rack after one month, and again as required. Allow to ferment out, then bottle.

This wine will be drinkable after a year but will benefit from at least two more years' aging.

Dried Rosehip Kompot

This recipe comes from my Russian friend Sasha and, like all kompots, is traditionally spooned into tea instead of sugar or diluted as a cordial. The dried leaves of rosebay willowherb (see p. 185) can be made into a tea that is traditionally drunk by Russians, and I find that this goes particularly well with it.

INGREDIENTS	EQUIPMENT
500g/1lb dried rosehips	2 large jars
800g/1.7lb sugar	colander
2 cinnamon sticks	muslin/cheesecloth
zest and juice of 1 orange	saucepan

METHOD ···

Soak the rosehips in 1.5 liters/1.5 quarts of warm water for eight to ten hours. Strain through a colander, then strain the liquor again through several layers of muslin, or a coffee filter. Leave the rosehips whole.

Pour the liquor into a saucepan and add the cinnamon, zest, and sugar. Slowly bring to a boil until all the sugar is dissolved. Add the rosehips and the orange juice, and remove from the heat. Allow to infuse for at least eight hours, or overnight.

Pour through a colander and place the rosehips in the sterilized jars. Bring the syrup to the boil and simmer gently for five minutes before pouring over the rosehips, filling the jars. Seal the jars.

ROSEMARY

Rosemary (*Rosmarinus officinalis*) is a fully hardy perennial shrub with needle-like evergreen leaves that can grow up to 2m (6ft) tall. It's in the same family as mint, and *Rosmarinus* roughly translates as "dew of the sea." It was known by the Greeks, who thought it aided recall. Scholars would wear garlands of it when taking examinations.

It is also considered a symbol of friendship, loyalty, and remembrance, and is often carried by mourners at funerals.

Foraging for rosemary

There is no need to grow a rosemary plant in order to have a steady supply of rosemary. Take a walk round your neighborhood and you will no doubt find some growing semi-wild. In Bristol there's some rosemary growing in one of the local parks, and some outside a massive supermarket. It still strikes me as odd that people go into that supermarket and buy rosemary that has been flown in from miles away—madness! If you end up picking from someone's front garden, be sure to ask first.

Rosemary is at its most aromatic when it's in flower as it's higher in essential oils, which will make for a better, more flavorsome ale, tea, or wine.

Growing rosemary

In bygone times young maidens would take cuttings of rosemary and give each a name. The cutting that grew the most vigorously would be the name of the maiden's future husband. I'm not sure if he had a choice in the matter, nor if there was a test that men could use.

Rosemary can be sown direct from seeds but germination can be sporadic at best. Start indoors in a dark room at a temperature of 15°C (60°F). Results should appear within three months.

It is easier to grow from cuttings. Take a cutting of 7cm (3in), pull off the bottom leaves, dust with hormone rooting powder, and plant in a compost/coir/grit mix. Don't overwater and don't allow to dry out.

Plant out when established in well-drained neutral-to-alkaline soil in full sun. Prune to encourage new growth and protect during harsh winters.

Rosemary Ale ——————————————————

Rosemary has several traditional associations, and one of them is with weddings. The word "bridal" derives from "bride ale," an ale traditionally made from rosemary and presented to the bride at her wedding.

INGREDIENTS	EQUIPMENT
1kg/2.2lb malt extract	large saucepan/cauldron
10 large rosemary sprigs	fermentation bucket

750g/1.5lb sugar (brewing sugar
  preferably, otherwise granulated)
13 liters/13 quarts of water
2 tbsp golden syrup or honey
ale yeast

muslin/cheesecloth
hydrometer (optional)

METHOD

Bring half the water to the boil then strip the rosemary needles into it and keep boiling for twenty-five minutes. Add the malt extract and sugar toward the end of the boil and stir until they have fully dissolved.

Strain the liquid into the fermentation bucket.

Pour over the rest of the cold water and make sure the wort is about room temperature before pitching your yeast. The gravity (if using a hydrometer) should be roughly 1030.

Allow to ferment out. Keg using two tablespoons of golden syrup as a primer, or one teaspoon per bottle if using bottles.

Rosemary and Yarrow Ale

This recipe makes a light and complex herbal ale and is an excellent step into making beer using grains. As with all herbal ales it does not keep for very long and should be drunk soon after it has been made. The addition of the hops will of course impart flavor, but if you want a traditional ale don't use them. If, however, you wish your ale (or rather beer) to last a bit longer the hops will work as a preservative—which is the reason brewers started using them in the first place.

INGREDIENTS

20 liters/20 quarts of water

1.8kg/4.4lb crushed pale malt

200g/7oz crushed crystal malt

150g/5.2oz black malt

500g/1lb dry malt extract

50g/1.7oz rosemary

28g/1oz yarrow

28g/1oz hops (optional)

ale yeast

sugar

EQUIPMENT

mash tun

large saucepan

thermometer

sparging equipment

fermentation bucket

siphoning tube

hydrometer (optional)

METHOD

Mash the grains (see p. 85) at 65–67°C (149–152°F) for an hour in 10 liters/10 quarts of water. Sparge (see p. 86) using 10 liters/10 quarts of water.

Bring the 20-liter/20-quart wort to a boil, add the rosemary and yarrow (and hops if using), stir in the dried malt extract, and boil for thirty-five minutes. If using a boiler with an element in the bottom of it, make sure that you stir from time to time to stop anything from sticking to the element.

Transfer into a fermentation bucket, cool to room temperature, and pitch the yeast. Gravity should be around 1032. Put in a warm place for seven to ten days or until it has fermented.

Siphon into bottles primed with one teaspoon of sugar per 500ml/1-pint bottle.

Rosemary (Infused) Wine

If you have made a white wine as an experiment and it doesn't really taste of much, or if you have been given a bland white wine as a gift, infusing it with a herb such as rosemary can give it the boost it needs and turn it into something quite drinkable. You could even give it back to the person who gave it to you as a much-improved gift!

INGREDIENTS

90g/3.5oz softwood rosemary

750ml/3 cups of white wine

EQUIPMENT

750ml/1.5 pint sealable jar

rolling pin (optional)

METHOD

Bruise the rosemary with the rolling pin (or even the wine bottle) and place in the sealable jar. Cover with wine and leave to infuse for three days. Strain back into the bottle, cork, and age for a couple of months. Serve chilled.

Morning tea

You open the curtains in the morning, it is still dark, and the best you can hope for is a day that is slightly less gray than a rain-sodden housing project deep in the most eastern part of the former eastern bloc during a food shortage. The closing days of winter can be the most miserable of all, but luckily nature can help out with some natural pick-me-ups. My herbalist friend Max Drake swears by this little mix to get him through the dark months.

INGREDIENTS

1 sprig of rosemary

nettle tops

1 tsp of honey

250ml/1 cup of water

EQUIPMENT

kettle

teapot

strainer

mug

METHOD

Pick the rosemary while in flower. The nettles too should be picked when young. Both should be at their best in late winter/early spring, and both can be dried for later use.

Boil the water, put the herbs in a teapot, pour over the hot water. Allow to infuse for at least five minutes before straining into a mug.

Other uses

Medicinally used for migraines, poor circulation, and digestive problems. Not to be taken by pregnant mothers.

Stripped woody stems make great kebab skewers for a barbecue as they impart a hint of rosemary flavor to the meat.

SEA BUCKTHORN

Sea buckthorn (*Hippophäe rhamnoides*) is a spiny shrub that grows up to 3m (9ft) tall. It lives, as you might imagine, by the sea, often forming impenetrable thickets on dunes and cliffs. The silvery-gray bushes with their rough black bark support orange berries that grow profusely on second- and third-year female bushes from late summer right through to early spring. The berries are highly nutritious, brimming with vitamins C and E, omega 3 and 6, iron, boron, potassium, and manganese.

Foraging for sea buckthorn

When harvesting sea buckthorn you have to beware of spiky branches. Prune off heavily laden branches and place into a large tough bag. The berries are very tender and explode to the touch so putting whole branches into the freezer is by far the easiest way to solidify the berries and make them easier to pluck off. In fact you can just knock them off the branch when they're frozen.

Sea Buckthorn Gin ——————————

Given to me by Emma Ball from the Eden Project, this unusual recipe makes use of a berry that would have been well known to our ancestors but is almost unheard of now. Every forager who uses sea buckthorn raves about it afterward, and Emma is no exception. Nor am I for that matter, for it has a truly unique flavor that's well worth trying.

INGREDIENTS

600g/1.5lb sea buckthorn berries

300g/11oz sugar

1 liter/1 quart of gin

EQUIPMENT

1-liter/1-quart jar

muslin/cheesecloth

METHOD ....

Pour half the gin into the jar. Plop the frozen berries into the gin bottle and jar until the liquid reaches near the top. Add half the sugar to each. Shake fairly regularly and after about four to six weeks strain into bottles. It will be ready to drink immediately.

The orange berry mush and gin tend to separate so will require a shake before serving.

SLOES

Sloes are known to most people in the UK, as they grow everywhere; unfortunately they are not as commom in the United States. They have, however, been naturalized in North America, and you will be forgiven for thinking they are just very big blueberries. After sharing gathering experiences with various people, it certainly seems that sloes will grow more abundantly every other year, so if this autumn you find a blackthorn bush (*Prunus spinosa*) close to your home with no sloes on it, don't despair, just have a bit of patience.

Foraging for sloes

Sloes grow on the blackthorn bush, which is very common not only throughout Europe but on all the (non-frozen) continents of the Earth. They are often used in traditional hedge-planting schemes and as ground cover for game birds.

I have heard it suggested that you should beat the blackthorn to get the sloes. To do this you need to put a sheet under the bush, beat with a large stick, then simply wrap up the sheet and walk away with your bounty. I prefer to be a lot more Zen than this and individually pick each sloe.

There is a small recreation ground close to where I am writing this (my house) and last month I was very busy with this and that and I could feel my stress levels rising. For a spot of meditation I wandered off to this recreation ground, which is brimming with sloes, and picked a carrier bag full. I arrived home after some time had passed feeling refreshed and relaxed and able to carry on with the day. So I say keep the sloes slow!

Sloe Wine

If you are fed up with sloe gin (you must be mad) or just fancy something different, this recipe makes a great sweet wine.

INGREDIENTS	EQUIPMENT
1.5kg/3.3lb sloes	fermentation bucket
250g/9oz raisins	potato masher
1.5kg/3.3lb sugar	sieve
4 liters/4 quarts of boiling water	muslin/cheesecloth
1 tsp yeast nutrient	4.5-liter/1-gallon secondary
1 tsp pectolase	airlock and bung
1 Campden tablet (optional)	siphoning tube
champagne yeast	

METHOD

Make sure that all bits of leaf and other matter have been removed from the sloes and place in a fermentation bucket. Cut up the raisins and put them in the bin too. Cover with 3 liters/3 quarts of boiling water and mash them up a bit with a potato masher until the water turns a lovely almost blackcurrant color. Allow to cool, then add the pectolase and Campden tablet (if using). Leave for a day, then return, and the must will have turned to a thicker blackcurrant color.

Boil 500ml/2 cups of water, dissolve two thirds of the sugar in it, and add this to the must. Now add the yeast and nutrient and stir well. Lightly cover and leave at room temperature for ten days.

After the ten days is up the wine must be strained into a secondary. Don't be tempted to push the sloes as this will make the resulting wine hazy.

The whole thing needs a little bit of a kickstart, so boil another 500ml/2 cups of water, pour that over the last 500g/1lb of sugar, and stir until it dissolves. Use this to top up the secondary. You will no doubt need to finish off with a little bit more water; it just depends on how much liquid you get from your must. Affix an airlock to the secondary.

Rack after one month, and again if necessary. Allow to ferment out before bottling.

This wine will benefit from a year's aging.

Sloe Gin

If sloe wine really does seem to be too much of a bother then stick with sloe gin. It has to be one of the easiest methods of getting a taste of the wild into your tipple.

INGREDIENTS
500g/1lb sloes
750ml/3 cups of gin
340g/12oz sugar

EQUIPMENT
large sealable jar
muslin/cheesecloth

METHOD

Wash the sloes and put in the freezer. Older books will state that you have to prick each one, and if you haven't got a freezer this may well be your only option. After giving a talk once, someone came running up to me and said, "I have a much lower-technology and cheaper way of pricking sloes." She paused for effect, then exclaimed "Children!" before scampering off laughing to herself.

Put the sloes into a large jar and cover with sugar. Top up with gin and shake, returning to the jar every time you remember it is there to shake it. Keep up this routine for the next three months.

Strain into clean bottles. It can be drunk right away but will mellow with age so is best left for as long as you can manage. My advice is to make as much as is humanly possible every year so it is impossible to drink it all in a few weeks. That way you should always have a bottle of vintage stashed away. I have never managed not to drink it, but it is a good theory.

Rumtopf

The word *rumtopf* (pronounced "romtoff") in Germany and Swiss-German areas is synonymous with Christmas, and literally translated means "rum pot." The glazed earthenware rum pot is set up in a cool dark place in the spring and as they come into season different ripe fruits are added throughout the year, along with a generous helping of sugar and a big glug of rum. A similar method of fruit preservation is adopted by the French but they use brandy instead of rum. Over the months the fruit becomes more and more saturated and thus preserved. It is eaten at Christmas with pancakes, as a condiment to rich meat, with hot apple strudel, or even on its own. The strained liqueur is a cocktail of delicious fruit flavors.

INGREDIENTS

Suggested: strawberries, raspberries, apricots, cherries, redcurrants, cherry plums, gooseberries, peaches, damsons, sloes, grapes, pears, plums

Not recommended: rhubarb, all citrus fruits, blackberries, blueberries, watermelon, apples and bananas

half the weight of fruit in white sugar

overproof rum

EQUIPMENT

a *rumtopf*, or large casserole with lid

muslin/cheesecloth

METHOD ···

Start by adding to your *rumtopf* the first ripe (but not overripe) fruits to come into season. Wash, seed, and pit the fruit if necessary. Bigger fruit such as pears or peaches should be cut into small slices. Pour over the sugar and completely cover the fruit and sugar with rum.

Keep adding fruit, sugar, and rum through the year as and when the fruit comes into season. Take a sneaky spoonful now and then— obviously just to check that it's OK, not for enjoyment. Also, keep an eye out for signs of fermentation. Unlike with the rest of the recipes in this book, you don't want that to happen. If it does, add some more rum.

The final layer is added in the autumn, and it'll be ready for Christmas, or roughly four to six weeks after the final layer is added.

On Christmas Day, take out your *rumtopf* from its hiding place and strain the liquor into a bottle, or glasses for all if you have a house full of guests. The fruit can be and should be eaten right away.

Holy Water!

The first of two booze recipes that aren't strictly winter drinks. Mike Griffiths from north Nottinghamshire introduced me to this very interesting tipple, which helps highlight that you can ferment practically anything. It's a great recipe for the beginner to try as the focus is not on producing subtle flavors, just on making alcohol. It makes a relatively tasteless, colorless alcohol, which in my experience is a little bit dangerously easy to drink.

INGREDIENTS

2kg/4.5lb sugar

4.25 liters/just over 1 gallon of water

1 tsp citric acid

1 tsp yeast nutrient

1 tsp Marmite

1 tsp all-purpose wine yeast

EQUIPMENT

saucepan

4.5-liter/1-gallon secondary

airlock and bung

METHOD

Heat half the water to just before boiling point and stir in the sugar and Marmite until fully dissolved. Pour into a secondary and add the rest of the water. Allow to cool to room temperature, then add the citric acid, yeast nutrient, and yeast. Attach the airlock and bung and allow to ferment out, which it should do rather quickly (ten to four-teen days).

Serve with cordials to make them alcoholic.

Prison Booze

A prison sentence need not signal the end of your brewing career, and inmates often make their own. Many different prison booze recipes (also known as "hooch" or "pruno") exist, and are indicative of what is served as "food" in each prison.

This is a basic recipe that can be followed at home using house-hold ingredients. If you do happen to be reading this in the slammer and find it difficult to get hold of the ingredients, tomato ketchup or biscuits can be substituted for sugar, leftover bits of fruit salad saved over a few days for fruit juice, and the bread can be any bread really. In fact don't worry if you can't get hold of bread as it's only used to get the yeast. You might be lucky enough to have some wild yeasts floating around your cell, in which case follow the instructions below but mix the ingredients together in a trash bag or carrier bag and leave the bag open to catch the wild yeast. Prison booze has even been fermented in toilet bowls.

Depending on what ingredients you use, the taste will vary. The ingredients below will make a passable wine, the substitutes suggested above will make alcohol.

INGREDIENTS

1 long prison sentence

1 liter/1 quart of water

as much pure orange juice as you can
   get your hands on (1.5 liters/
   1.5 quarts)

6 slices of whole-wheat/brown bread

500g/1lb sugar

EQUIPMENT

a place that is hidden from the screws

3-liter/3-quart plastic bottle(s) with lid

old T-shirt

bowl

bucket of warm water *or* radiator

METHOD

Place the bread into a bowl of warm water and leave it to soak for ten minutes. Squeeze each slice so that the water turns a light brown hue.

Pour the sugar into the plastic bottle(s), cover with 1 liter/ 1 quart warm water and shake vigorously until it dissolves. Strain the bread mixture through the T-shirt into the bottle(s), add the orange juice, and shake again. Making sure the lid is attached, put the bottle in a very warm place, such as by a radiator or in a bucket of warm water with a pillow or towels wrapped around it. If using warm water, the water will need to be changed every five to six hours.

Carbon dioxide will build up in the bottle so you'll need to loosen the lid occasionally (three times a day) to let it escape. Failure to do this will result in a rather messy and smelly explosion.

The hooch will be ready in five days and goes well with a cigarette rolled using the ends of other cigarettes.

PROBLEM-SOLVING

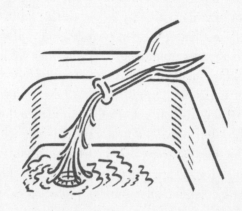

I HAVE THIS IMAGE of a would-be drink-maker picking up this book and trying on three occasions to make the perfect tipple. Every time something goes wrong: either the wine does not ferment at all, resulting in a rather sweet-tasting cordial-like wine that is, frankly, awful, or the wine or beer goes moldy, smelling out the house and therefore dooming the fermentation bucket to sit unused in a shed/garage or store room until the whole thing is embarrassingly chucked out. Or everything seems to go well—the wine clears and looks fine, it is bottled up, labeled, and proudly given to friends as Christmas presents—only for everyone to discover that it tastes like vinegar, thus forever clouding your and, worse, your friends' attitude toward homemade alcohol forever more. This book is put back on the shelf and all the drink-making equipment is put on eBay or given to thrift shops. New tastes remain unexplored, wine- or beer-tasting parties are never hosted, and friendships are not cemented over a shared bottle or two of homemade booze.

As with anything, it's easy to get things wrong when you first start. It's always better to persevere than to give up. Imagine if infants gave up potty training just because they got it wrong the first few times. I have made my fair share of mistakes over the years. On a couple of occasions I tried to make beer while celebrating the success of a previous batch. Under the influence, I ended up with a wort full of broken glass, which later turned into moldy beer. My first steps in wine-making were also far from assured. I have ended up with broken glass and sticky patches on more than one occasion.

Good practice should minimize problems (see Best Practice, p. 39) but it's inevitable that something will go wrong. And when it does, it helps to know why it went wrong, and if anything can be done to rectify the situation.

FERMENTATION WILL NOT START

This can happen for a number of reasons. First, your yeast may no longer be viable—check the date on the packet. (Not a problem if you make a starter—see p. 33.)

High sugar levels may also be a culprit as this will inhibit the yeast. Remember, yeast needs specific conditions to survive. Check your hydrometer and adjust accordingly.

Too little acid will also inhibit the yeast. The ideal pH is between 3.5 and 5.5. If lower then adjust by adding some citric acid.

The temperature of the wort or must may also need adjusting.

Temperatures over 30°C (86°F) or below 18°C (64°F) will affect the performance of yeast. Remedy: move to a cooler or warmer spot, and you may have to add more yeast.

STUCK FERMENTATION

Stuck fermentation is when the wine or beer tastes overly sweet and when tested with a hydrometer the reading suggests some sugar has not fermented out.

The first thing to check is the temperature (see above). If moving your booze doesn't work, try shaking it vigorously as this can often do the job. Next, try racking to add oxygen to your liquor.

Perhaps too much sugar has been put into your must or wort, in which case dilute it.

No nutrient is the next culprit—did the recipe call for some, and did you add any? If not, add some.

If none of these remedies works you can try buying a stuck ferment yeast from your homebrew stockist. Pitch this, and keep your fingers crossed.

EXPLODING BOTTLES

In his infinite wisdom our landlord decided to paint our kitchen white. Not the best color for someone who loves drink-making, the outdoors, and cooking, I thought, but I was assured it would make the place seem bigger so I agreed. Indeed, after they had filled the backyard with the moldy old kitchen and replaced it with a new gleaming white one I had to concede the point: it did look much

better and brighter, and even a bit bigger. I filled the kitchen with all our stuff, including a wine rack with a few bottles of elderberry wine. The wine rack was put up on the highest shelf, away from everything.

Two days passed, and while I was busy writing away in my office I heard a bang. I live in an inner-city area so at first I thought it was a gunshot. Naturally, I was somewhat reluctant to investigate. Then I heard a dripping noise. I ran downstairs to find that a bottle of the elderberry wine had exploded. Wine was dripping out of our cookbooks and the inside of the bread machine, but worst of all, one of the kitchen walls from ceiling to floor was totally covered in the stuff.

When booze has ceased fermenting it will have ceased releasing carbon dioxide. Remember, the whole process of fermentation is in very basic terms the yeast "eating" sugar, farting out carbon dioxide, and pissing alcohol; when it has eaten the sugar it has nothing else to eat and dies off. When you take consecutive hydrometer readings and you deduce your booze is not producing CO_2 and is safe to bottle, it's easy not to take any more precautions. Ideally you should put your secondaries in a warmer place for a few days to monitor them for more activity, before you bottle them. A step I missed out when making my effervescent elderberry wine. The move to the warmer kitchen was enough to restart fermentation. The rise in temperature during spring can also cause explosions.

Broken bottles can be the result of overpriming beer; one teaspoon of sugar per 500ml/1-pint bottle is plenty. Watch out too for exploding bottles when making "champagnes." These are best stored in the fridge as a preventative measure: the yeast will become sluggish and stop producing CO_2. Occasionally cordials will also start spontaneously to ferment. They should also be kept in the fridge.

ROTTEN EGG SMELL

Lack of nutrients, too much sulphite, leaving your wine on the lees (sediment) for too long, and bacterial contamination can all lead to excessive amounts of hydrogen sulphite in your must. If you encounter this problem early enough it can be dealt with. Your wine will need to be racked several times to get air into it—a process known as aeration.

MEDICINAL FLAVORS

This is generally down to a lack of acid in the must. If caught quickly enough you can add some. However, if the wine has fully fermented there isn't much you can do other than use it to cook with.

I've also found this problem occurring as a result of my own laziness, or at least taking shortcuts, which can have other detrimental effects. Once you have washed and sanitized a hundred beer bottles, or you're decanting in a hurry, you might think a quick rinse will do the job of getting rid of the sterilizing solution. Chlorine-based sanitizers react with compounds found in yeast and can lead to medicinal flavors, which will overtake the taste of anything you have made, so always rinse thoroughly.

MOUSY SMELLS AND FLAVORS

A horrible odor not unlike the smell of hemlock. It means your booze is off and there is no cure—sorry! Unsanitary equipment is the reason.

WINE OR BEER IS TOO SWEET

A high level of sugar causes an overly sweet drink, and can be due to there being too much sugar for the yeast to turn to alcohol or a stuck ferment (see above). You could try using less sugar next time. You could even dilute and try to re-ferment, although you will be at risk of ending up with a wine without much taste or body.

Another reason may be that it hasn't yet fully fermented. Move to a warm place and see if fermentation restarts.

HAZY WINES

Hazes can be caused by a number of things. Here are the two most common.

Pectin haze, due to a high level of pectin in the fruit or

vegetables. To test if your haze is due to pectin, drop some of the wine into methylated spirits. After fifteen minutes hold up to the light and look for spots or chains of jelly. If present, you have a pectin haze. To cure, add a teaspoon of pectolase per 4.5 liters/1 gallon, stir in, and keep warm. The use of pectolase in the first place should lessen the likelihood of a haze. Also, avoid boiling pectin-rich fruit and vegetables before fermenting them.

Starch haze. Normally this happens with beer, but also sometimes cider. It can be a result of mashing at the wrong temperatures or using unripe apples. To cure, add amylase.

Other hazes can be treated using bentonite, as directed on the packet.

DARKENING OF WINE OR LIQUEUR

This is caused by oxidation, which can be beneficial if a sherry-like flavor is the order of the day but in most circumstances it ruins the drink. It happens when wine is exposed to the air for more than twenty-four hours and it is not stable. Add two Campden tablets per 4.5 liters/1 gallon. Also, could be due to the presence of iron, in which case add ½ teaspoon of citric acid per 4.5 liters/1 gallon.

ACETIFICATION

The process of acetification is when wine, beer, or cider turns to vinegar. If caught early on it can be stopped by adding one Campden tablet per 4.5 liters/1 gallon of liquor. In general it can't be stopped, and you will end up with loads of vinegar. You will need to sterilize everything that has come into contact with this liquid.

Taste your fermenting booze at every stage of the game to make sure it doesn't taste vinegary, and if it does add one Campden tablet. The vinegar bacteria need air, which is one reason for keeping secondaries topped up at all times.

PART THREE

Further Information

DIRECTORY OF HOMEBREW EQUIPMENT SUPPLIERS

Alabrew Homebrewing Supplies
8916 Parkway E., Ste. A
Birmingham, AL 35206
(205) 833-1716
www.alabrew.com

All Seasons Gardening and Homebrewing Supply Co.
924 8th Ave. South
Nashville, TN 37203
(800) 790-2188
www.allseasonsnashville.com

Amazing Grains Food Co-Op
214 Demers
Grand Forks, ND 58201
(701) 775-4542
www.amazinggrains.org

American Brewmaster
3021-5 Stoneybrook Dr.
Raleigh, NC 27604
(919) 850-0095
www.americanbrewmaster.com

American Home Brew Supply
9295 Chesapeake Dr., Ste. E
San Diego, CA 92123
(858) 268-3024
www.redkart.com/ahbs

Annapolis Home Brew
836 Ritchie Hwy, Ste. 19
Severna Park, MD 21146
(410) 975-0930
www.annapolishomebrew.com

Barley Haven
1050 S. Wadsworth Blvd., Ste B
Lakewood, CO 80226
(720) 269-4278
www.barleyhaven.com

Barley and Vine
1445 Rock Quarry Rd., Ste. 204
Stockbridge, GA 30281
(770) 507-5998
www.barleyNvine.com

Barry's Homebrew Outlet
1447 N. American St.
Philadelphia, PA 19122
(215) 755-4556
www.barryshomebrew.com

Basin Brewing Supply
915 Klamath Ave.
Klamath Falls, OR 97601
(541) 884-1743
www.basinbrewingsupply.com

Beer, Beer and More Beer
3 Locations: Concord, Riverside, and Los
Altos, California
(800) 600-0033
www.morebeer.com

Beer Necessities
9850 Nesbit Ferry Rd.
Alpharetta, GA 30022
(770) 645-1777
www.beernecessities.com

Beer and Wine Makers of America
755 E. Brokaw Rd.
San Jose, CA 95112
(408) 441-0880
www.beerandwinemakers.com

The Beer and Winemaker's Pantry
9200 66th St.
North Pinellas Park, FL 33782
(727) 546-9117
www.beerandwinemaking.com

Beer and Wine Maker's Warehouse
290 Murphy Rd.
Hartford, CT 06114
(860) 247-2960
www.bwmwct.com

Beer and Winemaking Supplies, Inc.
154 King St.
Northampton, MA 01060
(413) 586-0150
www.beer-winemaking.com

Ben's Homebrew
327 E. 6th Ave.
Tarentum, PA 15084
(724) 409-4101
www.benshomebrew.com

Best Damn Home Brew Shop
1036 7th Ave.
San Diego, CA 92101
(619) 232-5175
www.bestdamnhomebrewshop.com

Bitter Creek Homebrew Supply
206 Slinger Rd.
Slinger, WI 53086
(262) 644-5799
www.bittercreek.com

**Black Dragon Brewery (Woodland
HomeBrew Supply)**
175 W. Main St.
Woodland, CA 95695
(530) 668-HOPS
www.blackdragonbrew.com

Blackstone Valley Brewing Supplies
407 Park Ave.
Woonsocket, RI 02895
(401) 765-3830
www.blackstonevalleybrewing.com

Black Swamp Bootleggers
228 North Main St.
Bowling Green, OH 43402
(419) 353-7126
www.blackswamp-bootleggers.com

Booth's Brewing
333 Falkenburg Rd.
N. Suite B-223
Tampa, FL 33511
(813) 685-1909
www.boothsbrewing.com

Brew Connoisseurs
3894 West State St.
Boise, ID 83703
(208) 344-5141
www.brewcon.com

Brew Gadgets
339 S. Lincoln Ave.
Lakeview, MI 48850
(616) 604-6553
www.brewgadgets.com

Brew Hut
15120 E. Hampden Ave.
Aurora, CO 80014
(800) 730-9336
www.thebrewhut.com

Brew It Yourself
25770 I-45 North, #107
Spring, TX 77386
(281) 367-2739
www.biy-tx.com

The Brew Shop OKC
3624 N. Pennsylvania Ave.
Oklahoma City, OK 73112
(405) 528-5193
www.thebrewshopokc.com

Brew and Wine Hobby
98 Pitkin St., Ste. C
East Hartford, CT 06108
(860) 528-0592
www.brew-wine.com

Brewers Connection
1425 E. University Dr., Ste 103
Tempe, AZ 85281
(480) 449-3720
www.brewersconnection.com

Brewer's Corner
800 Park Ave., E
Murfreesboro, TN 37129
(615) 849-7797
www.brewerscorner.com

Brewmasters of Michigan
1085 S. Milford Rd.
Highland, MI 48357
(248) 887-3400
brewmastersofmi.com

Brewmasters Warehouse
2145 Roswell Rd., Ste 320
Marietta, GA 30062
(770) 973-0072
www.brewmasterswarehouse.com

Brewstock
3800 Dryades St.
New Orleans, LA 70115
(504) 208-2788
www.brewstock.com

The CHI Company
6070-K Enterprise Dr.
Diamond Springs, CA 95619
(530) 622-8265
www.chicompany.net

Country Wines
3333 Babcock Blvd., Ste. 2
Pittsburgh, PA 15237-2421
(412) 366-0151
www.countrywines.com

Dave's Homebrewing Supplies
122 East Main St.
Belleville, IL 62220
(618) 277-2550
www.daveshomebrewgourmet.com

Deep South Brewing Supply
1283 Newell Pkwy.
Montgomery, AL 36110
(334) 260-0148
www.deepsouthbrew.com

DeFalco's Home Wine and Beer Supplies
9223 Stella Link
Houston, TX 77025
(713) 668-9440
www.defalcos.com

Delmarva Brewing Craft
24612 Wiley Branch Rd.
Millsboro, DE 19966
(302) 934-8588
www.delmarvabrewingcraft.com

DIY Brewing Supply
79 East St.
Ludlow, MA 01056
(413) 459-1459
www.diybrewing.com

Do Your Brew
9050 W. 88th Ave.
Westminster, CO 80005
(303) 476-3257
www.doyourbrew.com

Docs Homebrew Supplies
451 Court St.
Binghamton, NY 13904
(607) 722-2476
www.docsbrew.com

E. C. Kraus
PO Box 7850
Independence, MO 64054
(800) 353-1906
www.eckraus.com

Even You Can Brew
3402 N. Blackstone, Ste. 124
Fresno, CA 93726
(559) 681-8672
www.evenyoucanbrew.com

Fairview Homebrew
1012 E. Fairview Ave.
Montgomery, AL 36106
(334) 322-3143
www.fairviewhomebrew.com

Fermentables
3915 Crutcher St.
North Little Rock, AR 72118
(501) 758-6261
www.fermentables.com

F. H. Steinbart Company
234 S.E. 12th Ave.
Portland, OR 97214
(503) 232-8793
www.fhsteinbart.com

Fifth Season Gardening Company
900 Preston Ave.
Charlottesville, VA 22903
(866) 998-1782
www.fifthseasongardening.com

Foreman's Home Brewery (Texas)
3801 Colleyville Blvd.
Colleyville, TX 76034
(800) 817-7369
www.homebrewerysupply.com

Grape and Grains
104 Mauldin Rd.
Greenville, SC 29609
(864) 940-2938
www.grapeandgrains.com

The Grape and Granary
915 Home Ave.
Akron, OH 44310
(800) 695-9870
www.thegrape.net

Hearts Home Brew.Com
6190 Edgewater Dr.
Orlando, FL 32810
(800) 392-8322
www.heartshomebrew.com

Homebrew Adventures
209 Iverson Way
Charlotte, NC 28203
(888) 785-7766
homebrew.com/index.shtml

Homebrew Emporium
45 Sterling St.
West Boylston, MA 01583
(508) 835-3374
www.modernbrewer.com

Homebrew Exchange
1907 N. Kilpatrick
Portland, OR 97217
(503) 286-0343
www.homebrewexchange.net

Homebrew Haus
1201 US Hwy 70 E
New Bern, NC 28560
(252) 636-8970
www.homebrewhaus.biz

**Homebrew Heaven Brewing
Supplies**
9109 Evergreen Wy.
Everett, WA 98204
(425) 355-8865
www.homebrewheaven.com

Homebrewing Mexico
Chicago 25-170C
Mexico DF, Mexico 03810
(55) 55-36-66-80
www.homebrewingmexico.com

Home-Sweet Homebrew
2008 Sansom St.
Philadelphia, PA 19103
(215) 569-9469
www.homesweethomebrew.com

Home Wine, Beer & Cheesemaking Shop
22836 Ventura Blvd.
Woodland Hills, CA 91364
(818) 884-8586
www.homebeerwinecheese.com

Home Winery Supply Company and River Raisin Brewing Company
208 Main St.
Dundee, MI 48131
(734) 529-3296
www.homewinery.com

Hop Tech
6398 Dougherty Rd., Ste 7
Dublin, CA 94568
(800) DRY-HOPS
www.hoptech.com

Hops & Berries
125 Remington St.
Fort Collins, CO 80524
(970) 493-2484
www.hopsandberries.com

How Do You Brew?
203 Louviers Dr.
Newark, DE 19711
(302) 738-7009
www.howdoyoubrew.com

Humboldt Beer Works
511 6th St.
Eureka, CA 95501
(707) 442-MALT
www.humboldtbeerworks.com

Hydrobrew
1319 S. Coast Hwy.
Oceanside, CA 92054
(760) 966-1885
www.hydrobrew.com

Jim's Home Brew
2619 North Division
Spokane, WA 99207
(800) 326-7769
www.jimshomebrew.com

Just Brew It
1924 Highway 85
Fayetteville, GA 30214
(770) 719-0222
www.justbrewit-ga.com

Kennebec Home Brew Supplies
662 Maine Ave.
Farmingdale, ME 04344
(207) 623-3368
www.kennebechomebrew.com

Keystone Homebrew Supply
599 Main St.
Bethlehem, PA 18018
(610) 997-0911
www.keystonehomebrew.com

Let's Brew
8235 SE Stark St.
Portland, OR 97216
(503) 256-0205
www.letsbrew.net

**Listermann's Brewing Supplies and
Manufacturing**
1621 Dana Ave.
Cincinnati, OH 45207
(513) 731-1130
www.listermann.com

**Main Street Homebrew Supply
Company—Mainbrew.com**
23596 NW Clara
Lane Hillsboro, OR 97124
(503) 648-4254
www.mainbrew.com

Main Squeeze
124 Xenia Ave.
Yellow Springs, OH 45387
(937) 767-1607
www.mainsqueezeonline.com

Malty Dog Brewery & Supplies
29215 Northwestern Hwy
Southfield, MI 48034
(248) 595-8809
www.maltydogbrewery.com

Miami Valley BrewTensils
2617 South Smithville Rd.
Dayton, OH 45420
(937) 252-4724
www.americanbrewmaster.com

Midwest Homebrewing Supply
5825 Excelsior Blvd.
St. Louis Park, MN 55416
(888) 449-2739
www.midwestsupplies.com

Modern Brewer
2304 Massachusetts Ave.
Cambridge, MA 02140
(617) 498-0400
www.modernbrewer.com

**Mountain Homebrew & Wine
Supply**
8530 122nd Ave NE, B2
Kirkland, WA 98033
(425) 803-3996
www.mountainhomebrew.com

Mr. Steve's HomeBrew Supplies
2944 Whiteford Rd., Ste 5
York, PA 17402
(717) 751-2255
www.mrsteves.com

Mr. Steve's Homebrew
4342 N. George St.
Manchester, PA 17345
(800) 815-9599
www.mrsteves.com

My Brew Heaven
Browns Bridge Rd.
Gainesville, GA 30504
(770) 534-5517
www.mybrewheaven.com

Niagara Tradition Homebrew
1296 Sheridan Dr.
Tonawanda, NY 14217
(716) 877-8767
www.nthomebrew.com

Nor Cal Brewing Solutions
1768 Churn Creek Rd.
Redding, CA 96002
(530) 243-2337
www.norcalbrewingsolutions.com

North Jersey Homebrew
354 Lafayette Rd.
Sparta, NJ 07871
(973) 383-2739
www.njhomebrew.com

Northern Brewer Homebrew Supply
1150 Grand Ave.
St. Paul, MN 55105
(800) 681-2739
www.northernbrewer.com

Oak Barrel Winecraft
1443 San Pablo Ave.
Berkeley, CA 94702
(510) 849-0400
www.oakbarrel.com

O'Connor's Homebrew Supply
613 Lyon St. NE
Grand Rapids, MI 49503
(616) 635-2088
www.oconnorshomebrew.com

Old Goat Winery
640 North Tennessee St.
Cartersville, GA 30120
(770) 383-3100
www.oldgoatwinery.com

Old West Homebrew Supply
229 E. Pikes Peak Ave.
Colorado Springs, CO 80903
(719) 635-0211
www.oldwestbrew.com

Original Gravity Homebrew Supplies
6920D Lakeside Ave.
Richmond, VA 23228
(804) 264-4808
www.oggravity.com

Paradise Brewing Supplies
7766 Beechmont Ave.
Cincinnati, OH 45255
(513) 232-7271
www.paradisebrewingsupplies.com

Point Brew Supply
1816 Post Rd.
Plover, WI 54467
(715) 342-9535
www.pointbrewsupply.com

Rebel Brewer
105 Space Park
North Goodlettsville, TN 37072
(615) 859-2188
www.rebelbrewer.com

Red Arrow Hobbies and Homebrew Supplies
5095 Red Arrow Hwy
Stevensville, MI 49127
(269) 429-8233
www.redarrowhobbies.com/
homebrewsupplies.htm

Red Barn Winemaker Supplies
6181 W. 1350 N.
Demotte, IN 46310
(219) 987-WINE
www.redbarnwinemakersupplies.com

Rocky Top Homebrew and Beer Emporium
1617 Harrison Ave., NW
Olympia, WA 98502
(360) 956-9160
www.rockytopbrew.com

Salt City Brew Supply
750 E. Fort Union Blvd.
Midvale, UT 84047
(801) 849-0955
www.saltcitybrewsupply.com

Santa Fe Homebrew Supply
6820 Cerrillos Rd., #7
Santa Fe, NM 87507
(505) 473-2268
www.santafehomebrew.com

Somethings Brewn'
401 E. Main St.
Galesburg, IL 61401
(309) 341-4118
www.somethingsbrewn.com

Scotzin' Brothers
65 N. 5th St.
Lemoyne, PA 17043
(717) 737-0483
www.scotzinbros.com

Sound Homebrew Supply
6505 5th Place S.
Seattle, WA 98108
(206) 743-8074
www.soundhomebrew.com

Southern Brewing & Winemaking
4500 N. Nebraska Ave.
Tampa, FL 33603
(813) 238-7800
www.southernbrewingwinemaking.com

Southern Homebrew & Supply
634 N. Dixie Freeway
New Smyrna Beach, FL 32168
(386) 409-9100
www.southernhomebrew.com

Southwest Grape & Grain
9450 Candelaria Rd. NE, Ste. D
Albuquerque, NM 87112
(505) 332-2739
www.beer-brewing-wine-making.com

Stein Fillers
4160 Norse Way
Long Beach, CA 90808
(562) 425-0588
www.steinfillers.com

Still H2O
14375 60th North
Stillwater, MN 55082
(651) 351-2822
still-h2o.com

The Thirsty Brewer
13522 Long Green Pike
Baldwin, MD 21013
(410) 592-2843
www.thirstybrewer.com

Thomas Creek Brewery—Homebrew Supplies
2054 Piedmont Hwy
Greenville, SC 29605
(864) 605-1166
www.thomascreekbeer.com

U2CANBREW
15121 87th Ave. E.
Puyallup, WA 98375
(253) 321-1728
www.u2canbrew.com

Weak Knee Home Brew Supply
1300 N. Charlotte St.
Pottstown, PA 19464
(610) 327-1450
www.weakkneehomebrew.com

Weekend Brewer
4205 West Hundred Rd.
Chester, VA 23831
(804) 796-9760
www.weekendbrewer.com

Williams Brewing
2594 Nicholson St.
San Leandro, CA 94577
(800) 759-6025
www.williamsbrewing.com

Windy Hill Wine Making
10998 Perry Hwy.
Meadville, PA 16335
(814) 337-6871
www.windyhillwine.net

Winemakers and Beermakers Supply
9475 Westport Rd.
Louisville, KY 40241
(502) 425-1692
www.wine-beer-makerssupply.com

Worm's Way
1225 North Warson Rd.
Creve Coeur, MO 63132
(314) 994-3900
www.wormsway.com/missouri.aspx

Zok's Homebrewing and Winemaking Supplies
24 North St.
Willimantic, CT 06226
(860) 456-7704
www.homemadebrew.net

CANADA HOME BREWING SUPPLIERS

Ambleside Brewing Company
1531 Clyde Ave.
West Vancouver, British Columbia
Canada
(604) 926-6636
www.amblesidebrewing.com

Beer Grains Supply Co.
8 Frontenac Crescent
Deep River, Ontario Canada K0J1P0
(888) 675-6470
www.beergrains.com

Brew Time Brewery & Winery
1638 Upper James St.
Hamilton, Ontario Canada L9B 1K4
(905) 385-2739
www.brewtime.ca

Brewery Lane
286 Torbay Road
St. John's, Newfoundland Canada
(709) 754-4090
www.brewerylane.com/index.html

Brewhaven
820 Wharncliffe Road South, Unit 24
London, Ontario Canada N6J 2N4
(519) 680-0164
www.brewhaven.on.ca

La Cachette du Bootlegger
90 rue Morgan Baie-d
Urfe, Quebec Canada
(514) 457-1455
www.lacachettedubootlegger.qc.ca

Canadian Home Brewing Supplies
3347 Mainsail Cres.
Mississauga, Ontario Canada L5L 1H3
(877) 568-2739
www.canadianhomebrewing.ca

Custom Brew Niagara Falls
4129 Stanley Ave.
Niagara Falls, Ontario Canada L2E 7H3
(905) 374-2337

Ein Stein Brewhouse
481 North Service W
Oakville, Ontario Canada
(905) 825-2337

Grains Maltés Heine
707 Saint-Ephrem
Upton, Quebec Canada
(450) 549-5061
www.grainsmaltes.com

Grape & Grain
726 Osborne St.
Winnipeg, Manitoba Canada R3L 2C2
(204) 257-6770
www.grapeandgrain.ca

Grapes & Hops
11 Paisley Ave.
South Hamilton, Ontario Canada L8S
1T8
(905) 777-1717
www.grapesandhops.ca

Mout International
8191 Metropolitain Est
Montreal, Quebec Canada
(514) 354-6281
www.biereetvin.com

Noble Grape Burnside
95 Akerley Blvd. Burnside Industrial Park
Dartmouth, Nova Scotia Canada
(902) 468-9463
www.noblegrape.com

Noble Grape Halifax
362 Lacewood Dr.
Halifax, Nova Scotia Canada B3S
(902) 457-9463
www.noblegrape.com

Vin Maison V.T. (Vinothèque)
1129, rue Jogues
Drummondville, Quebec Canada
(819) 474-5588

FURTHER READING

BEER

Berry, C. J. J., *Homebrewed Beers and Stouts* (Amateur Winemaker, 1984)

Bickerdyke, John, *The Curiosities of Ale and Beer—An Entertaining History* (Swan Sonnenschein and Co., 1889)

Brown, Pete, *Hops and Glory: One Man's Search for the Beer that Built the British Empire* (Macmillan, 2009)

Buhner, Stephen Harrod, *Sacred and Herbal Healing Beers: The Secrets of Ancient Fermentation* (Siris Books, 1998)

Campbell, Andrew, *The Book of Beer* (Dennis Dobson, 1956)

Jackson, Michael, *Great Beer Guide* (Dorling Kindersley, 2002)

Line, David, *Brewing Beers Like Those You Buy* (Amateur Winemaker, 1984)

Papazian, Charlie, *The Complete Joy of Homebrewing* (Collins, 2003)

—— *The Homebrewer's Companion* (Collins, 2004)

Parkes, John, *Homebrewing Self-sufficiency* (New Holland, 2009)

WINE

Ball, Ian, *Wine Making the Natural Way* (Elliot Right Way Books, 1998)

Berry, C. J. J., *First Steps in Wine Making* (Amateur Winemaker, 1987)

Hardy, Ben, *Adventures in Wine Making* (The Good Life Press, 2011)

Harris, Mollie, *A Drop O' Wine* (Chatto and Windus/The Hogarth Press, 1983)

Paterson, Wilma, *Country Wines and Cordials* (Omega, 1983)

Vargas, Pattie, and Rich Gulling, *Making Wild Wines and Meads: 125 Unusual Recipes Using Herbs, Fruits, Flowers and More* (Storey Publishing, 1999)

WINE AND BEER

Bravery, H. E., *Home Booze—A Complete Guide for the Amateur Wine and Beer Maker* (Macdonald, 1976)

Tayleur, W. H. T., *Homebrewing and Wine-making* (Penguin, 1977)

Turner, Ben, *1000 Wine and Beermaking Hints and Recipes* (Marks and Spencer, 1985)

—— *The Complete Home Winemaker and Brewer* (Emblem, 1976)

CIDER

Pooley, Michael, and John Lomax, *Real Cider Making—On a Small Scale* (Nexus Special Interest, 1999)

Weaver, Graham, *Growing Your Own Cider* (Pelham, 1978)

SOFT DRINKS

Cresswell, Stephen, *Homemade Root Beer, Soda and Pop* (Storey Publishing, 1998)

DRINKS IN GENERAL

Standage, Tom, *A History of the World in Six Glasses* (Atlantic Books, 2007)

FORAGING

Brill, "Wildman" Steve, and Evelyn Dean, *Identifying and Harvesting Edible and Medicinal Plants in Wild (and Not So Wild) Places* (Harper Resource, 2002)

Coombes, Allen, *Pocket Nature Trees* (Dorling Kindersley, 2010)

De Mauduit, Vicomte, *They Can't Ration These*, Perspone Book 54 (Perspone Books, 2004)

Gibbons, Euell, *Stalking the Wild Asparagus* (Hood and Company, 1962)

Hamilton, Andy and Dave, *The Self-sufficientish Bible* (Hodder and Stoughton, 2009)

Hawes, Zoe, *Wild Drugs—A Forager's Guide to Healing Plants* (Gaia, 2010)

Henderson, Robert K., *The Neighborhood Forager—A Guide for the Wild Food Gourmet* (Chelsea Green, 2000)

Houston, Fiona, and Xa Milne, *Seaweed and Eat It: A Family Foraging and Cooking Adventure* (Virgin Books, 2008)

Irving, Miles, *The Forager Handbook* (Ebury Press, 2009)

Johnson, Owen, and David More, *Tree Guide: The Most Complete Field Guide to the Trees of Britain and Europe* (Collins, 2004)

Lewis-Stempel, John, *The Wild Life: A Year of Living on Wild Food* (Black Swan, 2010)

Mabey, Richard, *Food for Free: A Guide to the Edible Wild Plants of Britain* (Fontana, 1975)

—— *Weeds: How Vagabond Plants Gatecrashed Civilisation and Changed the Way We Think About Nature* (Profile Books, 2010)

Mears, Ray, and Gordon Hillman, *Wild Food* (Hodder and Stoughton, 2007)

Phillips, Roger, *Wild Food* (Fontana, 1972)

Press, J. R., et al, *Field Guide to the Wild Flowers of Britain* (Readers Digest, 1981)

Sterry, Paul, *Complete British Trees—A Photographic Guide to Every Common Species* (Collins, 2007)

Thanyer, Samuel, *The Forager's Harvest: A Guide to Identifying, Harvesting and Preparing Edible Wild Plants* (Foragers Harvest, 2006)

Wink, Michael, and Ben-Erik Van Wyk, *Mind-Altering and Poisonous Plants of the World—A Scientifically Accurate Guide to 1200 Toxic and Intoxicating Plants* (Timber, 2008)

GROWING YOUR OWN

Bird, Richard, *Growing Fruit and Vegetables—The Complete Practical Guide to Kitchen Gardening, from Planning and Planting to Care and Maintenance* (Hermes House, 2003)

Blackburne-Maze, Peter, *Organic Gardening—Natural Ways of Growing Fruit, Vegetables and Herbs* (Marshall Cavendish, 1988)

Bradley, Steven, *What's Wrong With My Plant?—Expert Information at Your Finger Tips* (Hamlyn, 2003)

Brand, Liz, *The National Trust Fruit from Your Garden* (Unwin Hyman, 1987)

Brickell, Christopher, *RHS Encyclopedia of Gardening—The Definitive Guide to Gardening Techniques, Planning and Maintenance, and to Growing Flowering Plants, Fruits and Vegetables* (Dorling Kindersley, 1992)

Greenwood, Pippa, and Andrew Halstead, *RHS Pests and Disease* (Dorling Kindersley, 1997)

Guerra, Michael, *The Edible Container Garden—Fresh Food from Tiny Spaces* (Gaia, 2000)

Hall, Jenny, and Ian Tolhurst, *Growing Green* (Vegan Organic Network, 2006)

Hamilton, Andy and Dave, *The Self-sufficientish Bible* (Hodder and Stoughton, 2009)

Hamilton, Dave, *Grow Your Own Food for Free—Well Almost* (Green Books, 2010)

Harrison, John, *Vegetable Growing Month by Month—The Down to Earth Guide that Takes You Through the Vegetable Year* (Right Way, 2008)

Pears, Pauline, *RHS Encyclopedia of Organic Gardening—The Complete Guide to Natural and Chemical Free Gardening* (Dorling Kindersley, 2005)

Seymore, John, *The Self Sufficient Gardener* (Faber and Faber, 1978)

Shepherd, Allan, *The Organic Garden—Green Gardening for a Healthy Planet* (Collins, 2007)

Spence, Ian, *RHS Gardening Throughout the Year* (Dorling Kindersley, 2009)

Toogood, Alan, *RHS Propagating Plants—The Definitive Practical Guide to Propagating over 1500 Garden Plants* (Dorling Kindersley, 2006)

Waddington, Paul, *21st-Century Smallholder—From Window Boxes to Allotments: How to Go Back to the Land Without Leaving Home* (Eden Project Books, 2006)

Wickers, David, *The Complete Urban Farmer—Growing Your Own Fruit and Vegetables at Home* (Fontana, 1976)

USEFUL WEBSITES

BEER-MAKING

www.sormbrewing.wordpress.com—a UK brewer influenced by US brewing

www.homebrewersassociation.org—huge resource

www.homebrewtalk.com—thriving online community

www.byo.com—website for the brilliant *Brew Your Own* magazine

www.brewersassociation.org—a passionate voice for craft brewers

www.petebrown.blogspot.co.uk—author of *Three Sheets to the Wind*'s blog

www.thebrewsite.com—the longest-running American beer blog full of articles and recipes, a cracking read and recourse

www.howtobrew.com—John Palmer's great, highly informative site

www.craftbeer.com—celebrating the best of American beer

www.bjcp.org/index.php—resource for would-be beer judges

www.homebrewersassociation.org/pages/directories/find-a-supply-shop—find a homebrew shop near you

www.thefullpint.com—craft beer news

www.thebrewingnetwork.com—beer radio!

WINE-MAKING

www.winepress.us/forums—American wine makers and grape growers association

www.ebacchus.com—wine making information site

www.brsquared.org/wine—improve your wine making (getting geeky)

www.winemaking.jackkeller.net—one of the most comprehensive wine-making sources on the net

www.downsizer.net—not a dedicated forum, but some resident experts and a great resource

www.selfsufficientish.com—a friendly and growing community of seasoned wine- and beer-makers

www.winemakingtalk.com/forum/—good US-based site

FORAGING

www.naturessecretlarder.co.uk—Kris Miner's wild food site

www.pfaf.org—Plants for a Future: database full of highly detailed information about plants collected by former bus driver Ken Fern during his time off

www.selfsufficientish.com—foraging courses run by Andy Hamilton or Dave Hamilton, information and interactive forum

www.wildmanwildfood.com—highly comprehensive foraging information and courses, by Fergus Drennan (forager extraordinaire)

www.woodland-ways.co.uk—bushcraft supplies and courses

www.foragersharvest.com—US forager extraordinaire Samuel Thayer's site

plants.usda.gov/java—excellent plant database

tech.groups.yahoo.com/group/ForageAhead—Yahoo! foraging group

www.wildfoodadventures.com—John Kallas's site

GROWING YOUR OWN

www.growinghopsyourself.com—hop-growing blog

www.gardenadvice.co.uk—advice on growing grapevines, among many other things

www.realseeds.co.uk—great for unusual seeds

www.yougrowgirl.com—lovely site from a lovely person

carletongarden.blogspot.co.uk—veg growing journal

www.thisgardenisillegal.com—a gardener in the suburbs of Cleveland, Ohio, waxes on and off about her garden

www.timssquarefootgarden.com—make the most of a small area

www.helpfulgardener.com—various forums and blogs to keep you happy for hours

GLOSSARY OF
BREWING TERMS

AAU Alpha acid unit. A measurement of the potential bitterness of hops, expressed by their percentage of alpha acid. Low = 2–4%, medium = 5–7%, high = 8–12%.

ABV Alcohol by volume. Standard measure of how much alcohol (ethanol) is contained in an alcoholic beverage, expressed as a percentage of total volume.

Acetic acid Formed when beer is exposed to the air, and it goes all vinegary. Also carried by vinegar flies.

Acetification When some or all of the alcohol oxidizes to acetic acid.

Acid The acids found or added to country wines are citric, malic, and tartaric. The correct acid level is important to obtain a good flavor and help act as a preservative.

Acidity The sourness, pH value, or total acid content of wine or (generally Belgian) beer, measured by its hydrogen ion concentration. A pH reading of between 3 and 3.4 is the desirable level.

Adjuncts Anything other than malt, hops, water, and yeast that is added to beer; examples include corn, rice, wheat, sugar, syrup, even unmalted barley.

Aerobic fermentation Also known as the first ferment. The quick, intense ferment when the yeast multiplies like mad. "Aerobic" denotes the involvement of air, and this ferment is what is happening at the stage when the wort or must is covered loosely, allowing air to get in.

Aftertaste The taste that develops on the uvula at the back of the throat after you have swallowed your drink. Also known as the "farewell" of a wine.

Airlock Also known as a fermentation lock. An often plastic device (in former times glass) that is affixed to a secondary and allows carbon dioxide to escape but doesn't allow in any air from the outside.

Alcohol The lovely stuff that gets you tiddly. Also defined as the by-product (along with carbon dioxide) of yeast eating sugar. There are different types of alcohol but the most common in brewing is ethyl alcohol.

Ale Defining ale could cause a riot among CAMRA members, historians, and general pedants. I intend to add to this debate and define it using the antiquated notion that it is only an unhopped beer, never a beer with hops in it.

All-grain brewing Brewing with just grain and no malt extract.

Alpha acid The bittering acid of hops (see AAU).

Ammonium phosphate Yeast nutrient.

Amylase An enzyme group that converts starches to sugars.

Anaerobic fermentation Also known as the second ferment. Slower than the initial stages in the absence of air.

Antioxidant A substance such as ascorbic acid normally added at the bottling stage that will prevent the wine from oxidizing.

Aperitif A drink taken before a meal, thought to stimulate an appetite.

Aroma The smell of drink, also known as the "bouquet" when talking about wine.

Attenuate The action of the yeast fermenting the sugars in a must or wort.

Autolysis The decomposition of dead yeast cells by enzymes previously secreted by them. It is what happens when wine comes into contact with the lees (sediment). In some wines this means off flavors and spoilage, but in other cases, such as in champagne-making, it is very desirable.

Balling A scale of measurement used to assess the density of a liquid in comparison to water.

Barm The now antiquated term for the scum on the top of wort when fermenting. Once used to make bread, and the ancestor to many yeast cultures. This is perhaps why it was also once used in place of the word "yeast." As a verb it can also mean to add yeast, or to pitch.

Barrel During the war people used to roll out barrels in order to have a barrel of fun. The modern equivalent would be 136.274824 liters (of fun).

Bead The bubbles in wine or beer.

Beer God's greatest gift to man, and according to the great Homer (Simpson), The Cause of and The Solution to all of life's problems. Less emphatically described as any alcoholic beverage made from the fermentation of sugars that have derived from grain.

Bentonite Diatomaceous earth or clay used as a clarifier.

Bitter wort Wort with bittering agents (such as, but not exclusively, hops).

Bladdered To be drunk after imbibing too much alcohol.

Bloom The waxy dust coating on fruit such as grapes and plums.

Body The texture or fullness of wine or beer.

Bottom fermenting The process of fermenting normally but not exclusively by a lager yeast, which ferments on the bottom rather than producing a beer cap. Bottom fermenting normally occurs at lower temperatures.

Bottoms In strictly brewing terms, the deposits of yeast and other solids formed during fermentation.

Bouquet The aroma normally of wine, also known as "nose."

Brew Another word for "ferment" when used to describe beer fermentation. Also used to refer to the final product.

Bung A stopper for a keg or secondary.

Calcium sulphite One of the chemicals that give water permanent hardness. Commonly called gypsum or Plaster of Paris.

Campden tablet A tablet about the size of an aspirin that contains about 7g of potassium metabisulphite. When dissolved it releases sulfur dioxide. It is used to sterilize, and as an antioxidant.

Cap Either the lid used to seal a beer, such as a crown cap, or the mass of solids pushed to the top of a fermenting wine by carbon dioxide.

Caramel Sugar syrup darkened by heat and used as a coloring for dark beers.

Carbon dioxide The gas formed during fermentation. It is what gives beer head and champagne its fizz. It is said that during the fermentation process, yeast pisses alcohol and farts carbon dioxide.

Carboy 20–60-liter glass or plastic container with a narrow opening at the top. Also known as a demijohn and usually fitted with a rubber bung and airlock. Comes from the Persian *qarabah* meaning "big jug."

Cask ale Also known as cask-conditioned beer. Unfiltered, unpasteurized beer conditioned in and served from a cask without adding carbon dioxide or nitrogen pressure. This is the type of ale CAMRA (Campaign for Real Ale) has very successfully campaigned for.

Casks Small oak barrels used to store wine or beer. A cask must hold at least 27 liters.

Casse Haze due to metallic taint.

Cellar A cool, dark place used to store wine. It does not have to be under a house, but the site must maintain an even temperature and have no light entering it.

Chambré At room temperature.

Champagne Officially, "champagne" should only be used to describe sparkling grape wines from the Champagne region in France. Unofficially, it's a term used to describe sparkling, semi-fermented, and generally very low alcohol soft drinks made from flowers.

Cheese Layers of apple pulp wrapped in press cloths.

Citric acid The primary acid from citrus fruits.

Clarify The clearing of any nasty floating bits from wine/beer/drink—often referring to wine hazes caused by excessive pectin or cloudy beers. A clarified beer can also be called a bright beer. Some call Jeremy Clarkson's world view unclarified.

Conditioning An aspect of secondary fermentation during which the yeast refines the flavors of the final beer. An immature beer lacks taste and aroma, and can also be flat. Conditioning happens in three steps: maturation, clarification, and finally stabilization. It can happen in the cask or bottle.

Copita Traditional sherry glass.

Copper Also known as the kettle. The third vessel used in beer brewing where the hops and the wort are boiled prior to fermenting. So named because kettles always used to be made of copper.

Country wine Any wine made from something other than grapes.

Craft brewer A homebrewer who makes beer to a professional standard.

Crown cap The metal stopper whose edges are crimped over the mouth of a beer bottle.

Cutting Stopping fermentation.

Decant To pour liquid from one container to another without disturbing the sediment.

Dessert wine Strong, full-bodied, full-flavored wine. Legally defined as any wine over 14% volume made without fortification, though due to modern yeast strains and viticulture this could now become antiquated as many normal wines can be produced to that level.

Dextrin A short starch molecule produced during malting and mashing. Residual dextrins contribute to the body of a beer.

Dextrose Glucose.

Diastase A complex of enzymes that convert starch to sugar.

DME Dry malt extract. See malt extract.

DMS Diastatic malt syrup. Malt extract containing some diastase used to convert the starch in the adjuncts to sugar.

Draft Beer from a wooden cask rather than from a bottle. Used to determine a beer on a pump.

Drop clear To clarify spontaneously.

Dry The taste of wine when very little or no sweetness can be detected.

Dry hopping Adding dry hops or pellets to a beer during fermentation (rather than the boil) to enhance the hop flavor. A practice adopted by many American IPA makers that leaves a grassy aroma.

Dumb Lifeless wine, normally lacking acid or tanning.

EBU European bittering units. See IBU.

End point When mashing grains, this is the moment when all the starch has been converted into maltose and dextrins.

Enzyme A protein that helps a complex molecule to change into a simpler one. Enzymes are essential in the fermentation process.

Esters Produced during maturation and often give fruity flavors to beers and wines.

Feeding Adding fermentable materials to the must during fermentation rather than at the start.

Ferment out Fermenting until final gravity has been reached.

Fermentation The production of alcohol when yeast eats sugar, pisses alcohol and farts carbon dioxide.

Fermentation bucket Brewing bucket, normally plastic with a lid. Used for fermenting wines and beers.

Fermentation lock See airlock.

Final gravity (FG) After all fermentation has ceased, FG is deduced when the hydrometer gives consistent consecutive readings over a period of time (normally a couple of days), even when moved to a warmer spot.

Finings Any substance mixed to the wort or must that clarifies.

Finishing hops Hops added in the final moments of boiling to impart flavor or aroma to beer.

Flat A bubble-free lifeless beer, or a wine that tastes dull and insipid.

Floater A minute particle of debris floating in wine—just as unwanted as what's left in the toilet that won't flush away.

Flocculation The clumping together of yeast once the sugar in a beer has fermented.

Flogger Wooden tool once used to bang corks into bottles.

Fobbing When a lively beer foams continuously out of a bottle after being overprimed or kept too warm.

Fortification The adding of a spirit to a wine to increase the alcohol level.

Fret To re-ferment in the bottle, cask or barrel.

Fructose Fruit sugar.

Gelatin A translucent, colorless, brittle (when dry) solid derived from the collagen inside animal skin and bones. Used as a fining agent, and sometimes spelled "gelatine."

Gelatinization The process of making starch soluble during mashing. Normally used in reference to boiling adjuncts.

Gin Drink that goes very well with most soft drinks.

Glucose A fermentable grape sugar also known as dextrose.

Glycerol Also known as glycerine. Produced during fermentation and often used as an additive in dessert wines to make them richer and smoother.

Goddesgoode An antiquated name for yeast, meaning "God's gift."

Goods The porridge-like mix of grist and hot liquor.

Gravity Abbreviated version of specific gravity.

Grist Ground malt and other adjuncts.

Gyle Unfermented wort that is put aside to be added later to a finished beer in order to condition it.

Hard water Water with a high mineral content, much sought after for brewing certain ales.

Haze A lack of clarity in wine due to tiny particles of matter that remain in suspension. Often caused by pectin, starch, or protein.

HBU Homebrew bittering units. A formula adopted by the American Homebrewers Association to measure the bitterness of beer, it means the same as AAU. There are often seasonal variations in the bitterness of hops so by specifying the alpha acid unit rather than the amount of hops in a recipe you can always impart the same amount of bitterness in a beer. So, for example, 1.5oz of fuggles hops at 5% alpha acid is 7.5 AAUs. If next year the alpha acid percentage in fuggles is 7.5%, you will only need 1oz rather than 1.5oz to arrive at the same bitterness contribution.

Head The foam on top of a beer.

Headroom The space between the top of the wine or beer and the cork, bung or cap. Sometimes referred to as the "ullage."

Helles German for "light," as in color.

Homebrew That which is brewed at home.

Homebrewer You (hopefully).

Hops Cones or flowers of the hop (*Humulus lupulus*) bine, used to add bitterness to and preserve beer.

Hydromel Antiquated word for mead.

Hydrometer Could also be called a sacchrometer as it's an instrument used to measure the sugar content of a liquid.

Hydrometer jar A narrow jar made of plastic or glass perfectly designed to float the aforementioned hydrometer.

IBU International bittering units. A system of bitterness measurement devised by brewing scientists and used as an accepted standard across the planet. One IBU is equal to 1mg of alpha acid in 1 liter of beer or wort.

Inhibit A fermentation is inhibited when the action of the yeast is prevented.

Invert sugar A mixture of the two monosaccharides glucose and fructose, obtained by splitting sucrose. It ferments immediately so is often used for priming or the final stages of brewing.

Irish moss A seaweed used to clear beer.

Isinglass A substance taken from the swim bladders of fish used to fine beer and wine.

Keeving Method of cider-making, often associated with the French, whereby very slowly fermented, clear, naturally sweet ciders are produced by promoting enzymic changes in the apple juice.

Keg A small barrel made from plastic, wood, or metal with a capacity of between 22 and 45 liters (five and ten gallons).

Kiln Building used to dry malt after germination, or hops.

Krausen The foamy head that develops on the surface of the wort in the open days of fermentation.

Krausening Priming beer using unfermented wort instead of sugar.

Lactic acid Also known as milk acid. Used in wine-making to promote maturation.

Lactose Milk sugar. Unfermentable sugar used to sweeten wine and beer.

Laevulose Fructose.

Lager Derived from the German "to store." Taken to mean a bottom-fermented beer brewed at comparatively (to ale) cold temperature and stored for a period of time.

Lager yeast *Saccharomyces uvarum*. A specific strain of beer yeast that ferments best at 0.5°C to 10°C (33°F to 50°F) and does not flocculate.

Lagering Aging a beer.

Lambic A Belgian style of beer infected with a bacteria that gives it a sour taste.

Lautering The process of removing spent grains or hops from the wort. It is done by sparging and straining.

Lees Sediment.

Liquor Brewer's term for water.

Log phase Period of rapidly accelerating yeast growth.

Lupulin The yellow powder found at the base of the hop flower that contains the oils and resins that give hops their bitterness.

Macerate To soften (fruit) by crushing and steeping.

Magnesium sulphite Also known as Epsom Salts. Added to water to improve the quality and increase the acidity of the liquor. Also used in recipes where fermentation can be a challenge. Not a great nutrient on its own, but when combined with other yeast nutrients it can enhance their rate of fermentation.

Malic acid Acid mostly found in unripe fruits.

Malt Also known as malted barley. Partially sprouted and then dried barley. During this process its starch changes to maltose by diastase.

Malt extract A syrup or dry form of concentrated maltose and dextrin. It is derived from mashing barley and dissolving evolved sugars in water. Both are made by evaporating water from mashed barley.

Maltase An enzyme that changes maltose to fermentable glucose.

Malted barley See malt.

Maltese Someone from Malta.

Maltose A sugar produced from starch by the action of diastase.

Mash tun Also known as a mashing bin. The vessel in which mashing takes place.

Mashing The process of converting grain starches to fermentable sugars by mixing grains with hot liquor, keeping the liquor at a regular temperature between 60°C and 71°C (140°F and 160°F) for a set time and then sparging.

Maturation The perfection of wine or beer through aging.

Metabisulphite Chemical used for sterilizing wine.

Mine sweeping The act of stealing beer from someone in a busy pub, bar, or nightclub. A despicable way of getting booze for free.

Mulled Heated but not boiled wine, cider, or ale with added spices. Often drunk during the winter months in the northern hemisphere.

Muselet The wire cage that fits around a cork and keeps it in place on a champagne, cider, or sometimes strong beer bottle.

Must Vegetable, fruit, or any other sugary solution that has been adjusted to ferment into wine.

Musty The off taste caused by mold in cask or bottle.

Nose All that can be learned from a drink by smelling it.

Nutrients Mineral salts, vitamins, and trace elements needed by yeast for most favorable fermentation. Also known as yeast nutrients or, at its most simplified, yeast food.

Oenophile A lover of wines but not a wino.

Original gravity The specific gravity of must or wort prior to pitching the yeast.

Osmotic shock Exposing yeast to too much sugar, often with fatal effects.

Oxidation Exposure to the air of wine, causing discoloration and sometimes off flavors. The high alcohol level in sherry-type wines makes oxidation a characteristic rather than a problem.

Pectin A carbohydrate that surrounds the molecules of fruit juices that gels and sets when heated and can often cause hazes in fruit wines.

Pectolase Also known as pectic enzyme or pectinaze. Compound that breaks down pectin and boosts juice extraction from fruit.

pH A measure of alkalinity or acidity on a scale of 1 to 14 where 7 is neutral.

Pitching Adding yeast.

Pith The white bit between the flesh and skin of a citrus fruit.

Plastering Adding gypsum to a sherry must.

Plato A more exact version of specific gravity used by commercial brewers.

Polishing A very suspect old method of filtering beer using asbestos.

Pomace The solid leftover after pressing apples or grapes.

Potassium carbonate Additive used to reduce tartaric acid.

Potassium metabisulphite Additive (see Campden tablet) used in beer and wine to inhibit growth of wild yeasts, bacteria, and fungi. When a wine bottle reads "contains sulphites" it often means potassium metabisulphite.

Potassium sorbate Used with the above to stop fermentation.

ppm Parts per million

Press cloth Squares of cloth used to wrap up apple pulp prior to pressing.

Primary fermentation The initial fermentation where between 60 and 75 percent of the sugar content is turned into alcohol.

Primary fermenter Vessel in which primary fermentation happens.

Primer Sugar or sugar solution that restarts fermentation in the bottle just enough to carbonate.

Priming The process of adding sugar or a sugar solution to a wine or beer in order to carbonate.

Proof The measure of alcohol in wine or spirits. 100% = 57.06% ABV.

Pulp Flesh, skins, and juice of fruit or vegetables.

Pulp fermentation Fermentation of the pulp to extract the flavor and color.

Punt The indentation in the bottom of a bottle of wine.

Quart Quarter of a gallon, or roughly 1 liter.

Rack(ing) The process of moving partially fermented wort or must from one fermentation vessel to another by siphon so that it is not fermenting on yeast sediment.

Respiration Metabolic and aerobic cycle performed by yeast before its fermentation cycle, during which oxygen is stored for later use.

Robe Normally used to describe red wines of outstanding color.

Ropiness An oily appearance in beer or wine caused by lactic acid bacteria. Thankfully, fairly rare.

Rouse Stirring thoroughly in order to bring air to the wort or must, normally to wake up sluggish yeast.

Saccharin A non-fermentable sweetener.

Saccharomyces Literally means "sugar fungi." Generic name for yeast.

Sacchrometer An instrument that determines the sugar concentration in a liquid.

St. Arnold of Metz Saint who said, "Don"t drink the water, drink beer."

St. Patrick Patron saint of homebrew—seriously!

Secondary A glass or plastic container used for the secondary fermentation of wine. In the UK they are normally a standard 4.5

liters (1 gallon) and are clear glass or plastic. In the US a 4.5-liter carboy is known as a "jug."

Secondary fermentation The slower second ferment, which for wine and beer normally occurs in a secondary. It is the stage that precedes bottling where the last 25 to 40 percent of fermentation happens. It is much less active and therefore does not create a protective layer of carbon dioxide so the wort or must is vulnerable to airborne contaminants and is generally kept airtight.

Sediment Insoluble substances that settle at the bottom of the wort or must or even beer or wine during fermentation and storage. Made up of dead yeast cells and decomposing ingredients.

Siphon A plastic tube used to remove wine or beer off the sediment. As a verb: the action of siphoning.

Sorbitol A natural fruit sugar that occurs in many fruits and berries of the *Sorbus* genus, used as a sweetener as it cannot ferment. Also used as a component of amateur rocket fuel.

Sparging A quick hot-water rinse at the end of the mash in order to remove all the maltose.

Sparkling wine A wine full of carbon dioxide caused by secondary fermentation in the bottle.

Specific gravity (SG) The weight of the must or wort compared specifically to water.

Stabilize To stabilize a wine is to cease fermentation. This is normally done by adding potassium sorbate and metabisulphite to kill the yeast.

Stable A stable wine is one that will not ferment.

Star-bright A most brilliantly clear wine or beer.

Starter A batch of already fermenting yeast added to wort or must to initiate fermentation.

Sterilize A process of cleaning that rids equipment of as much bacteria, wild yeast, and other contaminants as possible.

Straining Using a sieve or muslin cloth, or both, to remove solids.

Strike water Water that has been heated to approximately 72°C (162°F).

Stuck fermentation Fermentation that stops before it has finished.

Sucrose Ordinary cane sugar.

Sulphite See metabisulphite and Campden tablet.

Sweet Term used to describe a wine that contains some residual sugars, the opposite of dry.

Sweet wort Wort without bittering agents.

Tannin Astringent polyphenolic compound (substance) from the skins, pits, and stalks of grapes that acts as a preservative and gives a slight bitterness.

Tartaric acid The acid of grapes and bananas, which helps in the maturation process.

Thin A watery wine or beer that lacks body.

Top ferment Fermenting on the surface of the wort.

Trub Precipitated proteins from the wort during boiling.

Ullage See headroom.

Vinegar fly *Drosophila melanogaster*. Little bastard flies, also known as fruit flies, that are often the source of acetic infection.

Wort The mixture of malt and herb or hop essences in liquor prior to fermentation.

Yeast According to C. J. J. Berry, *First Steps in Winemaking*, that without which there would be no alcohol and the world would be all the worse for it.

Yeast nutrients See nutrients.

Zymase The name given to apo-zymase, a complex of enzymes secreted by yeast responsible for turning sugar into alcohol (fermentation).

Zymurgy The science of yeast fermentation.

GLOSSARY OF GARDENING AND BOTANICAL TERMS

Alien species Non-native plant normally introduced by humans.

Annual A plant that completes its lifecycle within one year.

Axil The angle between a leaf stalk and the plant stem.

Basal leaves Often rosette-shaped leaves at the base of a plant.

Biennial A plant that completes it lifecycle over two years.

Cloche A low-lying transparent temporary shelter for your plants.

Coir Coconut husk fiber used in potting compost.

Cold frame A kind of mini greenhouse that protects plants.

Crop rotation Rotating the area crops are grown in year after year to avoid pest and disease build-up.

Cultivar Type or variety of plant. Fuggles and Goldings, for instance, are cultivars of hops.

Deciduous Woody plants that shed their leaves in the winter to grow again in the spring.

Fruit The part of a plant that contains the seeds.

Germinate The process of growing a seedling from a seed.

Grafted When the tissues of one plant are encouraged to fuse with another. Normally, in the case of trees, the branches of one tree are fused to the rootstock of another.

Herb A plant without a woody stem.

Mulch Cover placed on soil to retard weeds and retain moisture. Grass clippings, hay, straw, and sawdust can all be used as mulch.

Native A plant that is indigenous to a given area.

Naturalized An introduced plant that has established in a given area.

Node The place on a plant stem where a leaf is attached.

Perennial A plant that completes its lifecycle over a few years, normally flowering every year.

Perlite Glassy globules used as part of a plant growth medium.

Pinnate Leaves arranged on a stem in opposite pairs.

Rhizome Swollen underground stem of a plant that sends out roots.

Rootstock A plant or stump that has been cultivated for its roots.

Shrub Woody perennial normally smaller than a tree and often without a trunk.

Stamen The male reproductive organ of a plant.

Stem The main axis of a plant.

Successional sowing Planting at intervals so that you can harvest over a period of time rather than in one go.

Thinning out The process of removing weaker seedlings when crops are bunched together so that the stronger ones can develop.

Umbel Umbrella-shaped part of a plant where groups of seeds grow on stems branching out from a central stem, as seen on plants such as alexanders and fennel.

Vein Thin strands that divide leaves.

ACKNOWLEDGMENTS

I am fairly positive that this book would not have got off the ground had it not been for Harry Man's enthusiasm for my work, so cheers, son, I know I'll buy you plenty more pints too, if you ever let me put my hand in my pocket! Praise too must be given to the two refreshingly frank and caring women who made this book possible: namely my agent, Araminta Whitley, and my editor, Susanna Wadeson. Credit is also due to my Emma, whom the words "patient," "wonderful," and "unquestionably supportive" don't even begin to describe.

Then there are the people who helped with the practical aspects of writing a book such as this. John and Garth for their initial enthusiasm and tasting of my homebrewing (and I will overlook your love of cherry Lambrini, Garth!). Francene for introducing me to Fergus Drennan and, of course, Fergus himself for his recipes. Max Drake, my herbalist, not only for his recipes and friendship but for his excellent knowledge of all things herbal. Alex Hughes for letting me crash and for taking the day off when our tasting session got the better of us (and his wonderful wife, Gemma). Bristol's most active good citizens, the Kocho-Williamses (master-brewer Ali and preserving-queen Sasha) for sharing their knowledge, food, booze, and home, and then even allowing me to use their finest recipes. Mike Griffiths for his encyclopedic knowledge of homebrewing, his recipes and, of course, his continued support on Selfsufficientish.com.

Leona Williamson for her excellent advice, company on forages, and enthusiasm for my booze! For the cider section, a debt of gratitude is due to Martin Cosgrove. Another Martin, from Brewers Droop, also deserves a nod for his occasional advice and, more important, his idle chats about anything from Go to mental health.

Thanks, too, to Jon Baldwin, Joy Mason, Gilly Wright, John Lewis Stempel, Emma Ball, Jeremy Daniel Meadows, and Stonehead (aka Dennis Johnson) for their recipes. Also thanks to the Selfsufficientish.com moderators past and present for their continued support throughout my career and for running the web forum and site.

As you can see, it's a labor-intensive business to write a book and more so publishing it. So my gratitude and thanks are not over. I'd also like to thank Becky Cole, my stateside editor, for making the "translation" as painless as possible; Kate Napolitano, not only for her hard work but for getting my subtle jokes; and the rest of the Plume team, namely Kathryn Court, Philip Budnick, John Fagan, Mary Pomponio, Lavina Lee, and the fantastic sales force headed by Norman Lidofsky.

I am truly sorry if you have been missed off the list; it has more to do with the extra glass of elderberry port I've just had than my lack of appreciation for what you have done. So if your name isn't here and it deserves to be, I owe you a pint—there, you even have it in writing!